Secure Android Design and Development

From App Layer to HAL – Aligned with Android 15

Mohammad Hossein Heydarchi

Secure Android Design and Development

From App Layer to HAL – Aligned with Android 15

Mohammad Hossein Heydarchi

ISBN 978-91-531-3120-5

First published in 2025 by Mohammad Hossein Heydarchi

Cover design by Mohammad Hossein Heydarchi

Tweet This Book!

Please help Mohammad Hossein Heydarchi by spreading the word about this book on Twitter!

The suggested hashtag for this book is #SecureAndroidDesign.

Find out what other people are saying about the book by clicking on this link to search for this hashtag on Twitter:

#SecureAndroidDesign

To my family— my heart, my home, my why.

Contents

Acknowledgments **1**

Brief **3**
The story of the book 3
No magic at all! 4
How to read the book 4
Who is the book written for? 4

The big picture **7**
Do We Need to Secure an Android Application? 9

Principles and Methodologies **11**
Gravity of principles (The rules of the game) 11
The Fail-Safe vs Fail-Secure Principle (Planning for the Unexpected) 11
Least Common Mechanism 14
Separation of Privilege and Least Privilege 15
The Zero Trust Principle: Trust No One, Verify Everything 17
KISS: The Principle of Least Complexity in Security 19
Defense in Depth 20
Defensive, Offensive, and Aggressive Programming 22
Notes on Modularity, cohesion, and coupling 28

Securing the Development Lifecycle **31**
Design Review 31
Code Review 32
Regular Security Assessments 40
Security Requirements 41
Integrating Security Testing 48

Threat Modeling, Standards and Guidelines **51**
Shostack's Four Question Framework 52
Threat Modelling frameworks 53
Security Standards and Guidelines 56
Some keywords to know 61

Attack and Defense **63**
We don't need to experience it again! 63
Why are we not learning from history? 63
How you will be attacked 66
How to Defend 68
Act as a chief 71

Common Programming Mistakes **73**
Memory safety 73
C and C++ 74
Java 81
Kotlin 85
Real world examples 89

Data Validation **93**
Untrusted Data Sources 93
Input Validation 96
Encoding Methods 103
Sanitizing user inputs 107

Android Security Model **115**
Let's open the onion layers 116
Application Sandbox and Android Runtime 118
Application Signing 119
Permission and Package Manager 122
SELinux 122
AndroidManifest and Components 124
Inter-process communication 124
HAL Layer 140
Play Integrity 143
Jetpack libraries 145

Protecting Data **147**
Data life-cycle 147
What Google has done to address insecure storage 150
File Integrity Verification 162
Private Space 162

Authentication, Network, and Protocols **163**
Android AccountManager for Access Control 163
Credential Manager 166
Android Biometric Authentication 170
Android Network Security Configuration 173
Sniffing 175

Certificate Pinning in Android Applications 178
Implementing SSL/TLS for Android Network Communications 185
OAuth and OpenID Connect for Android Applications 190
Bluetooth 196

Practical Scenarios **199**
Financial Android Application 199
Key Provider Service 204
Sensor HAL Layer Daemon 208
Vehicle Data Logger Application 212

Compilers and Tools **215**
Clang and GCC Security Features 215
Obfuscation 226
R8 232
Notes on hiding keys, secrets and credentials 232
Static and Dynamic Analysis Tools 234

Last word **243**

About the Author **245**

Abbreviations Glossary **247**

References **251**

Appendix **253**
Security Standards and Guidelines 253
A detailed STRIDE and TARA comparison 257
Useful tools 258

Acknowledgments

Writing this book has been an incredible journey, and I am deeply grateful to those who took the time to review my work, provide feedback, and help shape it into something better.

I would like to extend a special thanks to **A.Sh** for his feedback on **Threat Modeling** and **Security Principles** during the drafting stages of this work. His insights helped to improve the manuscript.Although I wasn't able to reach him for confirmation, I've used a shortened version of his name out of respect.

I am also deeply appreciative of **Sebastian Porst**, who provided detailed and invaluable feedback on multiple chapters. His guidance pushed me to bridge gaps, refine concepts, and ensure this book remains both practical and useful for developers.

Any errors or omissions remain my own.

Finally, to everyone who contributed—whether through direct reviews, discussions, or by sharing their knowledge and experiences—thank you. Your input has not only strengthened this book but has also deepened my understanding throughout this process.

This book is stronger because of your contributions, and I sincerely appreciate the time and effort you dedicated to helping me improve it.

To Readers

If you spot errors or have suggestions, please email me at:

feedback.heydarchi@gmail.com.

I warmly welcome your insights to refine this work.

Brief

"The road goes ever on and on" — J.R.R. Tolkien, The Hobbit

The story of the book

No one likes to put time into learning SELinux! That's true. Working with SELinux is not easy due to a lack of good documentation. Especially in Android, you can not find any easygoing resources. Most of us are satisfied with running some commands from Google Documents or *Stack Overflow*.

I was not satisfied with the in hand information. I was interested in learning more. So I started looking for good articles. You would not expect me to find that many resources for Android; however, the base is almost the same. Despite being introduced for Linux, Android has taken it more seriously. You might ask, "Why?". The answer is simple: "For the sake of user privacy & security!"

It was how the journey started for me, and many questions came to mind. There were lots of questions: Is SELinux enough? How can we develop more secure applications? Why do we hear a lot about Android malware? And many other questions. However, I needed help finding good resources that are exceptionally written for Android. I had two options: stick to the little scattered information and give up or continue to find a way forward. Any research, books, articles, courses, etc., could be a step forward. Besides, because of the previous study I did in cybersecurity at the beginning of my career, on some occasions, I had some understanding of cybersecurity that helped me to speedup the process.

My first step was to create a big picture of the journey. So, I started researching to clarify what I needed to know. The output was a rough roadmap that I still required to work on to fill the gaps. The good point was that I didn't have to reinvent the wheel, and I didn't try to do that. Borrowed the common concepts and practices from other domains could be a good option. I took courses, read books and article alongside having some hand on workshop to improve myself. Besides the common areas, I needed to work on Android-specific topics from Google's documents and the *Android Open Source Project (AOSP)*. The outcome was lots of notes that some articles have been published on *LinkedIn* and *AospInsight.com*. I had enough materials that were not in a good shape then. I thought publishing it as a book and sharing it with others would be a good idea.

A couple of years ago, automotive companies started migrating their infotainment systems to Android. Bringing Android into cars has unlocked many opportunities and brought many features to the users. Also, it means that companies must consider security and user privacy more seriously than before.

To explain the seriousness of the situation, I can give a simple example. If your phone is compromised, one of the worst cases could be losing money or sharing your private picture with attackers. :) But in the Automotive industry, it's terrifying. Thanks to Google and other reasons, vehicles have not been broadly targeted. Eventually, they will be, and the target might be safety then! I don't want to imagine a compromised car driving 80mph on a highway.

What next! I don't want to know.

For now, our job is to take it seriously in all phases of our products, from before designing the application or service to after publishing them. Let's focus on what we have control over instead of telling horrible stories.

No magic at all!

There's no magic spell to make the products secure. But we can think and work on that systematically through a simple and effective process in all the stages of our projects. We must collaborate with an open mind to deliver what our customers deserve.

I am still figuring out how much I could be successful, but the result of my efforts is in front of you. You can judge that by reading it and giving me feedback.

How to read the book

I have designed each chapter to be self-contained. It lets you read and explore them independently based on your interests. Although the chapters may have relationships and connections, you don't need to read them in order. As you progress through the material, you may find references to other chapters that provide additional context or information on a specific topic. In these cases, you can easily refer to the relevant chapter to deepen your understanding of the subject matter.

Who is the book written for?

"Is this book useful for you?"

It depends on your knowledge and experience. There is nothing to stop you from learning the concepts and applying them. However, to maximize the outcome, it is better to have a minimum understanding of Android components and IPC mechanisms and a few years of experience in software development. Here is some roles that could gain from the book:

1. **Android Developers** – Those building apps for mobile, automotive, and other Android-based systems.
2. **Cybersecurity Professionals** – Individuals focused on securing Android applications and platforms.

3. **AOSP Engineers** – Those integrating Android into embedded and automotive systems or developing at system level.
4. **Technical Leads, Team Leads & Architects** – Decision-makers responsible for secure system design and development.
5. **Students & Researchers** – Learners exploring Android security fundamentals and best practices.

You will find the topics and information cover different levels of Android development, from the application layer to HAL. Also due the the nature of Android the security concerns for various programming languages such as Java, Kotlin, and C/C++ are discussed. There has been an effort to provide a practical guide that you can use at any time, regardless of what you are developing in Android.

The books includes some real-world incidents linked to various vulnerabilities. By examining these case studies, along with their respective CWE (Common Weakness Enumeration) or CVE (Common Vulnerabilities and Exposures) codes, you will better understand the probable risks and threats that can occur due to inadequate input validation and handling, etc. This practical approach highlights the essence of secure coding techniques and shows how to apply them effectively in real-life scenarios.

Likewise, the chapters emphasize the importance of secure coding principles and their relationship with specific CWE codes. By doing that, I will give you a clear roadmap on how to apply these principles to mitigate potential vulnerabilities and improve the overall security of your applications. This book desires to provide you with the knowledge and tools needed to build resilient software that can withstand the ever-evolving challenges of the digital landscape. With a strong foundation in secure design &development you will be better prepared to safeguard your applications and protect your users from potential threats.

Though the title is *Secure Android Design and Development*, at least half of it could be used in different industries due to the common and general points provided in programming, especially in security principles. If you work in embedded areas, such as telecommunications, etc., you can still apply the principles and practical recommendations in your projects.

Hope it comes in handy!

The big picture

> “No matter how tall the mountain is, it cannot block the sun.” — Chinese Proverb

We need to start the security process at the beginning of the project. As a result, it should be included in the requirements that will influence the design and architecture as much as it can affect the test scenarios. Having more eyes on design, code, and development will help find the issues more efficiently than relying on one person. Protecting the application and its assets, such as data, will only be feasible with a better understanding of the principles that have been introduced and utilized for a long time. Any breaches could also compromise the system, which demands knowing the system and the environment in which our application is running.

We have the opportunity to learn from history. The commonly reported issues, best practices in design and development, and knowledge of operating systems, compilers, libraries, lint tools, etc., help us understand how an attack could occur. Once we have a good insight into how an attack happens, we can find a way to mitigate it. Here, you can see the big picture of what we will try to cover:

- Principles
- Development cycle
- Threat Modelling
- Attack & Defence
- Common issues
- Knowing the OS
- Data & Network
- Compiler and tools

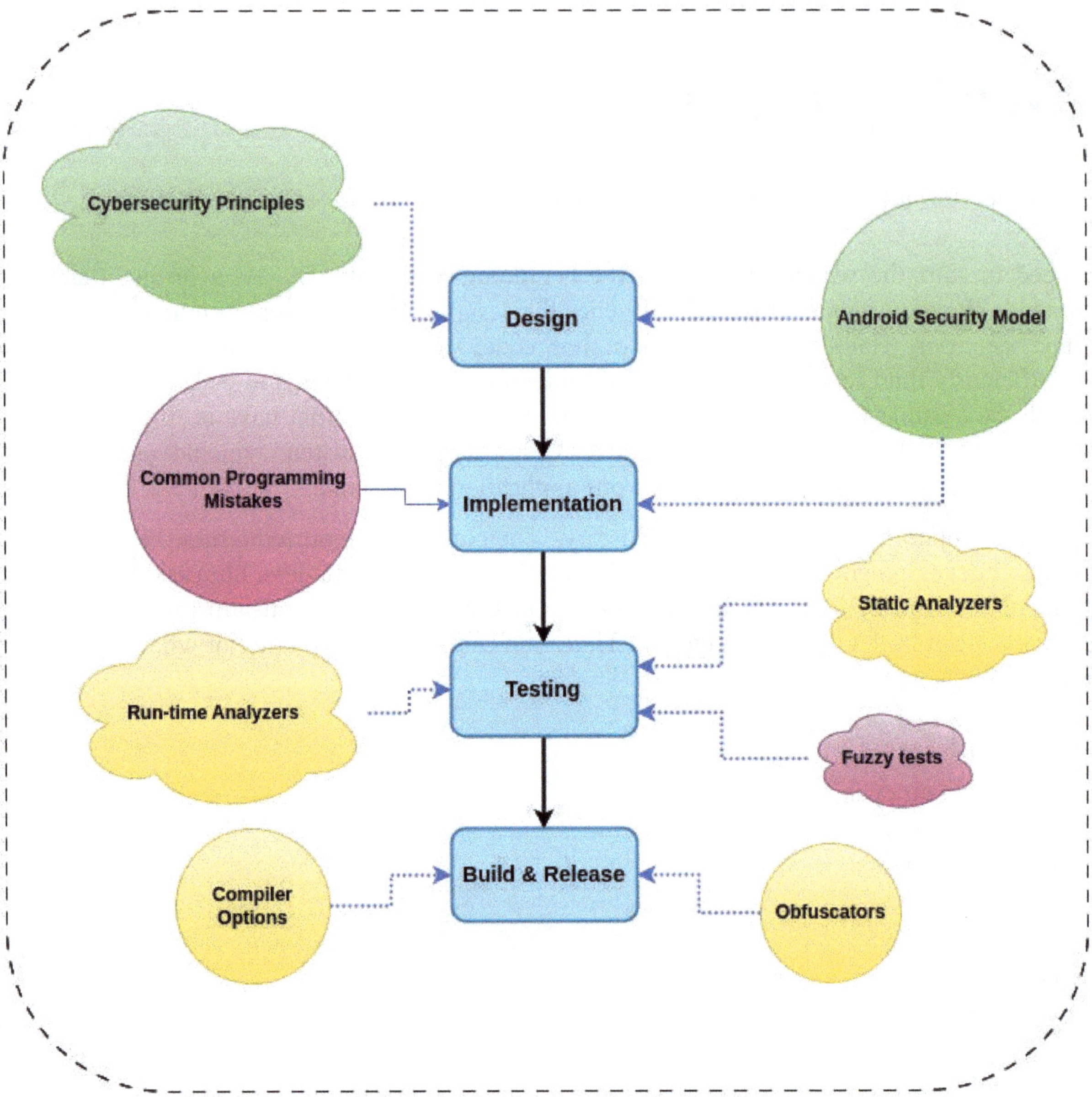

Figure 1. Big Picture Diagram

One more thing to mention here is the variety of programming languages. Android uses the Linux kernel, with some adjustments to fit it for Android's purposes and requirements. Linux kernel is developed by C, but C++ implements the Android HAL layer daemons/services. Going toward the upper layer, you will find that most system services and the framework are developed in Java. We still use Java for many reasons, while many developers and companies have utilized Kotlin for application-layer development. We could use it to build system services or extend the Android framework, which some companies are doing. If you're an Android system engineer, you need full-stack development knowledge, especially in a tech/team lead or architect role. We will discuss secure development in these languages in the chapter on common mistakes.

Do We Need to Secure an Android Application?

One crucial question we can ask ourselves—or that might be asked—is: Do we need to secure an Android application? In other words, is secure development for Android necessary?

At first glance, this question has no simple, immediate answer. The answer depends on multiple factors, including:

- The application's functionality
- The type and sensitivity of user data the app handles, accesses, or stores
- The level of permissions the application has
- The layer of the system where the application operates
- The type of device the application runs on

For example, securing an app designed for consumer smartphones and tablets fundamentally differs from securing an automotive application running in a vehicle's infotainment system.

Similarly, an application that only displays weather forecasts does not require the same security considerations as an application that handles banking or financial transactions. Likewise, social networking and news-reading apps belong to entirely different security categories.

Different Use Cases and Their Security Considerations

Let's consider different application domains:

- Healthcare applications: These apps handle highly sensitive personal data.
- Financial applications deal with critical monetary transactions and sensitive banking details.
- System applications: Apps running at the system level may have extensive access to device internals, making their security crucial.

For instance, consider an application that continuously listens to the surrounding environment, such as voice assistants like Siri or Google Assistant that activate when a wake word is detected. Such an app could raise privacy concerns in two ways:

1. It can monitor the user's surroundings.
2. Depending on its system-level access, it may perform unintended actions.

The language and layer at which the app is developed also influence its security risks. An app written in Java or Kotlin is subject to different risks than an app written in C++ at the native layer, where memory safety and manual memory management become more critical.

Similarly, the security requirements shift significantly when moving from consumer apps (for mobile, TV, and tablets) to the automotive sector. Previously, we discussed privacy concerns, financial security, and healthcare data security. However, safety is a primary concern in automotive software.

For instance, an application running on a vehicle's infotainment system can have varying levels of system access and data exposure, potentially affecting the user's privacy and passenger safety. In such cases, security breaches could lead to serious real-world consequences.

Security as a Spectrum, Not a Binary Choice

Ultimately, various factors and characteristics influence how much we should place on secure development.

Beyond these considerations, one critical takeaway is that many security best practices have little to no cost in terms of development effort or performance overhead. Throughout this book, I have highlighted guidelines and techniques that are easy to implement without requiring additional development time or complexity.

For example:

- Encrypting stored data
- Avoiding logging sensitive information
- Properly handling permissions

These simple yet highly effective measures require minimal effort but significantly improve security.

Thus, security is not a single fixed requirement. Instead, we deal with a spectrum of security needs shaped by various parameters such as functionality, data sensitivity, system access, and target device type.

Principles and Methodologies

"Even a poor plan is better than no plan at all." – Mikhail Chigorin [1]

Gravity of principles (The rules of the game)

Any game has its rules and principles developed from the day it was introduced. Let's look at chess. A chess game can be divided into three phases: the Opening, the middlegame, and the Endgame. Each phase has some specific considerations. In the opening, some general principles might be developing your pieces, taking control of the center, and following your plan. There are lots of documents, real games, and history behind chess. Of course, you can learn them at your own pace by learning from your failures and maybe your victories. Then, your progress will be based on your time playing, your opponent's level, how you document, etc. But you can speed up the process with a better approach! Taking courses and reading articles and books could save you from a month to a few years. Indeed, it would be best to practice whatever you have learned, but you don't need to reinvent the wheel.

That is the same in software development. We can get experience and learn slowly during our career or learn the principles and proven approaches to save time and resources. At the same time, they help us think clearly and systematically. It is totally up to us to select the path.

This chapter presents some principles that could help design more secure software. Each principle will give you a new perspective on how to look at your product. Each principle gives us a new perspective that can be applied to the development process, especially when we spend time designing the system, application, communication, etc.

At the end of each section, I have provided some questions to help you identify the subjects and verify how you have successfully applied the principles to your design and implementation.

The Fail-Safe vs Fail-Secure Principle (Planning for the Unexpected)

- What would happen if a security system were disconnected from some modules or sensors? Should we set off the Alarm or continue working in silence?
- What should be done if the electricity is cut off from an emergency door controlled from the center? Should it be open or be kept closed?

[1] Mikhail Chigorin was a Russian master and a world-class player. He tied for first place in the 1889 New York tournament and won the first three All-Russian tournaments from 1899 to 1903. (From chess.com)

These are some examples of the events of a failure in which the default behavior could make a considerable difference based on the industry, functionalities, and requirements.

That is where the difference between fail-safe and fail-secure will appear. The priority might be different in each situation. In an emergency door scenario, the door should be open to keep the people safe and let them exit. On the other hand, the security system should set off the alarm to guarantee security since there might be an intrusion!

Both principles are essential in various fields, including automotive, aviation, medical, and others. However, we must determine which comes first in the design and implementation phases.

The Fail-safe principle entails designing systems so that if they fail, they will fail in a manner that minimizes harm or damage. This concept is highly applicable in software development and security, where unexpected failures can have devastating impacts.

Fail-secure prioritizes security over safety since the system should be as secure as it is or even more in case of failures.

Fail-Safe Principle in Software Development

The Fail-Safe principle encourages software developers to anticipate potential failures and design systems that can gracefully handle them.

Similarly, we should design and develop software systems to prepare for and recover from failures. The Systems could heal or exit safely without causing further damage except for exception handling and logging, which can help catch and diagnose failures.

Companies invest heavily in safety to meet standards and confirm that systems accurately function when it matters most. However, we know that even overlooking a single condition in a complex system could happen because of a deadline, resources, etc. On the other hand, we are interested in finding unforeseen issues in the development phase since it is more resource-efficient than discovering them later.

Failures can have unredeemable consequences in industries such as the automotive and medicine industries. It emphasizes the significance of adhering to foundational principles throughout the design process.

Fail-Secure Principle

A security system must be designed to default to a secure state in case of failure. This means that if a system fails, it should fail in a way that does not expose the system to additional risk or allow unauthorized access. In general, there are three approaches to a security mechanism:

- Allow the operation
- Disallow the operation
- Throw an exception

Saltzer-Schroeder article

Jerome Saltzer and *Michael Schroeder* published "The Protection of Information in Computer Systems"[2], one of the most influential papers, and introduced some systematic information security principles. In this article, the definition of *Fail-Safe Defaults* pointed to the access permission, which from some point of view could cover both fail-safe and fail-secure definitions. For instance, access to the vehicle's doors should be granted by default in case of an accident, while disconnecting from the sensors should not open the doors. In both cases, the access to the doors is the subject, but the conditions and contexts could change the points of view.

I have separated them (as some others have done) to distinguish the situations and avoid any confusion.

Each approach will lead to a different outcome if incidents or failures happen. Let's have a look at some examples in security:

-Firewall: Consider a firewall as an example. If the firewall fails or loses power, a fail-secure design would default to blocking all incoming traffic rather than allowing all traffic to pass through. This way, the system remains secure in the event of a failure.

-Authentication system: What might happen if the authentication system fails? Will it grant access? Obviously, no! The system should default to denying access rather than granting it. For example, if a biometric scanner fails to read a user's fingerprint correctly, the system should deny access rather than mistakenly grant it.

The Fail-Safe and Fail-Secure principle encourages a proactive approach to potential failures in software and security systems. As developers or designers, we should plan for the worst to ensure that the systems are resilient and capable of handling unexpected events in a manner that minimizes damage and maintains security. Through careful design and anticipation of potential failures, we can create software and security systems that are robust and reliable in the face of the unexpected. We must pay attention to the fact that it's not just about preventing failures but also managing them effectively when they occur.

Fail-Safe as questions

- Do systems default to a safe operational state during unexpected failures?
- Are processes designed to prioritize safety over functionality in failure scenarios?
- Do I implement mechanisms to shut down or effectively isolate affected components during failures?
- Are there clear procedures in place for handling failures without escalating risks?
- Have I tested system responses to ensure failures do not propagate or cause harm to users or assets?

Fail-Secure as questions

[2] Saltzer, Jerome; Schroeder, Michael (April 17, 1975). "The Protection of Information in Computer Systems" (https://www.cs.virginia.edu/~evans/cs551/saltzer/)

- Do I default to denying access in case of system failure or error?
- Are systems configured to fail in a manner that maintains security rather than availability?
- Do I log failure events to identify patterns and improve system robustness?
- Are critical systems tested regularly to verify they fail securely?
- Do automated processes revert to secure states during interruptions or malfunctions?

Least Common Mechanism

The least common mechanism is among the various principles that form the bedrock of cybersecurity. It holds that mechanisms shared by more than one user or process should be minimized, influencing the architecture, design, and implementation of systems and protocols.

The principle of Least Common Mechanism stems from the idea that sharing mechanisms or resources among multiple users or processes can lead to potential security vulnerabilities. The more commonality among mechanisms, the greater the risk of one user's activities affecting another user, either inadvertently or maliciously. The standard mechanism could be a shared library, SDK, service, etc.; the users could be systems, processes, or even humans.

Sharing can lead to information leakage between users or processes, either by exposing sensitive data or providing avenues for one user to affect the operation of another. Shared mechanisms can also become a *single point of failure*, where an issue with a shared mechanism can affect multiple users or processes.

The Significance of the Principle

The Least Common Mechanism principle provides the system with robustness and reliability. Minimizing shared mechanisms reduces the attack surface and limits the potential for unauthorized access or data leakage, which enhances system resilience.

In practical terms, the Least Common Mechanism guides system designers in compartmentalizing or segregating system resources, limiting global variables or resources, and carefully managing and restricting the sharing of resources such as memory, network connections, and files.

Practical Examples

- Operating Systems: Modern operating systems have applied this principle by separating processes into their individual memory spaces. This prevents a bug or security vulnerability in one process from affecting others and avoids unintended information leakage between processes.
- Database Access: Consider an application that accesses a database. If every application component shares the same database access credentials, a compromise in one area could lead to unauthorized database access. Following the Least Common Mechanism principle, each element should have its credentials, with privileges restricted to only what that component needs. This limits the potential damage if one component's credentials are compromised.

- Microservices Architecture: In a Microservices Architecture, each service is isolated and runs its process, reducing the sharing of resources and limiting the scope of potential attacks. This is an example of the Least Common Mechanism principle in action, where the lack of shared mechanisms increases the system's overall security.
- Cloud Environments: In a cloud environment, the hypervisor is often used, which allows multiple virtual machines to share the same physical hardware. This can pose security risks. To mitigate this, some cloud providers offer dedicated hosts where a single user's virtual machines are the only ones running on a particular piece of hardware, eliminating the standard mechanism.

Least Common as questions

- Do I minimize shared mechanisms to reduce the attack surface?
- Are resources and processes segregated to limit unintended interaction?
- Do I ensure that shared systems have robust isolation controls in place?
- Are users, processes, and systems restricted from accessing shared services they do not explicitly need?
- Do I periodically review shared resources to identify and address potential risks?

Separation of Privilege and Least Privilege

The Separation of Privilege principle can be seen as an extension of the Principle of Least Privilege. While the Principle of Least Privilege ensures that users are granted the minimum levels of access necessary to complete their tasks, the Separation of Privilege takes it further by requiring two distinct privileges for specific actions.

The architecture of a system or product should provide an appropriate level of modularity to apply the Least Privilege principle. The architecture and design of your DB, services, and APIs could limit your use of the Least Privilege.

Assume you want to design and develop an Android application providing two main functionalities:

- Cloud-based photo printing
- Photo enhancement If you implement them as two separate services in your app, you can protect them from each other in case of any security flaws. Also, you might be able to keep your API keys or tokens safe. Besides, you can develop separate IPC mechanisms for each service to reduce the risk of data breach. It was a quick example of how the architecture and design of an application could empower you to apply security principles.

Separation of privileges is designed to prevent any single person from being able to compromise a critical part of the system. In essence, it's a strategy for reducing risk by spreading the ability to perform sensitive operations across multiple points.

Some of the benefits of Least Privilege

- Minimize the attack surface: By restricting the applications and processes to only the required accesses and the permissions
- Prevention of data breach: Limited access to sensitive data and resources reduce the incidental leaks

Some of the benefits of the Separation of Privilege

- Increased Security: Requiring multiple conditions or checks to operate significantly reduces the risk of malicious attacks or insider threats.
- Reduced Errors: When two or more parties are required to approve an action, the likelihood of mistakes is minimized.
- Enhanced Accountability: When more than one individual is involved, there is increased accountability, making it harder for malicious activity to go unnoticed.

Examples of Separation of Privilege & Least Privilege

Let's look at some examples of how the Principle of Separation of Privilege can be applied in practice:

- Financial Transactions: In many banking systems, significant transactions require approval from two separate individuals. This measure ensures that a single person cannot unilaterally move large sums of money, providing a check against fraud or mistakes.
- System Administration: In a corporate network, certain administrative functions, such as creating new user accounts or granting elevated privileges, could require approval from two administrators. This practice would guarantee that every administrator makes critical changes with oversight.
- Software Deployment: In a DevOps environment, deploying a new software version into production might require separate approvals from a developer and a system administrator. This separation of privileges ensures that no single individual can push changes to production without review.
- Android: In Android development, this principle can manifest in various ways, such as:
  - Running different components of an application under different user IDs to limit the scope of permissions. For example, an app feature that requires network access might run under a user ID that is allowed network access. In contrast, a different component that doesn't * require network access runs under a different user ID without such privileges.
  - Using Android's permission model to request only the permissions necessary for each component or feature within the app.

Implementing role-based access controls within the app so that different users have different capabilities, depending on their role.

These two security principles are powerful approaches for boosting security and accountability in systems with delicate procedures. Although putting this idea into practice may appear complicated, especially regarding operational effectiveness, its increased security makes it a crucial factor in designing safe systems and applications. Regarding security, remember that a second opinion is frequently preferable to one.

Separation of Privilege as Questions

- Are critical tasks divided among multiple individuals/roles could reduce the risk of fraud and error?
- Do I ensure that no single person, process, or system has end-to-end control over sensitive processes?
- Is there a system for regularly reviewing and monitoring roles and access?

The Zero Trust Principle: Trust No One, Verify Everything

The Zero Trust principle is a new approach to network security that assumes no trust by default. This principle is built on the mantra of "trust no one, verify everything," regardless of whether a request comes from within or outside the network. Zero Trust is a response to the evolving landscape of cybersecurity threats, where traditional network boundaries have become blurred and insufficient to protect against sophisticated attacks.

Traditional security models often assume that everything inside an organization's network can be trusted. However, this approach is no longer suitable in the age of advanced persistent threats, where attackers often find ways to infiltrate networks undetected.

The Zero Trust model assumes that threats can come from anywhere—inside or outside the network—and that every request and user must be authenticated and authorized.

While zero trust was introduced to verify requests coming from the network, we could use it as an approach in the architecture and design of applications as well. Though we might have network-based scenarios to apply the zero trust principle in Android, we have a lot of inter-process and within operating system communications to utilize this principle. For example, consider the system APIs in the Android framework, which regular applications cannot use. Alternatively, a service provided by a regular app that is only available to system apps or the applications signed with the same private key. These are examples of how we could apply zero trust to secure the system and applications.

Zero-trust security revolves around a few critical elements:

- Least Privilege Access: Grant users and systems only the access they need to perform their tasks and nothing more. This approach minimizes the potential damage in the event of a breach.

- Micro-segmentation: It reduces lateral movement in the event of an attack and divides the network into tiny, isolated segments.
- Continuous Verification: Continuously validate the security status of the systems and the users. In the zero-trust model, a single point of authentication is not enough.

Examples of Zero Trust

Let's look at some examples to understand the application of the zero-trust principle in security:

Access Control:

In a zero-trust environment, every user must authenticate and verify their identity, regardless of location (in the office or remote). For instance, an employee wants to access a sensitive company document. In that case, they must authenticate their identity, even if they access it from a company device inside the network.

Micro-segmentation:

Suppose a company has an extensive network comprising several services, including a payment system, a customer database, and an employee portal. In a zero-trust approach, these services would be separated into individual segments. If an attacker could access the employee portal, the attack would be confined to that segment and couldn't quickly spread to the payment system or customer database.

Multi-factor Authentication (MFA):

Zero Trust also includes the implementation of MFA, which requires users to provide two or more verification factors to access resources. For instance, after entering a password (something the user knows), they might also need to respond to a prompt on their smartphone (something the user has). MFA provides an extra degree of protection, preventing access even if a password is compromised.

Applying Zero Trust to Android Development

SELinux & App permissions

Android has been equipped with two methods that work in conjunction to offer adequate defense against unwanted access to protected resources and the system. The first line of defense at the application layer is permissions, which deny any attempt to access a system API or even a protected resource like a service that may require a specific permission and signature to function. The next layer that makes sure the request is approved and the program is given access is SELinux [3]. For

[3]Security-Enhanced Linux "(SELinux) is a security enhancement to Linux which allows users and administrators more control over access control". SELinux Project Wiki (https://selinuxproject.org/page/Main_Page)

the priv and system applications, the situation is a bit different since they could access system-level APIs. First, the permissions should be on the white/allowed list. Additionally, the requested access—which could be a file, API, etc.—should have the appropriate SELinux policy set up. Any request made to a system-level API will first be examined at the system level before being examined with SELinux at the kernel level. As you can see, SELinux needs to check; passing the system level won't be a free pass.

In today's complex and evolving cybersecurity landscape, the Zero Trust model could be a proactive approach to securing resources. By adopting a "trust no one, verify everything" stance, applications and services could ensure that every access request is fully authenticated and authorized, reducing the likelihood of unauthorized access and breaches. After all, in cybersecurity, it's better to be safe than sorry.

Zero Trust as questions

- Do I verify every access attempt, regardless of its origin (internal or external)?
- Are all processes, users, devices, and systems authenticated and authorized before granting access?
- Do I use least privilege principles with Zero Trust to limit access?
- Is data encrypted both in transit and at rest, even within the network?
- Do I continuously monitor and assess trust levels based on user behavior and context?

KISS: The Principle of Least Complexity in Security

The Principle of Least Complexity, also known as the KISS (Keep It Simple, Stupid) principle, could be considered a guideline in software design, particularly in cybersecurity. Less complexity in systems and design could lead to identifying and resolving the potential security issues more easily. Also, it reduces the likelihood of vulnerabilities and ensures better understanding, maintenance, and troubleshooting. Let's start.

This Principle emphasizes the need for simplicity in software and systems design. Let's take a look at some reasons that show how it could improve security:

- Reduced attack surface: An attacker can exploit a simpler system with fewer components and features.
- Increased maintainability: Simpler systems are easier to maintain, update, and patch, helping to keep security up to date.
- Enhanced understanding: A less complex system is more transparent and easier to understand, making it easier to identify and address potential security issues.
- Minimized human error: Complex systems are more prone to human error and misconfigurations, which can lead to security vulnerabilities.

Examples of the Principle of Least Complexity in Android

Android, the popular mobile operating system, provides several examples of how the Principle of Least Complexity can be applied to improve security:

- Minimizing permissions: Limiting the permissions requested by an Android app helps reduce the attack surface. By requesting only necessary permissions, you can ensure that an attacker cannot exploit the app to access sensitive user data or system resources.
- Using established APIs: Android developers should use well-established APIs and libraries provided by the Android platform to avoid introducing unnecessary complexity and potential security vulnerabilities.
- Limiting features and components: Android apps should be designed to include only the essential features and components required for their functionality. This helps reduce potential attack vectors and minimizes the risk of introducing security vulnerabilities.

Some KISS principle best practices

- Simplifying code: Writing clear, concise, and modular code can make it easier for developers and security experts to understand and audit the application. By decomposing complex functionalities into smaller, simpler components, developers can minimize the chances of errors and vulnerabilities.
- Simplifying user interfaces: Designing user-friendly and easy-to-understand user interfaces can empower users to follow security best practices, such as using strong passwords, granting only necessary permissions, and enabling two-factor authentication, etc.
- Streamlining the authentication process: Implementing a simple and secure authentication process using established libraries and protocols, such as OAuth or OpenID Connect, can help reduce the potential for vulnerabilities and make it easier for users to maintain security best practices.
- Reducing dependencies: Limiting the number of third-party libraries and frameworks used in an Android application can help minimize the attack surface and reduce potential security risks. By using only well-vetted, well-maintained, and necessary dependencies, developers can better manage the complexity and security of their applications.

KISS as questions

- Are my security policies and mechanisms easy to understand and implement?
- Have I avoided unnecessary complexity in system design that could introduce vulnerabilities?
- Do I use straightforward, well-documented solutions over intricate or custom implementations?
- Are users trained to follow simple, secure processes instead of overly complicated procedures?
- Have I reduced the number of components or dependencies in critical security systems?

Defense in Depth

The Defense in Depth (DiD) principle is another concept in cybersecurity, also known as layered security. It refers to managing risk with multiple defensive layers that aim to prevent security breaches and protect valuable data. This approach recognizes that no single protection method can completely safeguard against potential threats. Instead, it advocates using multiple security measures to provide a more comprehensive Defense.

The defense-in-depth principle is rooted in a military strategy that aims to delay rather than prevent an attacker's advance, buying time and reducing the chances of a direct hit on a single point of Defense. This strategy translates into implementing multiple layers of security controls throughout an information system.

These layers could include physical security, network security, application security, and more, each designed to protect information differently. If one layer is breached, others are still in place to protect the system.

Examples

Let's have a look at a few examples to understand the application of the defense-in-depth principle:

A Defense in Depth strategy in an ordinary IT system comprises several key elements:

- Access Control: Managing who has access to a network and to what extent.
- Firewalls: They are devices or software designed to block unauthorized access to a network.
- Intrusion Detection Systems (IDS): It monitors systems and networks for hostile activities or policy violations.
- Encryption: Preventing unauthorized access by transforming information into a code.
- Antivirus Software: Programs developed to detect and eliminate computer viruses.
- User Training: Educating users about safe practices, recognizing potential threats, and understanding company security policies.

Physical Security:

This is the first layer of defense. It involves securing the physical infrastructure housing the computer systems. Security measures can include locked doors, security guards, CCTV cameras, and biometric access controls.

Network Security:

This layer focuses on securing the network with firewalls that regulate incoming and outgoing traffic according to predefined security rules.

Application Security:

This layer is focused on protecting the apps that are used in a company. Measures can include regular software updates and patches, secure coding practices, and regular security testing.

Data Security:

In order to protect the data, this layer frequently uses encryption to make it unreadable by unauthorized parties. Additionally, it has backup and recovery features to ensure that data can be recovered if it is lost or corrupted.

User Training and Awareness:

Human-centered security incidents are still high, making users a vulnerable point in security. So, training users could be considered one of the most integral layers of a defense-in-depth strategy. As a result, training them to recognize potential threats (like phishing emails) and follow safe practices could reduce the number of incidents.

Example of an Android application Consider placing private data in an Android app for social media, banking, or other purposes. The first line of Defense is user authentication, which can be accomplished using a username-password combination, biometrics, etc. The server side's second step is to compare it to its hashes and encrypted database. However, a suitable protocol should be used to secure the network connection.

Following that, a credential might be obtained, which should be kept safe. Depending on the viewpoint, each layer may function as part of a defense-in-depth. In this case, even the first login method is defense-in-depth if you look at mobile devices. Afterward, storing the data properly and keeping it as safe as possible with different mechanisms could be the other layers of protection. (It was a simple example but not a complete solution to demonstrate how defense in depth can be used in practice.)

These days, we shouldn't rely solely on one layer of security and mechanism; rather, we need to combine several different mechanisms and apply them in layers.

Several levels of defense could develop a complete security posture that can resist a variety of threats. Although no security measure is perfect, systems and applications could build a robust Defense that can stop, detect, and react to a variety of assaults by integrating several security measures. Defense in depth is more than just a guiding philosophy in the dynamic field of cybersecurity—it's a requirement.

Defense in Depth as questions

- Do I have multiple layers of security controls to protect the critical assets?
- Are these layers independent, such that the failure of one does not compromise the system?
- Have I tested my layered defenses against potential attack scenarios?

Defensive, Offensive, and Aggressive Programming

Development stance

An approach to software development guided by an underlying philosophy or mindset is known as a "development stance". It influences the team's culture, decision-making, and development process. This approach is more flexible and abstract, allowing for customization based on the project's requirements and context.

Development method (methodology)

A development method is an organized and formalized collection of software development procedures, techniques, and equipment that provides a thorough, step-by-step plan for completing a project. It has clear rules and guidelines to ensure consistency and adherence to best practices, making it more prescriptive and strict. What is

Aspect	*Development Stance*	*Development Method*
Definition	Philosophy, mindset, or approach guiding software development.	Formalized set of processes, practices , and tools for software development.
Focus	Shaping approach, mindset, and culture.	Providing a detailed, step-by-step process.
Flexibility	More abstract and flexible.	More prescriptive and rigid.
Implementation	Embracing and internalizing principles and values; may require organizational changes.	Adopting specific practices, techniques, and tools; may require training and documentation.

Defensive programming

This approach aims to develop code that can run properly even in unforeseen states, user inputs, etc. The developer should anticipate different states and try to handle them to make the software continue properly. To make it happen, we should consider different terms:

- Handle unexpected user inputs, data, etc. comprehensively.
- Increase the code quality and reduce bugs through code review, static and dynamic analysis, etc.

- Develop and run different levels of tests, such as test units, functional tests, etc., as much as possible.

It also helps to ensure that any new revision can pass the last test, as it will pass the new tests, even the ones that should not happen. For instance, an empty list or a null pointer exceeding the expected length can lead to unexpected behavior from the method. Still, in defense programming, we will go further and cover the internal errors as well, which might not be efficient.

However, this approach has a paradox since we can not cover every possible state without making the code more complicated; it demands more resources, such as money, time, and energy.

When to use Defensive programming

Suppose you are interfacing directly with our world, especially hardware or any kind of communication or libraries that might have unforeseen behaviors. In that case, you need to consider handling the exceptions that might happen because of the timeout, failure, etc.

Handling exceptions is not a good approach during the development process since the developer will not be aware of the problem. The recommendation is to use the defensive approach for production rather than development. If there is any error or mistake, we need to know about it and fix it.

Pros

- Make the critical systems more stable & reliable as they continue working
- Cover even the not probable conditions

Cons

- Hiding the errors and problems
- It is hard to debug the code other than by logging any errors.
- Make the code more complicated to cover all the states

Example

```java
import java.util.Scanner;

public class DefensiveUserRegistration {

    public static String validateUsername(String username) {
        if (username == null || username.trim().isEmpty()) {
            throw new IllegalArgumentException("Error: Username cannot be empty or n\
ull.");
        }
        return username;
    }

    public static String validatePassword(String password) {
        if (password == null || password.length() < 6) {
            throw new IllegalArgumentException("Error: Password must be at least 6 c\
haracters long.");
        }
        return password;
    }

    public static void registerUser(String username, String password) {
        try {
            username = validateUsername(username);
            password = validatePassword(password);
            System.out.println("User registered successfully: " + username);
        } catch (IllegalArgumentException e) {
            System.out.println(e.getMessage());
        }
    }

    public static void main(String[] args) {
        Scanner scanner = new Scanner(System.in);

        System.out.print("Enter username: ");
        String username = scanner.nextLine();

        System.out.print("Enter password: ");
        String password = scanner.nextLine();

        registerUser(username, password);
        scanner.close();
    }
}
```

Offensive programming

Offensive programming can be considered a branch of defensive programming with a different attitude. While defensive programming stresses handling all kinds of exceptions due to external and internal reasons, offensive programming emphasizes leaving internal reasons to rise and trying to catch the external source. So, errors are divided into two categories: acceptable and preventable.

What is acceptable?

- Invalid (not improper) external inputs containing user inputs and other external sources
- Hardware-related errors/failures
- The system caused exceptions from system resources such as storage, network, and memory

What should be handled

- Out of defined conditions, input values for the internal functions (range, length)
- Undefined condition behaviors and return values
- Invalid function input parameters
- In simple terms, the offensive programming approach makes the errors bold and detectable.

Pros

- Nice approach for the development process
- Simpler code compared to defensive programming
- No hiding the bugs
- Force to deal with the bug but to let it be revealed. We need to Fail Fast

Cons

- Might influence the reputation because of the crashes
- Make the system unstable
- Can not be used in critical, real-time, or safety-critical services and systems
- It can't be ignored by customers if they appear repeatedly

Note: It is vital to have minimal offensive programming and not rely on the proper input for the system's critical modules, services, and applications.

Note: We will cover input validation (such as user input or external sources) later to secure the software but not to shut down the exceptions.

Example

```
public class OffensiveProgramming {
  public static int divide(int numerator, int denominator) {
      assert (denominator != 0) : "Denominator cannot be zero";
      return numerator / denominator;
  }


  public static void main(String[] args) {
      int result = divide(10, 0); // Will throw an AssertionError if assertions are \
enabled
      System.out.println("Result: " + result);
  }
}
```

Aggressive programming

In a time-critical project where delivery time plays a crucial role, we need to take another approach to make it possible to meet the deadline. It should focus only on the most essential features and functionalities of software rather than all aspects. Getting a prototype ready might happen once in the project's lifetime. At this moment, we put as much effort into feature development as possible while having an appropriate plan for testing. Aggressive programming is an approach suited for these times. However, after the delivery, we need to adjust the plan again to work on the other aspects skipped during the development. For instance, how we communicate, modules, etc., might change while we plan to return to normal development.

We can list other kinds of programming, such as functional, object-oriented, etc. We looked at those programming approaches more directly related to security; however, I cannot refute the idea that a clean architecture, modularity, etc., can lead to better quality that affects security.

Best practice

To take the best approach, we need to combine different techniques. In the development process, offensive programming helps to find bugs as soon as possible before delivering them to customers. Defensive programming for inputs from external sources is needed, especially hardware-related inputs. For the released version, it's better to report the bugs and errors silently. Then, the product continues working while we get feedback from the logs and fix them for the new versions.

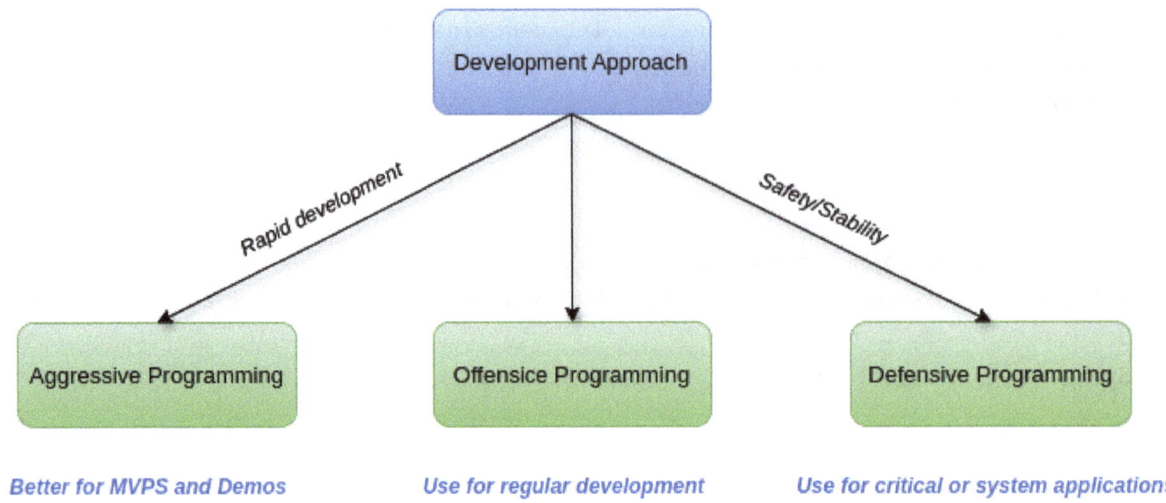

Figure 2. Software Development Methodologies

Notes on Modularity, cohesion, and coupling

We have gone through different principles, which have helped us to make better decisions in the design phase. You might have translated them to other design and architecture principles such as modularity, cohesion, etc. The truth is that how we design our applications and services will directly influence their security. Now, it is more apparent that even the regular design recommendations would be helpful. For instance, as much as we reduce the complexity of the implementation, it will be easier to tighten the fence over the app. Or we could consider splitting a service into multiple services so that they don't affect the functionality or performance by considering modularity. In that case, we can limit each service's access to the system resources. Plus, they probably won't be affected by a compromised service.

The Importance of Software Design and Implementation Beyond Platform-Specific Techniques

Here, I'd like to highlight an important point: Software design and implementation play a crucial role, regardless of the platform-specific techniques you use for development.

For example, in this chapter, we explored various principles, each offering a unique perspective on software development. Concepts like keeping software simple (KISS) or defense in depth directly influence architecture and software design.

There's a well-known term called Clean Architecture and Clean Code. Of course, there are different guidelines and methodologies available. Some are fundamental principles, while others are just best practices. For example, SOLID principles are widely discussed. However, there are two extremes when applying them:

1. Blindly enforcing them without understanding their impact can lead to over-complexity.
2. Ignoring them entirely can result in poor maintainability and scalability.

The key takeaway here is a general and universal principle that applies to almost every situation: Use the right tools and principles wisely and appropriately.

Principles and Software Complexity

Principles are just one set of tools at our disposal. Other important software design concepts include:

- Modularity
- Cohesion and Coherence
- Complexity management
- Architecture and its impact on implementation

Software architecture directly influences implementation and vice versa. At the implementation level, we have design choices that apply to modules, classes, functions, and even individual lines of code. Many of these concepts have evolved over the history of software engineering, and each provides valuable guidance.

For instance, understanding how to simplify conditions in code is crucial. Conditional statements are powerful but can also introduce unnecessary complexity. Some might even ask, *"Is it possible to write code without if-statements?"* In some cases, yes—but achieving that requires experience and practice over time.

Many books, articles, and videos explore these topics in detail when discussing SOLID principles, particularly the Single Responsibility Principle (SRP). Given their importance, I don't want to repeat those discussions unnecessarily, but I can't ignore them either.

For example, consider how SRP applies more to classes than functions when discussing complexity and modularity. If you try to enforce SRP at the function level, you might break tasks into too many smaller ones, some of which become shallow methods—functions that lack meaningful depth or reusability. Over-fragmenting functions doesn't necessarily improve maintainability.

Software Complexity and Security Risks

Understanding core programming principles remains essential in upcoming use-case-driven chapters focused on Android security.

You could apply every possible security technique to protect data storage, but if your software complexity leads to an unmanageable architecture or implementation, some execution paths or scenarios might go unnoticed.

Even with all the security techniques in place, a complex or poorly structured system might still introduce vulnerabilities, leaving potential entry points for unauthorized access.

Final Thoughts on Core Programming Concepts

As we progress, you'll notice that many problems can be solved at a higher level before reaching platform-specific or Android-specific techniques.

This is the key message I wanted to emphasize:
Before diving into platform-dependent security measures, focusing on sound software design and architecture can prevent many issues from arising in the first place.

Securing the Development Lifecycle

In the previous chapter, we discussed fundamental concepts and principles that can help us throughout a project, especially during the design and planning of our software, to ensure it is more secure and reliable. This applies to applications, services, or libraries. However, the key point here is that we follow a process known as the **software development process**, consisting of various stages and steps.

This process is not a straightforward, linear, and mechanical progression. Instead, it is complex, mainly because, at any stage, you may need to loop back, jump to a previous stage, and revise something overlooked or forgotten.

Typically, this process includes seven stages:

1. **Requirement Analysis**
2. **Planning and Feasibility Study**
3. **Software Design**
4. **Implementation and Coding**
5. **Testing and Quality Assurance**
6. **Deployment**
7. **Maintenance and Support**

Each stage plays a crucial role in the project's lifecycle and development, ultimately contributing to whether the software becomes more or less secure.

The **Requirement Analysis** phase typically leads to gathering more information and generating additional data based on the initial requirements analysis. This has a direct impact on the **architecture, design, and implementation** of the software. In fact, it can even influence other stages of the development process, such as:

- **Defining the level of testing**: determining at what levels testing should be conducted.
- **Planning the release strategy**: deciding how the project will be deployed and delivered.
- **Outlining maintenance strategies**: establishing how the project will be maintained and supported over time.

Since this phase establishes the foundation for the entire development process, any gaps or overlooked details at this stage can have cascading effects on later stages, potentially impacting the software's overall security, stability, and scalability. Now, I want to discuss these stages—or specific sub-components of them—that can help us develop more secure software.

Design Review

Now is a good time to connect to **Agile methodologies**. In Agile, we view the process as **incremental**, with the flexibility to accommodate changing requirements or features throughout the project's execution. This often leads to changes in **software architecture at a high level** or modifications in the **implementation approach**.

This is a natural occurrence because, as I mentioned earlier, in the **early stages of a project, our understanding is never complete**. Specific details—or even critical aspects—may remain hidden from us. That's why we must **incorporate design reviews** as a **non-continuous but essential activity** throughout the project.

For example, after the **Requirement Analysis phase**, we derive the **software characteristics and architecture** and proceed with the design. This design might be an **individual or team effort**, but even at this stage, a **design review** is necessary for aspects like **modularity, extensibility, stability, or maintainability**, but also for **security**.

Moreover, even after the **design phase**, when we enter the **implementation stage**, **design review remains relevant**. It is a valid topic that should be discussed, as design decisions can continue to impact security and overall software quality throughout development.

Code Review

The imperative role of code review

Software developers utilize a set of techniques and best practices known as secure coding to ensure that applications are developed and used to prevent unauthorized access, data tampering, and theft. Secure coding procedures must include security code reviews systematically examining software source code to find and correct flaws compromising the program's security.

Security code reviews can help developers create more secure applications and drastically lower the chance of security breaches by locating and correcting flaws and vulnerabilities in the code. Additionally, as these reviews frequently result in the discovery and correction of bugs and other problems unrelated to security but may nonetheless result in software instability, subpar performance, and other difficulties, they can also enhance the general quality of the product.

Due to the sensitive nature of the data and resources that Android applications frequently manage and the extensive range of attack vectors that bad actors can use to breach Android devices and user data, code reviews are critical in Android development.

Kick-off Meeting

A kick-off meeting between developers and reviewers should clarify the code review's objectives, expectations, and scope.

- Communicate the objective of the code review
- Agree on the timelines, milestones, and deliverables
- Clarify the roles and responsibilities of each team member
- Discuss any known areas of concern, potential risks, or challenges in the project

Code Review Checklist

Create a code review checklist to ensure that common problems, development standards, and best practices are effectively addressed throughout the review.

- Coding standards and conventions: language-specific coding standards, proper use of comments and documentation, consistent naming conventions, and proper indentation
- Architectural and design patterns: proper use of design patterns, separation of concerns, and adherence to the SOLID (Single responsibility, Open-closed, Liskov Substitution, Interface Segregation, and Dependency Inversion) principles
- Code Quality: efficient algorithms, optimized code, DRY (Don't Repeat Yourself) principle, and proper error handling
- Test coverage: unit tests, integration tests, and system tests
- Security: adherence to secure coding practices, proper authentication and authorization mechanisms, secure storage of sensitive data, proper input validation and output encoding, and proper handling of exceptions and error messages

Security Code Review Process

A proper security code review process should include the following stages:

Preparation:

Before the review can start, information must be gathered regarding the project being reviewed. This involves being aware of the technologies, the application's architecture, the project documentation, and the security specifications. At a minimum, a detailed explanation of what must be developed and how it interacts with other modules is required. The reviewer should also define the review's parameters and create an acceptable environment.

- Recognize the goals and specifications of the project.
- Familiarize yourself with the code architecture, modules, and components
- Be familiar with the languages, libraries, and frameworks utilized in the project
- Have a clear understanding of the security requirements of the project

Static Analysis:

During this step, the reviewer looks at the source code without running it, looking for any potential security flaws, coding errors, or departures from accepted practices. This can be done manually or automatically with tools like static code analyzers (such as linters, Clang Static Analyzer, and FindBugs for Java). Automated tools can save time by quickly locating problems in a big codebase. However, manual code reviews are still required to find more subtle vulnerabilities that automated tools can miss. Static analysis would be performed on the code before requesting a code review to save time and effort and avoid any team efforts. Then, before the manual review, any errors, issues, etc., can be fixed.

- Use static code analysis tools to identify common coding issues, such as unused variables, unreachable code, and overly complex functions
- Use security analysis tools to identify potential vulnerabilities in the code, such as SQL injection, cross-site scripting, and insecure encryption

We will discuss the static analyzers and introduce some of them later.

Dynamic Analysis:

In this stage, the reviewer concentrates on finding security flaws that can only be seen when the application is being used, such as runtime errors, inadequate input validation, or unsecured resource usage. This can be done manually using various testing approaches, such as penetration or fuzz testing, and dynamic analysis tools (such as debuggers, Valgrind, AddressSanitizer, etc.).

- Use dynamic analysis tools to detect run-time issues such as memory leaks, buffer overflows, and thread safety issues
- Use performance profiling tools to detect performance bottlenecks and resource-intensive operations in the code

Post-Review:

Following the static and dynamic analysis phases, the reviewer should list and rank the issues found, inform the development team about them, and help resolve them. The reviewer should also track how the problems were resolved to ensure they had been fully fixed and hadn't created any new vulnerabilities. This stage can lead to a request for change or code approval.

Manual Code Review

The reviewers must perform a manual code review using the provided code review checklist to review all updates and modifications to the code. At this phase, they should point out problems and offer suggestions to enhance the code's security, adherence to coding standards, and general quality.

- Go through the code changes and updates carefully
- Verify the code's compliance with the checklist
- Take notes on any identified issues and discuss them with other reviewers, if necessary
- Organize the feedback based on priority
- Provide transparent, respectful, and constructive feedback
- Provide examples or references if it is necessary
- Ensure that the feedback is actionable

Developer Updates and Follow-up

The developers should change the code according to the input after identifying faults and adding proposed enhancements. After the code upgrades, the reviewers should do another round of reviews to ensure that all problems have been fixed.

- Developers address the issues and update the code
- Reviewers perform a follow-up review to ensure all issues have been resolved
- Verify that the code review procedure has been completed.

Suppose we have a Java class for a simple calculator that performs basic arithmetic operations.

```java
public class Calculator {
    public int add(int a, int b) {
        return a + b;
    }

    public int substract(int a, int b) {
        return a - b;
    }

    public int multiply(int a, int b) {
        return a * b;
    }

    public float divide(int a, int b) throws IllegalArgumentException {
        return (float) a / (float) b;
    }
}
```

During the code review, the reviewer may identify the following issues:

- Typo in the method names "substract" that should be "subtract."
- Lack of input validation, for instance, large input values or negative numbers
- Lack of proper documentation comments for the methods

To address these issues, the developer updates the class as follows:

```
/**
* Represents a simple calculator that performs basic arithmetic operations.
*/
public class Calculator {
    /**
     * Adds two integers and returns the result.
     *
     * @param a - first integer
     * @param b - second integer
     * @return the sum of a and b
     */
    public int add(int a, int b) {
        return a + b;
    }


    /**
     * Subtracts two integers and returns the result.
     *
     * @param a - first integer
     * @param b - second integer
     * @return the difference between a and b
     */
    public int subtract(int a, int b) {
        return a - b;
    }


    /**
     * Multiplies two integers and returns the result.
     *
     * @param a - first integer
     * @param b - second integer
     * @return the product of a and b
     */
    public int multiply(int a, int b) {
        return a * b;
    }


    /**
     * Divides two integers and returns the result.
     *
```

```
     * @param a - dividend integer
     * @param b - divisor integer
     * @return the division result of a and b
     * @throws IllegalArgumentException if divisor (b) is zero
     */
    public float divide(int a, int b) throws IllegalArgumentException {
        if (b == 0) {
            throw new IllegalArgumentException("Division by zero is not allowed");
        }
        return (float) a / (float) b;
    }
}
```

Follow coding standards and best practices:

One of the best ways to ensure code security is to follow published coding standards and guidelines for the programming languages and frameworks being used. Awareness of the language nuances, security dangers, and the accompanying best practices can significantly decrease the likelihood of introducing security vulnerabilities.

Look for common security vulnerabilities:

While conducting the review, it is essential to be aware of vulnerabilities such as injection flaws, authentication and authorization issues, data storage and transmission problems, problems with using cryptographic components, and memory management problems like buffer overflows.

Understand the dependencies:

It is crucial to analyze the team's code and any external dependencies (such as libraries or frameworks) applied to the project. Ensure the dependencies are current, secure, and used according to best practices.

Conduct threat modeling:

Reviewers must know the application's threat model and comprehend potential dangers and attack vectors. Making a threat map can help the reviewer focus on the most important areas and set priorities for the study.

Use automated tools and perform manual reviews:

Automated tools help identify common vulnerabilities and concerns, but a manual review is necessary to find finer flaws that automated tools may miss.

Security Code Review Examples

Here are a few examples of common Android security issues in different programming languages:

```
public void saveToFileUnsafe(String fileName, String data)
        throws FileNotFoundException {
    FileOutputStream outputStream = openFileOutput(fileName, Context.MODE_PRIVATE);
    try {
        outputStream.write(data.getBytes());
    } catch (IOException e) {
        e.printStackTrace();
    } finally {
        try {
            outputStream.flush();
            outputStream.close();
        } catch (IOException e) {
                e.printStackTrace();
        }
    }
}
```

In the above kotlin example, the method *saveToFileUnsafe* uses *Context.MODE_PRIVATE* to store sensitive data in an internal storage file. While using it makes the file private and inaccessible to other applications, it might still be accessible by an attacker if the device is rooted and doesn't provide any encryption. A more secure approach would be to encrypt the data before storing it.

An example of URL Injection

```
...

class SecureWebViewActivity : AppCompatActivity() {
    override fun onCreate(savedInstanceState: Bundle?) {
        super.onCreate(savedInstanceState)
        val webView = WebView(this)
        setContentView(webView)

        val url = intent.getStringExtra("url") ?: return

        webView.settings.javaScriptEnabled = true  // JavaScript enabled (unsafe)
        webView.loadUrl(url) // No URL validation
    }
}
```

```
...
```

A more secure version

```
...


class SecureWebViewActivity : AppCompatActivity() {

    @SuppressLint("SetJavaScriptEnabled")
    override fun onCreate(savedInstanceState: Bundle?) {
        super.onCreate(savedInstanceState)
        val webView = android.webkit.WebView(this)
        setContentView(webView)

        val url = intent.getStringExtra("url")

        if (url.isNullOrBlank() || !isValidUrl(url)) {
            Log.e("SecureWebView", "Invalid URL provided!")
            finish()
            return
        }

        // Secure WebView setup
        webView.settings.apply {
            javaScriptEnabled = false // Disable JavaScript for security
            allowFileAccess = false
            allowContentAccess = false
            builtInZoomControls = false
        }

        webView.webViewClient = object : android.webkit.WebViewClient() {
            override fun shouldOverrideUrlLoading(view: WebView, request: android.we\
bkit.WebResourceRequest): Boolean {
                return false // Load URLs internally (secure choice)
            }
        }

        webView.loadUrl(url)
    }

    private fun isValidUrl(url: String): Boolean {
```

```
        return try {
            val uri = android.net.Uri.parse(url)
            (uri.scheme == "https" || uri.scheme == "http") &&
                    !uri.host.isNullOrBlank()
        } catch (e: Exception) {
            false
        }
    }
}

...
```

The activity gets a URL string through an intent and opens it in a WebView. However, the input URL has not been validated or cleaned up. A malicious party could potentially use the WebView to run JavaScript code. To reduce the possibility of this happening, use a secure WebView setup and validate and sanitize the input URL. Additionally, disable JavaScript execution.

Security code reviews are key to creating secure software, especially for Android apps, which often handle private data and have limited resources. To guarantee that our code is secure and resistant to common vulnerabilities and attack vectors, we must adopt a thorough and systematic approach to conducting security code reviews, including manual and automated analysis.

Regular Security Assessments

We live in an interconnected world, where attackers use software program weaknesses to obtain unauthorized access, retrieve sensitive data, or disrupt services and secure coding techniques. Having a regular security assessment could reduce security issues dramatically. We, as programmers, must act defensively when creating Android applications, ensuring our creations are solid and safe.

Android powers billions of devices with various hardware capabilities, and manufacturers and carriers worldwide present specific security difficulties and considerations. To safeguard users, data, and resources within their applications, we must be cautious in spotting potential dangers and employ secure coding techniques.

Importance of Regular Security Assessments

- Assessing vulnerabilities and weaknesses: Consistent security evaluations help you identify application shortcomings, such as inadequate access control or poor input validation. This allows you to address these problems before attackers exploit them.
- Ensuring compliance with regulatory requirements: Many sectors, such as finance and healthcare, have regulations requiring applications to adhere to particular security standards, such as PCI DSS or HIPAA. Regular security audits ensure your application follows these rules and stays out of trouble, legally or otherwise.

- Upholding a secure development lifecycle: By including security assessments in the development lifecycle, you can ensure that security issues are addressed uniformly during the program's design, development, and deployment phases.
- Gaining user trust: Users want to feel secure that using your application will not put their devices or personal information at risk. Regular security audits demonstrate your dedication to security and contribute to user trust.

Important Elements of Continual Assessments

- Code review: a comprehensive investigation of the application's source code to find security flaws and questionable coding techniques. Manual labor or automated technologies like code scanners or static analysis tools can do this.
- Vulnerability Assessment: You can find and assess your application's known security weaknesses by combining human and automated techniques, such as vulnerability scanners, penetration testing, and secure crash reporting tools.

Example A WebView component in an Android app may use the 'setJavaScriptEnabled(true)' command, which can lead to security problems such as cross-site scripting assaults. Evaluating such components and offering security standards to reduce hazards is crucial.

- Threat modeling: Identifying potential dangers to your application and figuring out how attackers can use the system to get in without authorization, interrupt services, or steal data. You can prioritize your security efforts and build suitable countermeasures with this procedure. An Android application, for instance, may be in danger of data leakage if it keeps private information in SharedPreferences without using the appropriate encryption. Threat modeling would recognize this risk and advise deploying encryption tools or employing more secure storage choices.
- Security Testing: Using various testing methods, such as functional testing, penetration testing, and fuzz testing, you may ensure that your application operates securely. For instance, in C++, fuzz testing libraries like libFuzzer or AFL can be used to find potential memory corruption defects in the code that could lead to security weaknesses like buffer overflows or use-after-free bugs.
- Incident Response Plan: Make a strategy to recognize, stop, and recover from security incidents by answering questions like: Who needs to be notified? And what corrective measures ought to be implemented.

Note: The next chapter will discuss threat modeling, standards, and organization.

Security Requirements

Secure coding is the process of creating reliable, effective software free from underlying codebase flaws. Security needs are increasing as Android development spreads and becomes more widely used. We should consider specific security standards to safeguard their applications, users' data, and the hardware on which they operate. The security specifications for secure coding in Android development, both low-level and high-level development, are described in this section.

Code Integrity

Booting Securely

Ensure that all Android-running devices have a secure boot procedure. This procedure checks the digital signatures of the firmware, kernel, and other essential system components before they are loaded onto the device. This guarantees that the device only loads and runs authenticated applications.

Example

```
fun verifySecureBoot(context: Context, alias: String) {
    try {
        val keyGenParams = KeyGenParameterSpec.Builder(
            alias,
            KeyProperties.PURPOSE_SIGN or KeyProperties.PURPOSE_VERIFY
        )
            .setDigests(KeyProperties.DIGEST_SHA256)
            .setAttestationChallenge("secure_boot_nonce".toByteArray())
            .build()

        val kpg = KeyPairGenerator.getInstance(KeyProperties.KEY_ALGORITHM_EC, "Andr\
oidKeyStore")
        kpg.initialize(keyGenParams)
        kpg.generateKeyPair()

        val keyStore = KeyStore.getInstance("AndroidKeyStore").apply { load(null) }
        val certificates = keyStore.getCertificateChain(alias)

        val attestationCert = certificates.firstOrNull() as? X509Certificate
        if (attestationCert == null) {
            Log.e("SecureBoot", "No attestation certificate found!")
            return
        }
```

```

        val parsedAttestationRecord =
            ParsedAttestationRecord.createParsedAttestationRecord(attestationCert)

        when (parsedAttestationRecord.verifiedBootState) {
            ParsedAttestationRecord.VerifiedBootState.VERIFIED -> {
                Log.d("SecureBoot", "Device boot verified (Secure Boot Enabled).")
            }
            ParsedAttestationRecord.VerifiedBootState.SELF_SIGNED -> {
                Log.w("SecureBoot", "Boot state: SELF_SIGNED. Possible custom ROM or\
 compromised boot chain.")
            }
            ParsedAttestationRecord.VerifiedBootState.UNVERIFIED -> {
                Log.w("SecureBoot", "Boot state: UNVERIFIED. Boot integrity unknown.\
")
            }
            ParsedAttestationRecord.VerifiedBootState.FAILED -> {
                Log.e("SecureBoot", "Boot state: FAILED. Boot verification failed!")
            }
            else -> {
                Log.e("SecureBoot", "Unknown verified boot state detected.")
            }
        }

        if (parsedAttestationRecord.teeEnforced.rollbackResistance()) {
            Log.d("SecureBoot", "Rollback resistance enabled (secure rollback preven\
tion active).")
        } else {
            Log.w("SecureBoot", "Rollback resistance not enabled.")
        }

        val osVersion = parsedAttestationRecord.softwareEnforced.osVersion
        Log.d("SecureBoot", "OS Version: $osVersion")

        val attestationVersion = parsedAttestationRecord.attestationVersion
        Log.d("SecureBoot", "Attestation Version: $attestationVersion")

        val keymasterVersion = parsedAttestationRecord.keymasterVersion
        Log.d("SecureBoot", "Keymaster Version: $keymasterVersion")

        val rootOfTrust = parsedAttestationRecord.rootOfTrust
        if (rootOfTrust?.isDeviceLocked == false) {
            Log.w("SecureBoot", "Bootloader is unlocked!")
```

```
        }

        val teeEnforced = parsedAttestationRecord.teeEnforced
        Log.d("SecureBoot", "TEE Enforced: ${teeEnforced.toString()}")

        val softwareEnforced = parsedAttestationRecord.softwareEnforced
        Log.d("SecureBoot", "Software Enforced: ${softwareEnforced.toString()}")

        val attestationChallenge = parsedAttestationRecord.attestationChallenge
        if (attestationChallenge.contentEquals("secure_boot_nonce".toByteArray())) {
            Log.d("SecureBoot", "Attestation challenge verified")
        } else {
            Log.w("SecureBoot", "Attestation challenge mismatch")
        }

    } catch (e: Exception) {
        Log.e("SecureBoot", "Exception during secure boot verification: ${e.message}\
", e)
    }
}
```

Compiler Optimizations

When generating your program, use the proper compiler optimizations to prevent exposing weaknesses in the produced code. It's essential to be aware that various compiler optimizations may delete or change the security checks that your code implements, making the application vulnerable.

Here is an example:

Original code

```
package com.example.myapplication

import android.util.Log

object SecurityUtils {
    fun isValidUser(password: String): Boolean {
        if ("superSecretPassword" == password) {
            return true
        } else {
            logFailedAttempt()
            return false
        }
```

```
    }

    private fun logFailedAttempt() {
        // Security logging method
        Log.e("SecurityUtils", "Unauthorized access attempt!")
    }
}
```

build.gradle configuration:

```
The optimized version by enabling the configuration blow:

    buildTypes {
        release {
            minifyEnabled true
            proguardFiles getDefaultProguardFile('proguard-android-optimize.txt'), '\
proguard-rules.pro'
        }
    }
```

A problematic ProGuard configuration:

```
# To keep the names
-keep class com.example.myapplication.SecurityUtils { *; }


# Problematic ProGuard config
-assumenosideeffects class android.util.Log {
    public static *** e(...);
}
```

Decompiled code by JADX

```
package com.example.myapplication;

import o2.c;

/* loaded from: classes.dex */
public final class SecurityUtils {
    public static final SecurityUtils INSTANCE = new SecurityUtils();

    private SecurityUtils() {
```

```
    }

    private final void logFailedAttempt() {
    }

    public final boolean isValidUser(String str) {
        c.e(str, "password");
        if (c.a("superSecretPassword", str)) {
            return true;
        }
        logFailedAttempt();
        return false;
    }
}
```

SecurityUtils is an empty method due to optimization by a problematic configuration.

Address Space Layout Randomization (ASLR)

ASLR reduces the likelihood of buffer overflow attacks by randomizing the memory layout of an application's address space. To prevent hackers from running code at known memory addresses, ASLR functionality should be implemented into programs.

ASLR can be enabled using the following compiler flag:

GCC

```
gcc -pie -fPIE file.c
```

Clang

```
clang -fPIE -pie -o file.c
```

Code Obfuscation

Obfuscate your application's code to make it more difficult for attackers to reverse engineer, modify, or tamper with your software. Code obfuscation techniques include renaming classes, methods, and variables, as well as encrypting string constants.

Data Protection

We can categorize data in different ways. I prefer to look at the data from their life cycle as listed below:

- In-Transit
- In-memory
- Temporary
- Persistive data

Each category has its specification, importance, and effect. We will come back to data protection later in detail.

Authentication and Authorization

Strengthened Authentication

Utilize strong authentication procedures to guarantee that only authorized users can access essential elements in your application. This might entail using the Android Keystore system's hardware-backed keys, biometrics, or multi-factor authentication (MFA).

RBAC or role-based access Control

Use role-based access control, which classifies people and resources according to roles and allows for the granting or revocation of access to secure resources based on roles. Limiting user access to select potentially vulnerable areas of the program can help lower the attack surface.

Incident Response

Monitoring and Logging

Install a reliable logging and monitoring system to track down forensic evidence during a security breach and identify real-time security occurrences. Avoid logging sensitive information, as an adversary might find it valuable.

Updates on Security

Use the most recent security patches, libraries, and best practices to keep your application and development environment current. Conduct regular security audits and assessments to find and patch any potential flaws in your code, dependencies, and device configurations.

Plan for Security Incident Response

Establish a thorough security incident response plan that outlines the actions to be taken in the event of a security issue. The plan should include roles and responsibilities, communication protocols, and post-incident analysis to prevent recurrences.

An all-encompassing strategy is needed for secure coding in Android development, considering many factors such as code integrity, data protection, authentication, network security, and incident response. You can ensure your Android applications are strong and resistant to frequent vulnerabilities and attacks by following these security standards and putting the right approaches into practice. To ensure your critical applications and user data are always secure, stay up-to-date with any new security advice or updates within the Android ecosystem.

Integrating Security Testing

Secure coding is creating apps that prevent security flaws and lower the danger of cyber attacks. Appropriate security controls, best practices, and procedures must be established during the software development process to protect the program from potential attacks.

One key component of secure coding is security testing, which aids in the early detection of vulnerabilities, hazards, and other potential problems in the program. The development process can be improved by incorporating security testing to protect apps from malicious attacks and unauthorized access.

Android devices are prone to several threats because of their extensive use and sensitive data. This section highlights the many testing approaches, strategies, and resources.

Security Testing Methods

To find and address vulnerabilities in Android applications, a variety of security testing techniques are utilized, including:

Static Application Security Testing and Static Code Analyzers (SAST)

This includes examining the application's source code without running the program. At the early stages of development, vulnerabilities, security problems, and departures from established practices are easier to spot. SAST tools can be linked to build systems or the linked development environment (IDE) to give developers real-time feedback. They search the source code for flaws, problems with its quality, and departures from recommended coding principles. To increase the quality and security of the code, the development process can incorporate tools like SonarQube, Checkstyle, PMD, or Android Lint. Lint is an invaluable tool for identifying potential security and API compatibility concerns in the context of Android. Usually, these tools could check for known vulnerabilities in third-party libraries and dependencies, including Dependency-Check, Snyk, and OWASP Dependency-Track.

Dynamic Application Security Testing (DAST)

DAST entails testing the application while actively running and frequently mimics real-world scenarios to find security flaws. DAST tools can automatically crawl applications, uncovering attack vectors and exploiting vulnerabilities. These technologies can be incorporated into the Continuous Integration (CI) pipeline and work well with black-box testing techniques.

Penetration Testing

To find vulnerabilities and evaluate the efficacy of current security controls, penetration testing simulates attacks on the application by a knowledgeable hacker or security expert. It can be carried out by hand or with mechanized tools.

Fuzz testing

A testing method involves giving the program random or unexpected inputs to cause crashes, memory leaks, or other unpredictable behavior. Due to the lack of memory safety measures included in C/C++ code, it is particularly helpful for identifying vulnerabilities in that code.

Security Testing Techniques and Tools

There are numerous techniques and tools available for security testing when designing Android, including:

Code Review

Automated and peer code review tools can significantly improve an application's security posture. A manual code review process should be implemented in addition to automated security testing technologies as part of the overall development workflow. Many open-source and paid technologies exist, including Crucible, Upsource, and Gerrit.

AI

The variety of AI-based tools in software development could be considered another automation tool that could be used to improve quality and security. Enabling AI tools to review the code on the repositories could save time and energy in the development process. At present, GitHub and GitLab offer AI code assistants that could help level up some software aspects. Also, we can consider other AI tools to enable them on private repos as a part of CI.

Secure Code Libraries

By offering thoroughly tested implementations of cryptographic primitives and other security-sensitive processes, secure code libraries like SafeNative, mbedtls, or libsodium can help developers avoid problems.

Integrating Security Testing into Android Development

There are various approaches to incorporating security testing into the Android development process, including:

Continuous Integration Pipeline

Security testing tools in the CI pipeline automate the discovery of security issues, enabling early detection. Software like Jenkins or GitLab CI can be configured to execute security tests automatically after each code commit. By receiving rapid feedback on the security implications of their changes, developers can correct problems before they are implemented in production.

Security Testing Examples

Checking for a buffer overflow vulnerability illustrates security testing done with C++ and the Android NDK. A buffer overflow, a common security issue, can occur when handling input data or strings due to faulty validation or copying of data. Developers can find code flaws where buffer overflows could happen by performing fuzz testing on the application.

Java programmers can increase the security of their code by incorporating SAST tools into their work environment, such as FindBugs or SpotBugs. These instruments can spot many security flaws, including unsafe HTTP connections and random number generation.

Developers may integrate Detekt, a static code analysis tool, into Kotlin to find potential security flaws, such as unsafe network timeouts, omitted SSL setups, or ineffective encryption techniques. This plugin-based solution enables developers to find and address security concerns early in development and integrates easily into the development environment or CI pipeline.

Integrating security testing tools into development environments and CI pipelines can also automate problem detection and enforce secure coding practices throughout the development process: the more automation, the less effort and human errors.

Threat Modeling, Standards and Guidelines

Now is the time to discuss an important activity in our software development process: threat modeling. Having some expertise within the development team could change the project's outcome in a sense of security. We know it is a wide topic, and we cannot cover it in one chapter. The idea of including it in the book is to provide preliminary information that familiarizes you with some of the important ones. You can find some books and courses to dig into each of them as a separate topic. Besides threat modeling, we will skim some standards and organizations that have a bold role in cybersecurity.

Before exploring these topics, it could be helpful to understand " why " we need to know them and " how " they are connected in a bigger picture.

There are various methodologies and frameworks for threat modeling, each with different use cases and levels of adoption. Some of them are still widely used, while others are specific to certain industries.
For example, the TARA methodology (Threat Assessment and Remediation Analysis) is commonly used in the automotive industry for security risk assessment in vehicles.

However, I have chosen to use a simpler and more practical model for identifying and categorizing threats. This model is called the Shostack's Four-Question Framework, introduced by Adam Shostack in his book Threat Modeling: Designing for Security, published in 2014.

I also noticed that this framework is becoming increasingly popular, which means it's not an obscure or overly complex methodology. Unlike some other frameworks that require hours of study just to understand their structure, this one is straightforward and easy to adopt.

Shostack's Four Question Framework [1]

This framework is based on four key questions:

1. What are we working on?
2. What can go wrong?
3. What are we going to do about it?
4. Did we do a good job?

- **What are we working on?**
  - This question ensures that we fully understand the product, service, or project we are working on.
  - It means we must have sufficient knowledge about what we are designing, developing, or implementing.
  - If we lack clarity on this, we won't be able to accurately assess security risks.
- **What can go wrong?**
  - This question identifies potential threats that could arise.
  - It requires understanding project details, assets, resources, and possible risks.
  - Essentially, this step involves threat identification—understanding what could go wrong and how it could impact security.
- **What are we going to do about it?**
  - Once threats are identified, the next step is to define mitigation strategies.
  - For example, if we determine that unauthorized access to locally stored files is a risk in an Android application, we must find solutions.
  - In Android, possible security measures include:
    * Storing sensitive data in private app storage
    * Encrypting local files
    * Implementing access control mechanisms
  - To effectively mitigate risks, we must also have a solid understanding of the platform and its security capabilities.
- **Did we do a good job?**
  - The final step is to evaluate whether our security efforts were effective.
  - This includes reviewing the entire process:
    * Did we properly identify the product or service scope?

[1] Shostack, Adam. Threat Modeling: Designing For Security. John Wiley & Sons, 2014

    * Did we identify and analyze potential threats?
    * Were the mitigation strategies sufficient?

  - This question ensures that the security measures are satisfactory and provide sufficient protection.

Despite being simple, these four questions are critical to threat modeling. They guide us through:

- Understanding the system we are working on
- Identifying security risks and potential threats
- Developing solutions to address those threats
- Evaluating our success in mitigating risks

This structured approach helps us detect, prevent, and mitigate security risks effectively while keeping the process practical and manageable.

Threat Modelling frameworks

Various threat modeling methodologies and frameworks take different approaches to identifying and mitigating security risks. In this chapter, we discussed the Four-Question Framework, which is straightforward, easy to follow, and not overly complex to work with.

Other threat modeling methodologies adopt a systematic approach, where the process unfolds in multiple structured steps, and the target system (whether software, a service, or an application) is assessed accordingly.

For example, some models focus on categorizing threats into specific types, such as:

- Phishing attacks
- Tampering
- Data breaches
  Others analyze attack surfaces to determine where vulnerabilities exist and how they could be exploited.

Each methodology comes with its own level of complexity and unique advantages, but in this case, I believe the Four-Question Framework allows us to proceed efficiently and effectively without unnecessary complications.

In an upcoming chapter, we will analyze four real-world applications and services, each representing different scenarios. We will:

1. Apply the Four-Question Framework to identify threats.
2. Assess the risks associated with each scenario.

3. Develop and implement security measures to mitigate the identified threats.
4. Evaluate the effectiveness of our security strategies.

This hands-on approach will help us understand the practical application of threat modeling and measure how well we can identify, mitigate, and prevent security risks.

As mentioned earlier, some industry-specific models and standards could be used to identify threats. Some of them are famous or more convenient, so it might be good to be familiar with them. Besides, some organizations actively provide useful information on the latest vulnerabilities or update their models. Combining different methods could reduce security issues.

There are one method/model that I would like to discuss here because of their importance during the last decade and their use as worldwide frameworks. That is TARA. TARA has a broader scope that could be used in any use case or domain. If you are working in industries such as automotive, it is crucial to know about TARA since it is usually used for ongoing organizational security assessment.

TARA

Intel developed TARA, or *Threat Agent Risk Assessment*, for risk assessment. It focuses on threat agents and identifies and assesses security risks. TARA prioritizes risks based on the type of probable adversary and their goals. The process is followed by creating a profile for the threat agent based on the risk likelihood and impact. TARA focuses on potential attack agents early and helps address issues before they become breaches.

The first step is to define the scope and list the assets to understand the system's big picture. In this step, we need to identify the assets that might need protection. Now that the picture is complete, we will determine the potential threats. Having a broad perspective and looking for threats from different perspectives will help us minimize the missing points.

We have the big picture and a list of potential threat agents. The next step is to analyze the threats to determine their motivations, capabilities, etc. To better understand them, we will analyze the attack vectors based on the agent to extract more details. After identifying the attack vectors, we must run a risk assessment to determine their severity and risk level. We can prioritize the attack vectors based on the risk score to create mitigation strategies. Together, all the steps and activities will enable us to eliminate or minimize the impact of the attacks.

Here is a simplified version of the TARA steps:

1. Define scope and assets

- Security objectives
- Model System

    - Functions
    - Data (Stored data, in communication data)
    - Component (hardware, communication participants)
    - Data Flow (actual communication)

- Identify Protection Needs

2. Identify Potential Threat Agents

- Internal
- External
- Environmental
- Physical
-

3. Analyze Threat Agents

- Motivations and goals
- Capabilities
- Tactics, techniques, ..
- etc.

4. Assess Attack Vectors
5. Risk Assessment

- Impact severity (1-5)
- Likelihood (1-5)
- Risk score = Impact * Likelihood

6. Prioritize Threats
7. Develop Mitigation Strategies
8. Monitor and Review

Figure 3. TARA Process Flow

What I need to highlight here is the common pitfalls. For instance, we usually consider threat modeling as a one-time activity while the threats are changing continuously. It demands to have an active approach. We should update the solutions and the mitigation in an iterative process during the project life-time. Besides, involvement of all the stakeholders in the threat modeling sessions/meeting will provide a wider perspective about the critical challenges and threats since each side might have a certain concerns, knowledge or insight in the project. It means that to provide a secure produce the cooperation from different parties is essential. Otherwise, the effectiveness of this process will be limited.

Security Standards and Guidelines

By searching the web, you can find a long list of the standards and guidelines in the different categories of cybersecurity; since each one was born for a specific reason, we need to pick the proper one based on our requirements. Some of them might be general and could be utilized in all industries. However, using industry-specific standards and guidelines could maximize the advantage. Here, you can see a short list of them included in the next page table that I have created out of the most important and used ones and tried to categorize them to help you find the right one quickly. (Appendix 1 provides a long list of the methods, models, and organizations that you can check for more information) We will get to know just some of them in this chapter to apply the advice throughout the rest of the book.

This short list includes only the models, standards, and organization that we are willing to utilize in the next chapters. You can skim it to get an idea of what we will discuss and cover later.

Category	Standard/Guideline	Description	Industry Focus
General	**CWE**	Database of common software weaknesses and vulnerabilities.	Software Development
General	**CVE**	List of publicly known cybersecurity vulnerabilities and exposures.	General
Core Security Frameworks	**MITRE ATT&CK**	Framework for describing attacker tactics and techniques.	Cybersecurity
Core Security Frameworks	**OWASP**	Best practices and guidelines for web application security.	Web Applications
Automotive Standards	**AUTOSAR**	Security framework for automotive systems.	Automotive
Automotive Standards	**ISO 26262**	Functional safety for road vehicles.	Automotive
Threat Modeling	**STRIDE**	Threat modeling framework	General

Category	Standard/Guideline	Description	Industry Focus
Risk Assessment	TARA	Threat Assessment and Remediation Analysis.	Software Development
Development Guidelines	MISRA C	Guidelines for safety-critical systems.	Embedded Systems
Development Guidelines	CERT C/C++	Secure coding standards for C and C++ languages.	Software Development

Some organization to know

Here, you can find a quick introduction to each organization. We will use their data to explain the security issues or even pick up their recommendations. Being familiar with these organizations could give us a broader landscape of security issues and recommended practices.

MITRE

MITRE ATT&CK® is a globally accessible knowledge base of adversary tactics and techniques based on real-world observations. The ATT&CK knowledge base is used as a foundation for the development of specific threat models and methodologies in the private sector, in government, and in the cybersecurity product and service community. [^cwe.org]

Basically, MITRE is an organization connecting to the CVE and CWE frameworks, which it maintains as a main player. These frameworks provide very useful information about vulnerabilities and weaknesses that are used widely by many developers and companies. The CWE database is being used in the STRIDE model to provide technical-level information on threat modeling. CVE supports the TARA model in determining risk levels, etc., at the organizational level.

MITRE's categorized tactics are based on real-world observations that provide valuable insight into attacker behavior and threat detection. They can enhance knowledge and understanding and serve as a guide for security monitoring and incident response.

CVE

The Common Vulnerabilities and Exposures (CVE) system provides a reference method for publicly known information-security vulnerabilities and exposures. [2]

The mission of the CVE® Program is to identify, define, and catalog publicly disclosed cybersecurity vulnerabilities. This program plays a crucial role in vulnerability management by offering standardized entries that make it easier to discuss and address security issues. [3]

[2] https://en.wikipedia.org/wiki/Common_Vulnerabilities_and_Exposures
[3] https://www.cve.org/About/Overview

CWE

The Common Weakness Enumeration (CWE) is a category system for hardware and software weaknesses and vulnerabilities. [4]

Common Weakness Enumeration (CWE™) is a community-developed list of common software and hardware weaknesses. A "weakness" is a condition in a software, firmware, hardware, or service component that, under certain circumstances, could contribute to the introduction of vulnerabilities. The CWE List and associated classification taxonomy identify and describe weaknesses in terms of CWEs.[5]

CWE is a community-driven list with a comprehensive database of known weaknesses. It includes information such as impact, detection methods, potential mitigation, and other useful information that developers could use to improve their development and testing processes.

OWASP

The Open Worldwide Application Security Project [7] (OWASP) is an online community that produces freely available articles, methodologies, documentation, tools, and technologies in the fields of IoT, system software, and web application security.[6]

The Open Worldwide Application Security Project (OWASP) is a nonprofit foundation that works to improve the security of software. [7]

Choosing the Right Framework

As mentioned earlier, each model or method might cover a specific domain and fulfill certain requirements. To save limited resources and maximize the outcome, we need to start by finding a proper framework based on the project requirements, industry, etc. Different factors could influence the selection of the appropriate framework based on the domain, security goals, requirements, etc. I have gathered some of them that you can use to decide. You can expand on these factors to have a broader perspective in your selection process.

1. Application domain (automotive, mobile, web)
2. Development phase
3. Security requirements
4. Available resources
5. Team expertise

Another reason to find a suitable model for your domain is to acquire enough expertise to apply it in the software development process. To be expert enough, we need to go through the process

[4]https://en.wikipedia.org/wiki/Common_Weakness_Enumeration
[5]https://cwe.mitre.org/about/index.html
[6]https://en.wikipedia.org/wiki/OWASP
[7]https://owasp.org/about/

multiple times in different projects. Each time, we might learn a new point, which, after some time, will make all the knowledge and experience we have gained valuable assets in securing the project.

We can not expect to reach the maximum possible security in our application only by selecting one method and applying it. Instead, we need to take action in different areas and aspects to upgrade the security level of our products. You can find some suggestions here:

1. Combine multiple frameworks where appropriate
2. Regularly update security knowledge
3. Maintain documentation
4. Train team members
5. Review and adjust implementation
6. Monitor effectiveness
7. Stay informed about new threats

Note If you need a quick and straightforward solution for mobile application development, I would recommend using the OWASP guideline, which is a compiled version of threat modeling and addresses the possible Android issues clearly.

Framework/Tool	Application Domain	Goal/Functionality
STRIDE	General (Web, Network, App)	Identify and mitigate threats like Spoofing, Tampering, Repudiation, Information Disclosure, Denial of Service, and Elevation of Privilege during design, implementation, and testing phases.
OWASP Threat Dragon	General (Web, Mobile, App)	Lightweight threat modeling tool for analyzing risks and integrating STRIDE during design and implementation.
NIST SP 800-30	General (Government, Enterprise)	Framework for risk management, assessing data security, and implementing controls during the risk management phase.

Framework/Tool	Application Domain	Goal/Functionality
MITRE ATT&CK	Network, Endpoint	Provides a comprehensive framework for identifying, understanding, and mitigating adversary tactics and techniques.
CWE (Common Weakness Enumeration)	General (Web, Network, App)	Database of common software weaknesses to address vulnerabilities during design, implementation, and testing.
CVE (Common Vulnerabilities and Exposures)	General (Web, Network, App)	Catalog of known vulnerabilities to support maintenance and testing phases with vulnerability tracking.
AUTOSAR	Automotive	Standard for ensuring system safety and security across the entire lifecycle of automotive systems.
ISO 26262	Automotive Safety	Focused on functional safety during the entire lifecycle of automotive systems.
TARA (Threat Analysis and Risk Assessment)	General (Web, Network, App)	Identifies and prioritizes risks by analyzing threats and creating mitigation strategies during design and implementation.
MISRA C	Embedded Systems	Guidelines for secure coding practices in embedded systems during the coding phase.
CERT C/C++	General (Web, Network, App)	Provides secure coding standards to mitigate vulnerabilities in C/C++ during the coding phase.
OWASP	Web, Application	Best practices and tools for secure application development at various phases, including coding and testing.

Some keywords to know

Vulnerability Severity Score

A CVSS score is a way to evaluate and rank the reported threats defined by CVSS. The scores have been split into five categories, as below, each covering a range of numbers out of 10. One advantage of the scores is that they allow you to prioritize the resources and responses according to them.

- Critical 9.0-10.0
- Hight 7.0-8.9
- Medium 4.0-6.9
- Low 0.1-3.9
- None 0

The score is the outcome of a formula that depends on several metrics. The metrics could be divided into three main factors, and each one has some parameters:

- Base Score Metrics
- Temporal Score Metrics
- Environmental Score Metrics

Vulnerability Risk

That is the impact of the vulnerability in case of happening.

Attack Vector

An attack vector is a specific method, pathway, or scenario by which an unauthorized user (attacker) could control or gain access to the system or its resources, such as data or the network.

Attack Surface

The attack surface is the sum of the possible attack vectors or points an unauthorized user can access to extract/enter/change data or control the system.

Privilege Escalation

That is, an attacker will gain illicit or illegal access to the system or its resources by exploiting a vulnerability in the system beyond what the user, application, etc., is entitled to.

Zero-Day Vulnerability

A zero-day vulnerability is an unknown or undiscovered vulnerability in a system or application for which no official path has been provided.

Note: We will see how threat modeling works in practice later through some real examples

Attack and Defense

We don't need to experience it again!

> "Those who do not remember the past are condemned to repeat it." – George Santayana [1]

Why are we not learning from history?

You might be shocked if you look into the common issues that have been reported by different organizations during the last decades. Some organizations, such as CWE, CVE, and OWASP, provide information about common vulnerabilities and the best practices we can follow to avoid the known issues that have been happening repeatedly. Security issues are usually common regardless of the industry, programming language, or operating system you're working with. You can easily find the use cases and the stories behind famous security reports through these organization websites. Eventually, you will end up in the known vulnerability category, which has been around for a long time. Of course, the applications, frameworks, etc., are different, but the vulnerability's concept and mechanism are the same. Now, the question is: " Why have not we learned from them?" That's a simple question but complicated to answer since that's the outcome of different causes combined.

Anyway, we will review the top known vulnerabilities and weaknesses to understand their characteristics and how we can avoid them.

You need to know that each has its own perspective and categories. While they look at security from different angles, they all provide invaluable information that together could give us a good grasp of security in the software industry. I will try to explain their points of view and combine them to clarify the different corners of the topics.

Let's simplify

> "Simplicity is the ultimate sophistication." -Leonardo da Vinci

If you start your journey without any destinations, you won't know where you will end up. But if you go without a map, you won't know where you're heading. We should have A map, or maybe we can say we need a road map. We would try to organize the information in a way that helps us have a systematic approach to securing the applications. This approach can include knowing

[1] George Santayana was a Spanish-American philosopher, essayist, poet, and novelist (1863-1952).

how an attack might take place, finding the architecture's weakest point, etc. As developers, team leaders, or architects, we should cover many grounds to ensure that the products are delivered with an acceptable level of security. That won't happen if we don't know where to look for them or, as mentioned in the earlier chapters, do not take security as an ongoing process, which we need to apply the principles from day one.

All the ways to get inside

I would like to give you an overview of the ways that your application can be attacked before explaining how CVE, CWE, MITRE, etc, have categorized the information. From this site, you can plan to tighten your seatbelt when securing the code. We will discuss the different ways that software, especially Android, could be compromised.

I need to add here that we need to understand different levels of attack. We might face different scenarios, and not all of them will try to compromise the application. In some cases, the attacker might look for useful information to use for a web-based attack. Therefore, we can not expect to see the same pattern. It will be helpful to list different scenarios before explaining the sequence of a general attack.

Different Scenarios

Behind any attack is a reason that makes it worthwhile. Knowing these reasons might not directly impact the way that you design or implement your system and application. But they will help you apply them to the context you're working on to find potential targets. Then, it will be easier to secure more interesting objectives. The general motivations for an attack could be:

- Financial gain
- Blackmail
- Data theft
- Espionage
- Sabotage
- Political or Ideological objectives
- Social engineering

Generally speaking, the attacker could follow one or multiple general scenarios:

- Looking for data
- Accessing to the devices on different levels

Now that you know that's all about data and access, you can formulate everything that way.

The combination of the categories above could lead to the detailed implementation of one or more scenarios, which we will examine later. I am interested in shedding light on security in this way to push our mindset beyond the technical details. Getting involved in the technical aspects will lead to losing the other angles. So, before discussing them, we need to have a general mindset about cybersecurity. You can fill in the gaps while we work in an evolving environment where, each day, we might deal with new concepts, requirements, or threats.

- Accessing insecure credentials, keys, etc.
- Monitoring user inputs
- Extracting private information
- Hijacking communication & network attack
- Inject code (mostly for the web-based apps)
- Denial of service
- Exploit applications, components, libraries
- Infecting device
- Ransomware
- Phishing

General steps

An insider

What if there's a trojan already in the castle? When you sleep, the intruders will enter and do whatever they want. Yes, that's serious. You should expect it, especially if you're blindly using a 3rd part library, service, or piece of code. We cannot develop everything independently due to the limited resources we have access to. Therefore, we will utilize the ready-to-use resource to accomplish the project. That is a wise decision and normal. We need to keep our eyes on the new news version and clearly understand how a 3rd part module is being integrated into our project. This will help determine how some vulnerabilities could affect us when unaware. In case of being compromised, the level of permission your application has been granted would be critical since they will directly impact the scope of the impact.

The plane is hijacked

What if an actor fakes their personality and hijacks the communication? That's what we call man-in-the-middle! There are several known solutions to keep communication through the network secure.

No guard watching the doors

If you leave the doors open, no one will ask who is entering. The same will happen to your inputs from outside, especially when you are dealing with an untrusted data source. Any data you receive from outside your application needs to be checked using known techniques. For instance, SQL injection is a well-known vulnerability that all applications using DB should take seriously. Input sanitization is an effective technique that could help confront SQL injection vulnerabilities.

Shaky building

Design and architecture are key players in security. For instance, a modularized architecture could limit the system's compromised scope. Increasing the cohesion within a module (a kind of SRP at the module level) will restrict the module's access level by granting only the required permissions.

Superhero is forbidden!

Like a god-object, we must be careful about the permissions we give to a service or application. Any added permission means we have increased the span of the system, which could be affected by a security issue. It is important to narrow down the permissions to the necessary ones to avoid future problems.

You don't know my language

The application assets include DB, configuration files, layouts, etc. They are important targets for hackers. Protecting them from unauthorized access by keeping them in a safe place is one solution. Android provides different mechanisms to protect our assets, such as private space and shared preferences. Additionally, we can protect the application components easily by not exposing them, which will help reduce the attack surface.

He has a mask

Due to Android's layers of security, privilege escalation is usually not the outcome of a single vulnerability. Therefore, security involves protecting as much as possible and reducing the impact of a compromise. However, there might be some situations in which the attacker has designed an in-depth, complicated scenario based on the target to gain full access to the system.

How you will be attacked

To start hardening your application or system, first, you need to know how an attacker will look at it. We won't be able to mitigate the risks without knowing how malware can compromise our application/system and having a big picture of the different steps and stages of an attack. Let's look at the general steps of an attack.

Unfold the target

The first crucial step of any attack is identifying the target by enumerating the technologies, the application structure, etc. This information will help the hacker/cracker understand the target well. Analyzing the gathered information leads to finding the probable vulnerabilities. This step can include different activities from the attacker that are listed below:

- App reverse engineering - Use of tools like Apktool, JADX, and Frida, etc.
- Reading the available document
- Monitoring the network traffic
- Check the public assets, such as created folders, etc.

After de-compiling the application and gathering information about it, we need to extract more information from the de-compiled app.

Extract information from the unfolded app

It is time to explore the generated source code and .class to find some helpful information. Some of the subjects could be:

- Permissions
- Databases
- Hardcoded keys, passwords, usernames, etc.
- Exposed components
- Type of storage
- 3rd party libraries
- Network protocols and addresses

Look for a vulnerability

If the application is obfuscated, finding the code vulnerabilities will be challenging. But if it's not obfuscated, the hacker could search for the potential vulnerabilities that are listed below:

- Look for any insecure storage
  - Keys
  - Tokens
  - Username & Password
  - Exported DB
- Analyze input data handling for:
  - Input validation
  - SQL injection
  - Buffer overflow
  - etc
- Searching for 3rd party insecure libraries
- Vulnerable network protocols
- Weak authentication
- Scan the app's backend APIs

Examine the founding

At this step, the hacker will start verifying what has been found by developing codes, checking the device, using tolls, etc.

Prepare to attack

In case of success in compromising the application, the hacker could prepare some code or application for that specific one.

Attack

Now that the tools are ready, the attack can take place.

Attack Steps Diagram

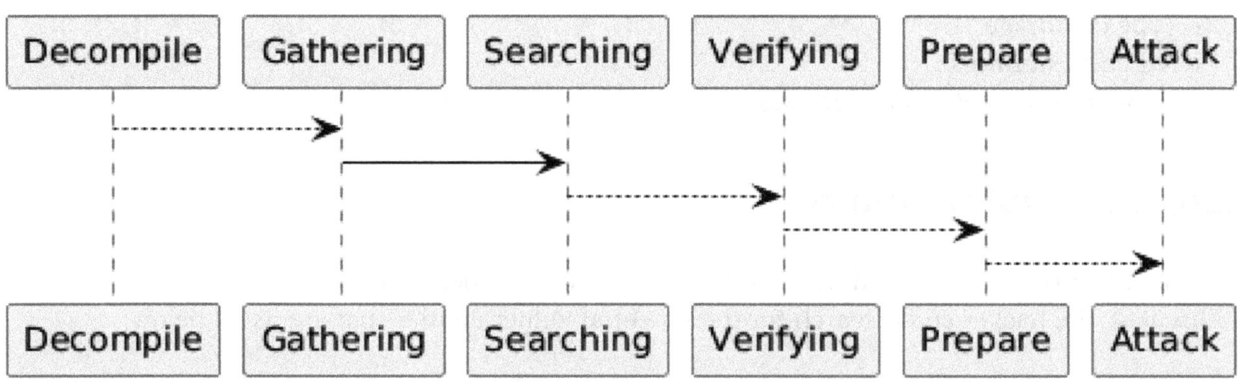

Figure 4. Attack Steps Diagram

How to Defend

Besides the big picture you have now, going through different attack scenarios gave us a better understanding of various parts of the puzzle. We have come here to find out how to protect our applications from threats at an acceptable level. We have a good grasp of how each step in the development process matters. Therefore, we would apply the principles alongside the best practices in Android. We must understand that all the techniques and protections might eventually be bypassed, but we will try to make it harder.

Defensive Techniques

Here you can find a short list of the techniques that we could utilize to deliver more secure products:

In the development process

- Utilizing security principles
- Design review
- Code review
- Threat Modeling
- Security Requirements Definition

Minimizing the surface attack

All the knowledge and techniques we could find about the attack and defense would reduce the attack surface, reducing the possibility of being compromised by an unauthorized actor. We are not able to remove the threats, but we could try to use some contrivance to limit the impact of an attack.

Compiler & tools

- Anti-Reverse Engineering Techniques
- Obfuscation
- Static Analysis Tools
- Dynamic Analysis Tools
- Automated Build Security Checks

Run-time

- Integrity Check by Signing
- Using Play Integrity API
- Installer Package Verification
- Root Detection Mechanisms
- Debug Mode Detection
- Runtime Application Self-Protection (RASP)
- Environment Verification

Implementation & Language Specific

- Input Validation
- Input Sanitizing
- Proper error handling
- Avoiding Common Mistakes
- Secure Memory Management

Data Protection

- Hard-code keys
- Encryption
- Android KeyStore
- Secure Shared Preference
- Database Encryption
- Secure Backup Practices

Network & protocols

- Use SSL/TLS
- Use encryption over network
- SSL pinning
- Short token valid period
- Secure API Design
- Network Traffic Monitoring

OS Mechanisms

- Limit Permissions
- Protect Inter-Process Communication (IPC)
- Use of SELinux Policies
- Regular OS Updates

Libraries

- Assess Third-Party Library Vulnerabilities
- Use Trusted Libraries
- Regular Library Updates
- Static Linking Avoidance

System level

- Disable USB Debugging (adb)
- Restrict Installation from Unknown Sources
- Enforce Secure Boot
- Use Verified Boot
- Implement dm-verity

Testing

- Fuzz Testing
- Penetration Testing
- Security Regression Testing

Act as a chief

A chef needs to prepare the exact ingredients to cook a delicious meal. Also, the order and process that should be used matters. Even a small deviation could lead to something different. And that's for a meal you might cook for hours, and if you fail, you have wasted the resources you have prepared, the time and energy you put in, and also *your reputation*!

What about developing an application for months with lots of interaction between the back-end, UX/UI team, developers, etc? Sounds like a lot of resources. Yeah, it's no surprise if a company collapses because of security breaches in the service or the application provided. Now the question could be: "Is it enough to know how an attack happens and how you can defend?" Of course not!

Security should be part of each stage, from designing to the time we release or even after that. The principles explained earlier could be helpful if we use them, especially in the design process, to ensure that we are not on the opposite side, which puts us in a weak position in the sense of security. Till then, we went through the high-level concepts and tried to look at the topic from different perspectives. However, we should not stop the effort at this point; instead, we should utilize other techniques to complete the process. The principles will help us have the right mindset when designing and caring for the architecture. However, during the implementation process, we need other tools. To provide a practical approach, in the next chapters, we will go through different areas:

- General techniques
- Language-specific topics (C/C++, Java, Kotlin)
- Understanding Android structure as an operating system
- Compilers & Static analysis tools
- etc.

Each area might require a book to be fully converted, though we will try to familiarize ourselves with important ones. You can then research them later using different resources, such as the Web, books, articles, etc.

Like a chef, we need to choose the right material and cook in order properly.

Common Programming Mistakes

Now that you are familiar with CVE, CWE, etc., we could examine the most common vulnerabilities in this chapter. Security vulnerabilities often arise from small but critical coding mistakes. These errors may be tied directly to known Common Weakness Enumerations (CWEs) or violate core secure coding principles (KISS, Fail Safe, Zero Trust, etc.). Here, we highlight frequent pitfalls and show how to address them with secure coding practices across C/C++, Java, and Kotlin.

Memory safety

Native software development on *Linux*, the *Android kernel*, and various layers of the system is typically done using **C and C++**. However, **Go and Rust** have also gained traction in this space. In this discussion, I want to focus specifically on Android.

In Android, we can develop processes, applications, or services using C and C++ at two layers:

1. **The Hardware Abstraction Layer (HAL)**
2. **The Android Kernel**, which is based on **the Linux kernel**

The Challenge of Memory Safety in C and C++

One of the most debated topics regarding **C and C++** is **memory safety**. By default, neither of these languages provide built-in memory safety, meaning that developers need to consciously manage memory throughout the development and implementation process.

While this is not an inherently complex task, it often gets overlooked, leading to memory leaks, dangling pointers, buffer overflows, and other security vulnerabilities. With experience, proper training, and adherence to guidelines, these issues can be mitigated—but this requires extra effort. Although it is not necessarily "hard" work, it does demand additional attention from developers.

Rust: A Safer Alternative?

On the other hand, **Rust** provides memory safety by default. Thanks to its built-in features and ownership model, it prevents memory leaks, dangling pointers, and similar issues at compile-time—without requiring manual intervention from developers.

That said, every language comes with **trade-offs**:

- **C and C++ offer higher performance** compared to Rust.
- **Rust provides built-in memory safety**, reducing security risks.

Why Hasn't Rust Been Widely Adopted Yet?

One major challenge is the limited number of Rust developers and the lack of extensive resources and sample projects, especially in Android development. Because of this, many companies are reluctant to invest in Rust, as it increases both development time and cost. Additionally, debugging and troubleshooting in Rust can require more effort compared to C++ in some cases.

A Potential Transition Strategy

Perhaps the best approach is to gradually transition Android's native processes and services toward Rust. This would help address memory safety concerns by default, reducing vulnerabilities over time. However, it's important to remember that choosing a programming language isn't just about security, safety, or cost—it requires evaluating multiple technical and business factors.

I wanted to share this thought because I believe Rust could solve some of the problems we face with C and C++, provided that we have the necessary expertise and experience within our team. If a team is capable of adopting Rust—or at least investing in it—it could be an available option for long-term security and stability in Android native development.

C and C++

C and C++ have long been used as high-performance and system-level programming languages. All critical operating systems, such as Linux, Unix, Windows, etc., are based on them. This performance and power come with specifications that make them vulnerable. If the developer has a good grasp of C and C++, it can produce a stable and intense application. In continuing, we cover some of the most common mistakes we might make while developing with them.

Buffer overflow & Out-of-bund write

C & C++ lets developers take advantage of pointers and memory addresses. While it removes lots of memory allocation and copy operations, it can lead to corrupting memory if it has yet to be used in a protected way. Here, we will discuss two similar weaknesses, *buffer overflow* (CWE-121) and *out-of-bound write* (CWE-787), that can be categorized as the same issue while different. Both focus on writing to unexpected and out-of-bound memory space, but the reasons vary. If not caused by a sequential copy of excessive data from a fixed starting location, it will be labeled by out-of-band write (CWE-787). On the other hand, if an allocated buffer in the stack is overwritten, it's called buffer overflow (CWE-121). Buffer overflow is usually caused by a lack of input validation, leading to exceeding the length of the allocated buffer. One of the most significant differences is out-of-band write, which includes buffer underwrite.

- **Buffer Overflow (CWE-121)**: Typically involves overwriting a stack-allocated buffer due to lack of input validation.

- **Out-of-Bounds Write (CWE-787)**: Writing beyond the allocated boundaries of a buffer, but not necessarily in a straightforward sequential copy scenario. Out-of-bounds write can also include buffer underwrite cases.

```
#include <stdio.h>
#include <string.h>
#include <stdlib.h>


int main(int argc, char *argv[])
{
  char password[8];
  char tempBuffer[8];
  /*if (argc < 2)
  {
          printf("You need to enter password\n");
          exit(0);
  }*/


  strcpy(password, argv[1]);
  printf("password= %s\n", password);
  printf("tempBuffer= %s\n", tempBuffer);


  return 0;
}
```

To see what happens, you can try to build and run the code above for the conditions below:

- Give it a parameter with at most eight characters
- Give it a parameter with at most 16 characters and less than 16
- Give it a parameter with more than 16 characters

The first and second conditions work fine. The second condition works thanks to tempBuffer. But you can see that the *tempBuffer* content is over-written by the input of more than eight characters. However, the third condition leads to crashing because trying to write out of defined memory means a buffer overflow is happening. Then, if the smashing detection is enabled, you will see the following:

Build normally(stack protection is enabled by default)

```
gcc   buffer_overflow.c -o buffer_overflow
```

Result

```
*** stack smashing detected ***: terminated
```

But you can see the result by disabling the stack protection. To disable the stack protector, you can use *-fno-stack-protector* parameter.

```
gcc  -fno-stack-protector buffer_overflow.c -o buffer_overflow
```

Result

```
Segmentation fault (core dumped)
```

Out-of-band write (buffer underwrite)

```
#include <stdio.h>
#include <string.h>
#include <stdlib.h>


int main(int argc, char *argv[])
{
  char fileExtension[20];


  if (argc < 2)
  {
          printf("You need to enter db file address\n");
          exit(0);
  }


  const char *extIndex = strchr(argv[1], '.');
  printf("extIndex: %s\n", extIndex);
  printf("length of extIndex: %ld\n", strlen(extIndex));
  strncpy(fileExtension, extIndex, strlen(extIndex));
  printf("fileExtension: %s\n", fileExtension);


  return 0;
}
```

If the input does not include '.', it will cause a *segmentation fault*, and the application will stop. This is an out-of-band write, but if the input includes '.' and the file extension exceeds 20 characters, it will be a buffer overflow.

Solution

- Check the input size
- Copy the exact number from the input
- Use stack protection

Expired pointer dereference (CWE-825)

If we use a pointer to a memory location that is no longer valid, it causes problems. This title can be broken into the items below.

Use after free (CWE-416)

Use after free (CWE-416) occurs when a variable is referenced or used after it has been freed. This can lead to an application crash, executing code, or using an unexpected value.

```
#include <stdio.h>
#include <stdlib.h>
#include <unistd.h>
#include <string.h>


#define BUFSIZER 100


int main(int argc, char **argv) {
char *buffer_1;
char *buffer_2;


if (argc < 2)
{
      printf("You need to enter a parameter\n");
      exit(0);
}


```

```
buffer_1 = (char *) malloc(BUFSIZER);
buffer_2 = (char *) malloc(BUFSIZER);
free(buffer_1);
buffer_1= NULL; // Removing/Disabling this line leads to unknown behavior
strncpy(buffer_1, argv[1], BUFSIZER-1);
free(buffer_2);
printf("buffer_1: %s", buffer_1);
return 0;
}
```

Result

```
Segmentation fault (core dumped)
```

If we remove *buffer_1= NULL;*, no error will occur, but the point is we are accessing the memory space that has been de-allocated. If it happens in a larger application, it might lead to overwriting another variable/object value.

Double free (CWE-415)

```
#include <stdio.h>
#include <stdlib.h>
#include <unistd.h>


#define BUFSIZER 100


int main(int argc, char **argv) {
  char *buffer_1;


  if (argc < 2)
  {
          printf("You need to enter a parameter\n");
          exit(0);
  }


  buffer_1 = (char *) malloc(BUFSIZER);
  free(buffer_1);
  free(buffer_1);
```

```
  return 0;
}
```

Result

```
free(): double free detected in tcache 2
Aborted (core dumped)
```

As you can see, we have freed the pointer, which is *buffer_1*, twice. The error doesn't provide a clear lead on what happened. But we know that the cause of the application crash was. In a simple application like this example, it might be easy to find the issue with skimming on the code; however, in a big code, it might not be so easy.

Out-of-Bounds Read (CWE-125)

Example:

```
#include <stdio.h>
#include <string.h>


int main() {
  char buffer[10] = "Hello";
  // Attempt to read beyond the allocated buffer
  for (int i = 0; i < 15; i++) {
      // Once i >= 10, we read beyond the buffer's end
      printf("Character %d: %c\n", i, buffer[i]);
  }
  return 0;
}
```

Verification: `buffer` is 10 chars, containing `"Hello\0"`, which fits comfortably. Once `i` reaches 10, `buffer[i]` goes out of the valid range `[0..9]`. This results in reading memory beyond the array boundary. This is a correct demonstration of out-of-bounds read.

Buffer Over-Read (CWE-126)

Example:

```
#include <stdio.h>
#include <string.h>


int main() {
  char source[] = "Short";
  char dest[10];
  // Copying 15 bytes from 'source' which has only 6 bytes (5 chars + '\0')
  memcpy(dest, source, 15);
  printf("Copied: %s\n", dest);
  return 0;
}
```

Verification: `source` = "Short" + '\0' = 6 bytes total. Using `memcpy(dest, source, 15)` attempts to read 15 bytes from `source`, which is more than it contains. After 6 bytes, `memcpy` reads beyond the source buffer. This accurately shows a buffer over-read scenario.

Buffer Under-Read (CWE-127)

Example:

```
#include <iostream>
#include <cstring>


int main() {
  char arr[5] = "Data"; // 'D' 'a' 't' 'a' '\0'
  char *ptr = arr + 2;  // Points to 't'


  // Move the pointer back by 3, which would place it before arr[0]
  ptr -= 3; // Now ptr points before the start of arr


  std::cout << "Reading memory before array: " << *ptr << std::endl; // Undefined be\
havior
  return 0;
}
```

Verification: `arr` has five elements: indices 0..4. Initially, `ptr = arr+2` points to `arr[2]` ('t'). Doing `ptr -= 3` sets `ptr = arr[-1]`, which is invalid. Attempting to read `*ptr` now reads memory before the buffer starts. This is a correct example of under-read buffers.

NULL Pointer Dereference (CWE-476)

Example:

```
fun main() {
  var str: String? = null
  // Using '!!' bypasses null safety and will throw NullPointerException if str is n\
ull
  println("Length of string: ${str!!.length}")
}
```

Verification: `str` is `null`. Using `!!` forces a dereference despite `null`, causing a NullPointerException at runtime. Correct demonstration.

Example:

```
#include <stdio.h>


int main() {
  char *ptr = NULL;
  // Dereferencing a NULL pointer leads to undefined behavior
  printf("First character: %c\n", *ptr);
  return 0;
}
```

Verification: `ptr` is `NULL`. Dereferencing `*ptr` is an undefined behavior and typically crashes. Correct demonstration.

Access of Uninitialized Pointer (CWE-824)

Example

```
#include <stdio.h>


int main() {
  char *uninitializedPtr; // Not initialized, contains garbage
  // Attempt to read or write through it is undefined behavior
  printf("Value: %c\n", *uninitializedPtr);
  return 0;
}
```

Verification: `uninitializedPtr` may point anywhere. Dereferencing it without assigning a valid memory address causes undefined behavior. Correct demonstration.

Java

Java provides memory safety through its managed environment and garbage collection, reducing certain classes of errors common in C/C++. However, Java is not immune to other mistakes that can lead to severe vulnerabilities if code is not properly secured.

Serialization Vulnerabilities (CWE-502: Deserialization of Untrusted Data)

Principle Violation: Zero Trust and Fail Safe. Using native Java deserialization with untrusted data can allow attackers to instantiate unexpected objects or execute code remotely.

Bad:

```
// BAD: Deserializing untrusted data directly
// CWE-502: Deserialization of Untrusted Data
// Violates Zero Trust - trusting input from unknown sources
ObjectInputStream ois = new ObjectInputStream(inputStream);
Object obj = ois.readObject(); // Potential RCE if attacker provides malicious object
```

Good:

```
// GOOD: Use a safe serialization format like JSON with a known schema
// or a whitelist of classes allowed for deserialization
Gson gson = new Gson();
MyClass obj = gson.fromJson(jsonString, MyClass.class);
// Validate obj fields before use to ensure it's safe
```

Ineffective Exception Handling (CWE-209: Information Exposure Through Error Messages)

Principle Violation: Fail Safe. Detailed stack traces can reveal internal logic, file paths, or credentials.

Bad:

```
// BAD: Logging full exception details to the user or in unsecured logs
try {
  processPayment(userData);
} catch (Exception e) {
  // CWE-209: Leaking internal error details
  System.out.println("Error: " + e.getMessage()); // Might leak sensitive info
}
```

Good:

```
// GOOD: Generic error messages for the user and detailed logs only in secure server\
 logs
try {
  processPayment(userData);
} catch (Exception e) {
  // Show the user a generic message
  System.out.println("An error occurred. Please try again.");


  // Log more details securely, without exposing them publicly
  logger.warn("Payment processing failed for user: {}, error: {}", userId, e);
  // Ensure logs are properly protected and not world-readable
}
```

Use of Reflection (CWE-470: Use of Externally-Controlled Input to Select Classes or Code)

Principle Violation: Separation of Privilege. Uncontrolled reflection can allow bypassing of normal access controls.

Bad:

```
// BAD: Directly using user input to select a method via reflection
// Could invoke methods not intended for user access
String methodName = request.getParameter("method");
Method m = targetObject.getClass().getMethod(methodName);
m.invoke(targetObject); // Attacker can call arbitrary methods if not filtered
```

Good:

```
// GOOD: Whitelist allowed methods
Set<String> allowedMethods = Set.of("safeMethod1", "safeMethod2");
String methodName = request.getParameter("method");
if (allowedMethods.contains(methodName)) {
  Method m = targetObject.getClass().getMethod(methodName);
  m.invoke(targetObject);
} else {
  // Fail safe: deny request
  logger.info("Attempted call to disallowed method: {}", methodName);
}
```

Insecure Configuration and Hard-Coded Credentials (CWE-798: Use of Hard-coded Credentials)

Principle Violation: Security Through Obscurity, Zero Trust.

Bad:

```
// BAD: Storing credentials directly in code
// CWE-798: Hard-coded Credentials
String dbUser = "admin";
String dbPass = "SuperSecret123";
connectToDatabase(dbUser, dbPass);
```

Good:

```
// GOOD: Retrieve credentials from a secure vault or environment variables
String dbUser = System.getenv("DB_USER");
String dbPass = System.getenv("DB_PASS");
if (dbUser == null || dbPass == null) {
  // Fail safe: do not proceed
  throw new SecurityException("Database credentials not set!");
}
connectToDatabase(dbUser, dbPass);
```

Unchecked Input Leading to Injection (CWE-89: SQL Injection, CWE-79: XSS)

Principle Violation: Zero Trust.

Bad:

```
// BAD: Using string concatenation for SQL queries with user input
String userParam = request.getParameter("id");
String query = "SELECT * FROM users WHERE id='" + userParam + "'";
Statement stmt = conn.createStatement();
ResultSet rs = stmt.executeQuery(query); // Vulnerable to SQL injection
```

Good:

```
// GOOD: Use prepared statements
String userParam = request.getParameter("id");
String query = "SELECT * FROM users WHERE id=?";
PreparedStatement pstmt = conn.prepareStatement(query);
pstmt.setString(1, userParam);
ResultSet rs = pstmt.executeQuery(); // Safe against SQL injection
```

Integer Overflow/Underflow (CWE-190 / CWE-191)

Example

```
public class IntegerOverflowExample {
  public static void main(String[] args) {
      int maxVal = Integer.MAX_VALUE; // 2147483647
      int overflowed = maxVal + 1;    // Wraps to a negative number
      System.out.println("Overflowed value: " + overflowed);
  }
}
```

Verification: In Java, `Integer.MAX_VALUE + 1` wraps around to `Integer.MIN_VALUE`, demonstrating overflow. This is correct.

Example

```
public class IntegerUnderflowExample {
  public static void main(String[] args) {
      int minVal = Integer.MIN_VALUE; // -2147483648
      int underflowed = minVal - 1;   // Wraps around to a positive number
      System.out.println("Underflowed value: " + underflowed);
  }
}
```

Verification: `Integer.MIN_VALUE - 1` wraps around to `Integer.MAX_VALUE`, demonstrating integer underflow. This is correct.

Kotlin

Kotlin's safer type system and null-safety features reduce some risks, but developers must still be aware of common pitfalls in concurrency, object copying, and extension functions.

Null Safety Misconceptions

Principle Violation: Fail Safe. Using the `!!` operator blindly can cause unexpected crashes.

Bad:

```
// BAD: Using !! On nullable data without checks
val input: String? = null
println(input!!.length) // NullPointerException at runtime
```

Good:

```
// GOOD: Use safe calls and elvis operator
val input: String? = null
println(input?.length ?: "No data") // Gracefully handles null input
```

Improper Coroutines Usage (Race Conditions and Data Races)

Principle Violation: Zero Trust and Defense in Depth. Failing to synchronize data can lead to unpredictable behavior.

Bad:

```
// BAD: Shared mutable state without synchronization can lead to race conditions
var counter = 0
repeat(1000) {
  GlobalScope.launch {
      counter++ // Not thread-safe
  }
}
```

Good:

```kotlin
// GOOD: Use Mutex or other synchronization primitives to prevent data races
val mutex = Mutex()
var counter = 0
runBlocking {
  repeat(1000) {
      launch {
          mutex.withLock {
              counter++
          }
      }
  }
}
// Now increments are atomic and safe
```

Extension Functions Misuse

Extension functions can improve code readability but might unintentionally expose internal details or break encapsulation if used carelessly.

Bad:

```kotlin
// BAD: Extension exposing internal state
class SensitiveData(private val secret: String)


fun SensitiveData.getSecret(): String {
  // Violates Separation of Privilege: exposing internal secrets via extension
  return this::class.java.getDeclaredField("secret").also { it.isAccessible = true }\
.get(this) as String
}
```

Good:

```kotlin
// GOOD: Only provide safe operations as extension functions
class SensitiveData(private val secret: String) {
  fun canReveal(userRole: String) = (userRole == "admin")
}


fun SensitiveData.safeReveal(userRole: String): String? {
  // Check authorization before revealing any internal data
  return if (canReveal(userRole)) "Some redacted info" else null
}
```

Data Class Copy Functions

Data classes have a `copy()` function that can inadvertently duplicate sensitive objects without checks.

Bad:

```
data class UserToken(val token: String, val expiry: Long)


// BAD: Blindly copying sensitive data
val original = UserToken("secret-token-123", System.currentTimeMillis() + 3600_000)
val copy = original.copy() // Duplicates sensitive token
```

Good:

```
data class UserToken(val token: String, val expiry: Long) {
  fun safeCopy(): UserToken {
      // Maybe omit the token or replace it with a masked version
      return UserToken("masked", expiry)
  }
}


val original = UserToken("secret-token-123", System.currentTimeMillis() + 3600_000)
val safeCopy = original.safeCopy() // Avoid duplicating sensitive data directly
```

Default Parameters and Overloading

Using default parameters incorrectly could lead to unexpected behaviors, which allows unauthorized actions if security checks are skipped.

Bad:

```
// BAD: A function with a default parameter that bypasses checks if not specified
fun performAction(userRole: String = "guest") {
  if (userRole == "admin") {
      println("Performing sensitive action")
  } else {
      println("Insufficient permissions")
  }
}


performAction() // Defaults to "guest", but what if logic changes and guest acts as \
admin by mistake?
```

Good:

```
// GOOD: Explicitly require a role and validate it
fun performAction(userRole: String) {
  when (userRole) {
      "admin" -> println("Performing sensitive action")
      else -> println("Insufficient permissions")
  }
}


// Always specify role explicitly
performAction("admin")
```

NULL Pointer Dereference (CWE-476)

Example

```
fun main() {
  var str: String? = null
  // Using '!!' bypasses null safety and will throw NullPointerException if str is n\
ull
  println("Length of string: ${str!!.length}")
}
```

Verification: `str` is `null`. Using `!!` forces a dereference despite `null`, causing a NullPointerException at runtime. Correct demonstration.

Real world examples

Below are some examples of CVEs related to the typical vulnerabilities discussed in this chapter. While not comprehensive, these illustrate how mistakes like buffer overflows, use-after-free errors, and insecure configurations have manifested in both Linux and Android ecosystems. You can check them on your own to see some of the operating system-related vulnerabilities. They will give you a better perspective on the actual scenarios that could happen.

Linux-Related CVEs

1. **CVE-2022-0847 (Dirty Pipe)**:

- **Context**: A vulnerability in the Linux kernel's pipe implementation allowed attackers to overwrite read-only files.
- **Relation to This Chapter**:
  - **Principle**: Violates "Least Privilege" and "Fail Safe" because it allowed unauthorized modification of files from processes that shouldn't have that capability.
  - **Weakness**: Out-of-bounds write or improper kernel memory handling leads to privilege escalation.

2. **CVE-2020-8597 (pppd vulnerability)**:

- **Context**: A buffer overflow in the PPP daemon (pppd) on Linux-based systems allowed remote code execution.
- **Relation to This Chapter**:
  - **CWE**: Maps to buffer overflow weaknesses (e.g., CWE-121).
  - **Principle**: Violates "Zero Trust," as the daemon did not properly validate untrusted network input.
  - **Impact**: Attackers could gain remote access due to unsafe handling of incoming packets.

3. **CVE-2019-14615 (Intel Graphics Driver on Linux)**:

- **Context**: A flaw in the Intel i915 graphics driver in the Linux kernel permitted reading out-of-bounds memory.
- **Relation to This Chapter**:
  - **CWE**: Out-of-bounds read (CWE-125).
  - **Principle**: Violates "Minimize Attack Surface" and "Fail Safe," as improper boundary checks allowed leakage of sensitive kernel memory.

Android-Related CVEs

1. **CVE-2019-2215 (Android Binder Use-After-Free):**

- **Context:** A use-after-free vulnerability in the Android kernel's binder driver allowed local privilege escalation.
- **Relation to This Chapter:**
  - **CWE:** Use-after-free (CWE-416).
  - **Principle:** Violates "Fail Safe" and "Least Privilege." The kernel should never let unprivileged users gain escalated privileges due to incorrect memory lifecycle management. Impact: Attackers could exploit this bug to root devices or execute arbitrary code at the kernel level.

2. **CVE-2021-0920 (Android Kernel Memory Corruption):**

- **Context:** Memory corruption vulnerability in Android's kernel leads to potential privilege escalation.
- **Relation to This Chapter:**
  - **Weakness:** Similar to buffer overflows or out-of-bounds writes (CWE-787) and potentially other memory-safety issues.
  - **Principle:** Violates "Fail Safe," as a kernel memory error provided attackers with an avenue to break out of the restricted environment.

3. **CVE-2017-13218 (Android Media Framework):**

- **Context:** A vulnerability in Android's Media framework allowed remote code execution by sending specially crafted media files.
- **Relation to This Chapter:**
  - **CWE:** Could map to CWE-119 (Buffer Overflow) or other memory corruption issues in complex media parsing code.
  - **Principle:** Violates "KISS" since complex media parsing logic without strict validation leads to buffer overflows.
  - **Impact:** Attackers could potentially take control of the device by tricking users into opening malicious media files.

4. **CVE-2022-20465 (Android System Vulnerability):**

- **Context:** A vulnerability in the Android system component allowed attackers to execute arbitrary code or gain higher privileges.
- **Relation to This Chapter:**
  - **Principle:** Violates "Zero Trust" and "Least Privilege."
  - **Weakness:** This could be due to unsafe handling of system calls or an integer overflow leading to memory corruption.

Data Validation

Untrusted Data Sources

The safety and integrity of an application are critically dependent on how untrusted data sources are handled in secure programming. Untrusted data sources may contain malicious code, inaccurate information, or other flaws that pose various security threats, including code injection, data tampering, and data leakage. By ensuring that the application is deployed securely, these risks can be avoided. Also, it helps to safeguard sensitive data from the application's potential access. Handling untrusted data is even more vital for Android development since Android apps are part of a broad, varied, and open environment.

Here, we discuss different techniques for handling untrusted data sources, emphasizing Android programming. The Examples are supplied in multiple languages, including C, C++, Java, and Kotlin, and special attention will be given to the Android application development environment.

Types of Untrusted Data Sources

Before diving into handling untrusted data sources, it is necessary to understand the types of data sources that can be considered untrusted. Let's have a look at some common examples:

External storage:

Files stored on external storage, such as an SD card, can be accessed by any application with the appropriate permissions. Any data originating from external storage should be treated as untrusted.

User input:

Data that originates from or is entered by a user should be considered untrusted, as its integrity cannot be guaranteed.

Network connections:

Data obtained from servers, APIs, or other remote services can have varying levels of trustworthiness. In many cases, this data should be treated as untrusted.

Third-party libraries:

Although they might increase applications' capabilities, external libraries can also provide unforeseen security threats. When using third-party libraries, caution should be exercised, and their data should be regarded with suspicion.

Dealing with Untrusted Data Sources

The following are some techniques and best practices for securely handling untrusted data sources:

Input validation:

Validating input from various sources is at the core of handling untrusted data. Input validation checks the data against a set of predefined rules and constraints to help ensure it matches the expected requirements.

For example, consider a simple Java program that handles user input:

```
import java.util.Scanner;

public class InputValidation {
  public static void main(String[] args) {
    Scanner scanner = new Scanner(System.in);
    System.out.print("Enter your age: ");
    int age = scanner.nextInt();

    if (age < 0 || age > 120) {
      System.out.println("Invalid age!");
    } else {
      System.out.println("Your age is: " + age);
    }

    scanner.close();
  }
}
```

In this example, the user's input is checked to ensure it is within a reasonable range (0 to 120).

Encoding and escaping data:

Properly encoding and escaping data is another essential aspect of handling untrusted data. For instance, when displaying data from an untrusted source in an HTML context, escaping the data is necessary to prevent cross-site scripting (XSS) attacks. In Android, TextViews automatically escape HTML when set using the setText method, but you can escape HTML manually using the following in Java:

```
String untrustedData = "<script>alert('XSS')</script>";
String escapedData = Html.escapeHtml(untrustedData);
textView.setText(escapedData);
```

In Kotlin:

```
val untrustedData = "<script>alert('XSS')</script>"
val escapedData = HtmlCompat.escapeHtml(untrustedData, HtmlCompat.TO_HTML_PARAGRAPH_\
LINES_CONSECUTIVE)
textView.text = escapedData
```

Limiting third-party library usage:

Nowadays, many third-party libraries are available that can help add functionalities more efficiently, faster, and cheaper. However, adding new libraries might also introduce vulnerabilities. We should use and select those libraries carefully and only when necessary to reduce the potential risks.

Sandboxing and isolation:

If the untrusted data needs to be processed in a potentially harmful manner, consider using an isolated environment which separates processes to mitigate the risk of damage to the primary application.

Handling untrusted data sources securely reduces code injection risks, data tampering, and data leakage. Several precautions can be taken to ensure the application and its data's confidentiality and integrity, such as validating input, encoding and escaping data, storing and transmitting it properly, limiting third-party libraries, and sandboxing or isolating it. By following these best practices, application developers can better protect their applications against security threats from untrusted data sources.

Example

```
<!-- AndroidManifest.xml -->

...

<service
    android:name=".TheIsolatedService"
    android:process=":isolated_service"
    android:isolatedProcess="true">
</service>

...
```

This configuration run *TheIsolatedService* in a separate process which is isolated from the rest of the system. This process doesn't have any permission on its own. The other activity or services could communicate through binding to it. It is a good option for running third party code/libraries in isolation

Input Validation

A key approach in safe programming is input validation, which confirms that user input data is reliable, accurate, and satisfies the application's specifications. It also ensures that the program does not process data that could result in security flaws like code injection, buffer overflows, or denial-of-service attacks. With people relying increasingly on mobile devices, particularly Android smartphones and tablets, the significance of input validation has significantly increased.

We will cover different input validation techniques applicable to Android development, from low-level to high-level programming with C, C++, Java, and Kotlin. We will also provide some examples to illustrate the use of these techniques.

Input Range Validation

The range of input data sometimes plays a key role in stability and security. If the code is not protected against out-of-range input, it can lead to a crash in the simplest situation, leak data, or create a vulnerability. For instance, if some data is out of range that the user should not access, it should be protected by comparing the data to a strict condition. Moreover, the range can cause an overflow or even be out of the index.

```
const int MAX_USER = 1000;


List<UserInfo> userInfoList;
void getUserInfoByIf(int userId)
{
  return  userInfoList[userId];
}
```

It was a straightforward illustration of what might occur if the userId is larger than the list's size. The minus index, on the other hand, can result in a similar issue. It can worsen in languages like C and C++ by triggering overflow or writing to or reading from a nearby, forbidden memory address.

Input Length Validation

One of the simplest yet essential input validations is checking the length and range of the user input, especially in languages such as C and C++. This technique helps prevent buffer overflow attacks, which occur when an attacker provides input exceeding the capacity of a variable, causing it to leak into adjacent memory locations. Using a strict approach leads to preventing exceptions in all languages. For instance, in other languages like Java and Kotlin, attempting to write/read out of bounds will raise an exception that can lead to an application crash if it's not managed properly.

For instance, a C++ example of input length validation can be:

Safe approach

```
void getUserName(char *userInput)
{
  char userName[20];
  strncpy(userName, userInput, 20);
}
```

Unsafe approach

```
void getUserName(char *userInput)
{
  char userName[20];
  for(int i = 0; userInput[i]!= null; i++)
    userName[i] = userInput [i];
}
```

The second approach is not safe. It leads to writing to memory addresses beyond the userName boundary, which can cause an application to crash or corrupt other data.

When you're coding for Android, keeping your app secure is super important, and one way to keep things tight is by putting a cap on how much input you allow. It's like bouncers at a club—you want to ensure you don't let in so much data that it causes chaos, like crashes, or worse, gives hackers a way in. Setting up these input limits creates a safety net that guarantees your app works smoothly without opening the door to cyber threats.

Importance of Input Length Restrictions

Length restrictions on user inputs demonstrate various benefits, including:

Prevention of Buffer Overflow Attacks

Buffer overflow is when a program messes up and writes more data than it's supposed to in a storage spot called a buffer. This can cause all sorts of chaos, like crashing the application or—even worse—letting some sneaky code run when it shouldn't. The trick to stopping this is for programmers to be strict about checking the size of the input they're getting, making sure it won't try to cram too much data into the buffer.

Protection Against Denial of Service (DoS) Attacks

Input length restrictions can also protect applications from being consumed by excessive data, which can result in a denial-of-service (DoS) attack. A DoS attack's primary goal is to overwhelm the target system, rendering it unavailable to users. Restricting input data length prevents this by limiting the processing power and resources required to handle input.

Data Integrity

Checking how much data is shoved into our apps is super important. Think about it—if you try to pack too much stuff into too small a space, something will get cut off or messed up, right? That's exactly what can happen with data. If we let it get too bulky and overflow the space we've got for it, we can end up with only half of what we need or a total data disaster on our hands. By being strict about how long the input can take, we developers can avoid these headaches and guarantee everything runs smoothly.

Usability

Applying input length restrictions can also improve an application's usability by guiding users to provide inputs that the system can handle properly. For example, an application might require users to enter specific information, such as their postal code or phone number, to complete a process. Creating length restrictions helps guide users toward entering valid and acceptable information, leading to a more satisfying user experience.

Implementation Techniques

There are various ways to enforce input length restrictions in different programming languages. Here are some practical examples using C, C++, Java, and Kotlin.

C In C, the developer can use the *fgets* function to read input up to a specific limit, preventing buffer overflow vulnerabilities. The following code demonstrates reading input restricted to a set length:

```
#include <stdio.h>
#include <stdlib.h>

#define BUFFER_SIZE 1024

int main() {
  char buffer[BUFFER_SIZE];
  printf("Enter some text: ");
  fgets(buffer, BUFFER_SIZE, stdin);
  printf("You entered: %s", buffer);
  return 0;
}
```

In this example, fgets reads the user input with a maximum limit of BUFFER_SIZE - 1 characters, preventing buffer overflow issues.

C++ In C++, one approach to restricting the input length is using the std::getline function from the string library. For example:

```
#include <iostream>
#include <string>

constexpr unsigned int MAX_LENGTH = 1024;

int main() {
  std::string input;
  std::cout << "Enter some text: ";
  std::getline(std::cin, input);

  if (input.length() > MAX_LENGTH) {
      input.erase(MAX_LENGTH);
      std::cout << "The input was too long, trimming to " << MAX_LENGTH << " charact\
ers.\n";
  }

  std::cout << "You entered: " << input << std::endl;
  return 0;
}
```

Here, std::getline reads user input as a string, and the input length is compared to the defined maximum limit. It trims the string to the desired length if it exceeds the limit.

Java Java provides various techniques for restricting input length. A standard approach is to use the substring method. Here's an example:

```
import java.util.Scanner;

public class InputLengthExample {
  public static void main(String[] args) {
      final int maxLength = 1024;
      Scanner scanner = new Scanner(System.in);

      System.out.print("Enter some text: ");
      String input = scanner.nextLine();

      if (input.length() > maxLength) {
          input = input.substring(0, maxLength);
```

```
            System.out.println("The input was too long, trimming to " + maxLength + " \
characters.");
        }

        System.out.println("You entered: " + input);
        scanner.close();
    }
}
```

In this snippet, the input string's length is checked to ensure it does not exceed the specified maximum limit. If it does, the substring method trims it to the desired length.

```
const int MAX_INDEX = 1000;
const int MIN_INDEX = 0;
UserInfo userInfoList[MAX_INDEX];

void getUserInfoByIndex(int index)
{
  return userInfoList[i];
}
```

In the previous example, sending an index number less than zero or bigger than 1000 causes ArrayIndexOutOfBoundsException.

Kotlin In Kotlin, the developer can leverage extension functions to create a custom inputLimit function. For example:

```
import java.util.Scanner

const val maxLength = 1024

fun String.inputLimit(length: Int): String {
  return if (this.length > length) {
      this.substring(0, length).also {
          println("The input was too long, trimming to $maxLength characters.")
      }
  } else {
      this
  }
}

fun main() {
  val scanner = Scanner(System.`in`)
```

```
    print("Enter some text: ")
    val input = scanner.nextLine()
    val limitedInput = input.inputLimit(maxLength)

    println("You entered: $limitedInput")
    scanner.close()
}
```

The inputLimit extension function limits the input string's length. The function trims the string to the desired length if the input exceeds the maximum limit.

Whitelisting and Blacklisting

Whitelisting is a technique that permits only specific or predefined input values, while blacklisting rejects specific or harmful input patterns. It is generally advisable to favor whitelisting, as it is a more restrictive approach. Because anything missed by blacklisting could result in a problem, we can easily compare user input against the white list depending on the kind of data the user provides.

A Java example of utilizing whitelisting is as follows:

```
public boolean isAllowedCharacter(char c) {
String allowedCharacters = "abcdefghijklmnopqrstuvwxyzABCDEFGHIJKLMNOPQRSTUVWXYZ";
return allowedCharacters.indexOf(c) != -1;
}
```

In this example, the code defines a set of allowed characters and checks if the input character exists within the set.

Input format

Sometimes, we need to obtain a specific data format from a user or through another source, after which we process the data to separate or extract different parts. In this situation, extracting or slicing data without verifying its format may result in an unexpected error, such as type casting, being outside of the range, being outside of the index, etc. To receive the appropriate information, we cannot rely on assumptions.

Regular Expressions

Regular expressions (regex) provide a robust mechanism to match patterns in input strings. They can be employed effectively to validate and sanitize user input.

A Kotlin example demonstrating the use of regular expressions for input validation is as follows:

```
fun main() {
  val emailPattern = Regex("""^[a-zA-Z0-9._%+-]+@[a-zA-Z0-9.-]+\.[a-zA-Z]{2,}$""")
  print("Enter your email address: ")
  val input = readLine() ?: ""


  if (emailPattern.matches(input)) {
      println("The email address is valid")
  } else {
      println("The email address is invalid")
  }
}
```

I just wanted to give you a heads-up on how to check if an email address is legitimate using a fancy regular expression.

Type-checking and Casting

Type checking and casting ensure that the variables are of the correct data type before using them in application logic. Type casting can lead to runtime exceptions if not performed correctly, making verifying the input data types essential. It's important to protect the application from type-casting exceptions. As you can see in the Java code below, it uses type checking and casting surrounded by try-catch:

```
public static Integer toInteger(String input) {
try {
  return Integer.parseInt(input);
} catch (NumberFormatException e) {
  return null;
}
}
```

Application Framework and Library Input Validation

In Android development, app frameworks and libraries with built-in input validation capabilities can significantly enhance security measures. For example, the Android framework contains numerous classes and methods that allow for secure input validation and handling, such as EditText and InputFilter.

Here is an example of using InputFilter in an Android app (Java):

```
EditText editText = new EditText(this);
InputFilter[] filters = new InputFilter[1];
filters[0] = new InputFilter.LengthFilter(10); // Maximum input length
editText.setFilters(filters);
```

Some libraries and methods for input validation:

- Using inputType, maxLength and android:pattern attributes to restrict the user input
- TextInputLayout & TextWatcher
- AwesomeValidation (supports regex)
- Saripaar v2 (needs to be excluded from ProGuard)

Note! Please remember that data encompasses a wide range of elements, including metadata, raw data, user input, XML, JSON, and more.

Real-life Incidents

Imposing limits on input length is required for application security. Failure to enforce these restrictions has precipitated a series of prominent security breaches.

The Morris Worm (1988):

One of the first computer worms was distributed via the Internet. It exploited a vulnerability in UNIX's finger program through a buffer overflow attack. The application's lack of input length restrictions allowed the worm to overwrite the stack and gain unauthorized access to the system.

The infamous Heartbleed bug that affected OpenSSL (2014):

This vulnerability enabled attackers to read sensitive data from a server's memory by abusing the lack of proper input validation and length restrictions, resulting in unauthorized access to private information.

These examples illustrate the significant impact on security when adequate input length restrictions are not implemented. Developers must consider this vital security measure to prevent similar incidents from occurring in their applications.

Encoding Methods

To guarantee proper data handling and avoid data injection attacks, output encoding is an essential approach in secure coding. To assure accurate interpretation and usage by various programming languages, systems, or applications, this approach refers to converting data from one form to another.

By correctly encoding data that is shown, communicated, or stored, output encoding techniques support the security of an application in the context of Android development.

Output encoding helps mitigate several security concerns, such as SQL injection,cross-site scripting (XSS), and command injection attacks. Furthermore, correctly encoded output data is required for processing Unicode characters, which are used in almost all current software programs and systems.

In this section, we'll discuss numerous output encoding techniques important for secure Android development in low-level and high-level programming, provide examples in Java and Kotlin, and explore relevant events and the background of output encoding.

HTML Encoding

HTML encoding is the process of converting specific characters into their corresponding HTML entities. This prevents the confusion of data and code and ensures that unauthorized code execution does not occur in a web context.

Example

```
import org.apache.commons.lang.StringEscapeUtils;


String unsafeString = "<html> Hello, <b>World</b>!";
String safeString = StringEscapeUtils.escapeHtml(unsafeString);
System.out.println(safeString);
```

The safeString variable will now contain the HTML-encoded version of the unsafeString:

```
&lt;html&gt; Hello, &lt;b&gt;World&lt;/b&gt;!
```

URL Encoding

URL encoding, also known as Percent Encoding, converts characters within a URL into a format that can be transmitted correctly over the Internet. Unsafe ASCII characters are replaced by a '%' followed by two hexadecimal digits. This encoding method is crucial when passing user-generated data in URLs.

Example

```
import java.net.URLEncoder;
import java.nio.charset.StandardCharsets;


String unsafeString = "Hello, World!";
String safeString = URLEncoder.encode(unsafeString, StandardCharsets.UTF_8);
System.out.println(safeString);
```

The safeString variable will now contain the URL-encoded version of the unsafeString:

```
Hello%2C+World%21
```

JavaScript Encoding

JavaScript encoding is essential when untrusted data is embedded within a scripting context. This process involves replacing the unsafe characters with their respective escape sequences.

```
import org.apache.commons.lang.StringEscapeUtils;


String unsafeString = "alert('Hello, World!');";
String safeString = StringEscapeUtils.escapeJavaScript(unsafeString);
System.out.println(safeString);
```

The safeString variable will now contain the JavaScript-encoded version of the unsafeString:

```
alert(\'Hello, World!\');
```

SQL Encoding or SQL Escaping

SQL encoding, also known as SQL escaping, is the process of converting data to a format that is safe to use within an SQL statement. This procedure mitigates SQL injection attacks by neutralizing certain characters to prevent them from being misinterpreted as SQL commands.

Example

```
import java.sql.Connection;
import java.sql.DriverManager;
import java.sql.PreparedStatement;
import java.sql.SQLException;


String unsafeString = "'; DROP TABLE Users;--";
try (Connection conn = DriverManager.getConnection(DB_URL, DB_USER, DB_PASS)) {
  String query = "INSERT INTO Users (username) VALUES (?)";
  PreparedStatement pstmt = conn.prepareStatement(query);
  pstmt.setString(1, unsafeString);
  pstmt.executeUpdate();
} catch (SQLException e) {
  e.printStackTrace();
}
```

By parameterizing the SQL query, the prepared statement ensures that the unsafeString is treated as data and not as an SQL command.

Unicode Encoding

Unicode encoding involves transforming a string into a sequence of bytes using a specific character encoding. Due to its widespread use and compatibility, UTF-8 is the typical choice in Android development.

Example

```
import java.nio.charset.StandardCharsets


val unsafeString = "Hello, □□!"
val safeString = unsafeString.toByteArray(StandardCharsets.UTF_8)
println(safeString.contentToString())
```

The safeString variable will now contain the Unicode-encoded version of the unsafeString as bytes:

```
[72, 101, 108, 108, 111, 44, 32, 228, 184, 150, 231, 149, 140, 33]
```

Incidents and History

Output encoding has gained significant importance in recent years, considering the rise in data breaches caused by injection attacks. Famous security incidents include the well-known Heartbleed vulnerability, which occurred because proper output encoding was not used when handling TLS heartbeat messages. The OWASP Top Ten Project, which outlines the most critical security risks in web applications, consistently includes injection attacks—whose mitigation relies heavily on output encoding methods—among its top risks.

Adopting rigorous encoding strategies is imperative for ensuring the security and integrity of applications. Appropriate encoding methods must be deployed to meet the distinct demands of data processing. HTML, URL, JavaScript, SQL, and Unicode encodings are among the critical techniques that must be utilized to fortify the security of Android applications. Applying these encoding practices significantly enhances the applications' robustness and concurrently diminishes the risk of security infringements occasioned by injection attacks.

Sanitizing user inputs

As the name implies, input sanitization is paramount to secure coding methods. It entails cleaning and validating user input data, particularly when the program uses it in crucial contexts like database queries or file manipulations. Sanitization ensures that the input is in the right format and free of dangerous data that can ultimately result in security problems.

Given the large user base and diverse sources of input that an application may face, especially when we need to secure back-end communication, user private data, etc., input sanitization becomes a crucial component in Android development. Thus, employing input sanitization libraries is essential to ensuring that programs meet security standards.

Input Sanitization Libraries are generally discussed, along with how they are used and examples in the C, C++, Java, and Kotlin programming languages for low-level and high-level development.

Importance of Input Sanitization

Being an integral part of any secure coding practice, input sanitization protects an application from various security issues, like:

SQL Injection:

This is caused when unescaped user input is used to craft SQL queries, which may lead to unauthorized access to application data. In an SQL injection attack, an attacker can execute malicious SQL queries in the application's database by manipulating user inputs. This could result in unauthorized access to or manipulation of data.

Take into account the following Java code fragment, which builds a SQL query using user input:

```
String userInput = ... // User-supplied input
String query = "SELECT * FROM users WHERE username = '" + userInput + "'";
Cursor cursor = db.rawQuery(query, null);
```

It's possible that an attacker exploit this vulnerability by feeding user input containing an SQL injection payload, such as admin'–, which would result in the authentication bypass.

To prevent SQL injection, use parameterized queries, which will handle user input in a safe manner:

```
String userInput = ... // User-supplied input
String query = "SELECT * FROM users WHERE username = ?";
Cursor cursor = db.rawQuery(query, new String[] { userInput });
```

Example: To find potential security flaws in the codebase, we can use a program like FindBugs in Java. A possible SQL injection vulnerability is included in the code snippet below:

```
String query = "SELECT * FROM users WHERE username = '" + userInput + "'";
Statement stmt = connection.createStatement();
ResultSet rs = stmt.executeQuery(query);
```

During a code review, developers would suggest parameterized queries or prepared statements to prevent SQL injection attacks.

```
String query = "SELECT * FROM users WHERE username = ?";
PreparedStatement pstmt = connection.prepareStatement(query);
pstmt.setString(1, userInput);
ResultSet rs = pstmt.executeQuery();
```

Cross-site scripting (XSS):

Cross-site scripting occurs when an attacker sends malicious code in the form of browser-side scripts through a web application to an end user.

Command Injection:

Unplanned commands on a host system are executed when unsanitized user input is incorporated into system commands, a process known as command injection.

Buffer Overflow:

If unchecked, long user input may overflow the memory buffer, potentially allowing an attacker to execute arbitrary code.

Why use Input Sanitization Libraries?

Instead of writing custom sanitization functions for every user input scenario, sanitization libraries curate a pre-built set of functions covering various input validations and encodings. These ready-to-use libraries could be used to cover a wide range of abstract use cases.

Some advantages include:

- Availability of secure and reliable functions to verify and sanitize user inputs
- Faster development by avoiding the need to write custom functions
- High assurance of security with constant updates and optimizations provided by the library
- Compliance with common security standards

Input Sanitization Libraries for C/C++

Various libraries are available for C and C++ languages that provide input sanitization functions. Some popular ones include:

Libinjection:

It is a small, MIT-licensed C library that detects SQL injection and cross-site scripting using lexical analysis. The library parses and sanitizes strings to check for SQLi or XSS payloads.

StringSan:

Another library that focuses on removing or executing malicious code in strings provides robust protection against all types of buffer overflows and other string-based attacks.

libtidy:

a C library to clean input HTML and clean it up

Example: Using Libinjection library in C

```
#include <stdio.h>
#include <stdlib.h>
#include "libinjection.h"


int main(){
  char input[] = "1 UNION SELECT * FROM users -- ";
  int is_sql_injection = libinjection_sqli(input, strlen(input));


  if (is_sql_injection) {
      printf("SQLi detected\n");
  } else {
      printf("Input valid\n");
  }


  return 0;
}
```

Input Sanitization Libraries for Java

For Java and Android development, popular sanitization libraries include:

OWASP ESAPI:

The OWASP "Enterprise Security API" provides input validation and output encoding functions to ensure data security in Java applications.

Apache Commons Validator:

It is a widely used library that provides a set of input validation functions for various common Java use cases.

Google Guava:

Although not specifically designed for input sanitization, Guava can be used as a utility library with essential sanitization classes, like the Escaper class, to prevent HTML injection.

Example: Using OWASP ESAPI for input validation in Java

```
import org.owasp.esapi.ESAPI;
import org.owasp.esapi.errors.ValidationException;


public class SanitizerExample {
  public static void main(String[] args) {
      String userName = "<script>alert('XSS Attack!');</script>";


      try {
          String cleanUserName = ESAPI.validator().getValidInput("User Input", userN\
ame, "SafeString", 100, false);
          System.out.println("Valid User Name: " + cleanUserName);
      } catch (ValidationException e) {
          System.out.println("Invalid input detected: " + userName);
      }
  }
}
```

Input Sanitization Libraries in Kotlin (Android)

For Kotlin and Android development, some popular libraries are:

Android Saripaar:

This is a simple annotation-based Android library that provides input validation. It checks for various input patterns according to the annotations added to the respective input.

Validators Kotlin:

A lightweight Kotlin library that offers predefined input validation functions for common scenarios. Example: Using Android Saripaar for input validation in Kotlin

```
import com.mobsandgeeks.saripaar.annotation.*
import com.mobsandgeeks.saripaar.ValidationError
class MainActivity : AppCompatActivity(), Validator.ValidationListener {
  @NotEmpty
  @Email
  private lateinit var emailEditText: EditText
  @NotEmpty
  @Password
  private lateinit var passwordEditText: EditText
  private lateinit var submitButton:Button
  private lateinit var validator: Validator
  override fun onCreate(savedInstanceState: Bundle?) {
      super.onCreate(savedInstanceState)
      setContentView(R.layout.activity_main)
      emailEditText = findViewById(R.id.email)
      passwordEditText = findViewById(R.id.password)
      submitButton = findViewById(R.id.submit_button)
      submitButton.setOnClickListener { validateInputs() }
      validator = Validator(this)
      validator.setValidationListener(this)
  }
  fun validateInputs(view: View) {
      validator.validate()
```

```
    }


    override fun onValidationSucceeded() {
        Toast.makeText(this, "Input data is valid", Toast.LENGTH_SHORT).show()
    }


    override fun onValidationFailed(errors: List<ValidationError>) {
        for (error in errors) {
            val view = error.view
            val message = error.getCollatedErrorMessage(this)


            if (view is EditText) {
                view.error = message
            } else {
                Toast.makeText(this, message, Toast.LENGTH_LONG).show()
            }
        }
    }
}
```

Using input sanitization libraries helps keep coding safe, especially when making apps, and especially when someone tries to insert harmful information.

Android Security Model

As smartphones continue to shape how people interact with the world—storing personal documents, facilitating financial transactions, and guiding our daily travels—the importance of a robust security model cannot be overstated. Users expect that their personal information will remain private, that their credentials and sensitive communications will not be hijacked, and that the operating system will resist the countless forms of attack that arise in a connected world.

Android, powering billions of devices worldwide, is constantly exposed to the threats associated with scale and openness. Yet, the platform is structured with a comprehensive security architecture that spans every system layer. This architecture begins at the hardware level and extends upward through the Linux kernel and SELinux policies, the frameworks and services that govern application behavior, and the user-level interfaces and permissions that directly impact daily usage.

The Android security model could be a multi-layered onion, each layer providing unique defenses. At the outermost layers, user-centric controls, application sandboxes, and runtime permissions ensure that malicious apps cannot trivially gain access to personal data or system resources. Beneath this layer, the platform relies on robust code signing, package management, kernel-level security measures, strict SELinux policies, and hardware-backed security features like ARM TrustZone. Together, these measures form a "defense in depth" approach. Even if one layer is compromised, the adversary must still bypass the protective measures of deeper layers to achieve a meaningful breach.

Android's multi-layered security architecture is supposed to fulfill confidentiality, integrity, and availability requirements. Android follows a safe-default model to ensure that the fundamental bases of information security are in place.

Now, that is the time to go through the protection layers from a system perspective rather than a user's view. We will move through the layers, examining how applications are isolated at runtime, how permissions and SELinux policies constrain what an app can do, how the system verifies the integrity of applications, how inter-process communication (IPC) is secured, and how hardware abstractions and integrity checks bolster the platform's resilience. We will also consider the special role of the Play Integrity API, network security, update mechanisms, and the importance of secure user interface practices. By understanding this architectural model, developers, security professionals, and informed readers can appreciate the sophistication behind Android's daily operations.

Let's open the onion layers

One common approach in software engineering is to consider some layers to create an easy-to-understand model. The layers are abstractions that explain how communication, control flow, or data flow happen. I would like to follow the same pattern and use this approach to explain the Android Security Model.

Before diving into the system layers, it is helpful to look at the security goals across the layers:

1. **Device Security**: The platform protects against physical and network-based threats using secure boot processes, Trusted Execution Environments (such as ARM TrustZone), and enforced encryption of user data.
2. **Data Security**: Encryption safeguards user data at rest, while carefully controlled access ensures that only authorized entities can read or modify it.
3. **User Security**: The system guards user interactions, privacy, and credentials. This includes preventing malicious overlays on critical UI elements and ensuring that biometric and credential-based authentications are resistant to tampering.
4. **Application Security**: Android uses application sandboxing, permission checks, and code signing to contain untrusted or malicious software, which cannot easily escalate privileges, tamper with other apps, or access sensitive APIs without explicit user consent.
5. **Network Security**: Android enforces secure communications protocols such as TLS and HTTPS by default. VPN integration and a trusted set of system-wide Certificate Authorities strengthen the reliability of encrypted data in transit.
6. **Hardware Security and TrustZone Integration**: Hardware-backed key storage and secure execution environments protect cryptographic keys, verify device integrity at boot-time, and support DRM frameworks for content protection.
7. **Update Mechanisms**: Regular over-the-air (OTA) updates, monthly security patches, and a responsive incident response system keep devices resilient against newly discovered vulnerabilities.
8. **Preventing Remote Exploits**: Past threats like Stagefright have led to more stringent memory protections, standardized encryption, stronger sandboxing, and improved communication handling.

What could be added here is how Zero Trust and Defense in Depth have been implemented in Android. As can be seen, the multilayer in Android provides powerful protection against various types of attacks. No one can claim that the castle is impenetrable, but it is possible to pass the gates easily!

The Big Picture of the Android Security Model*

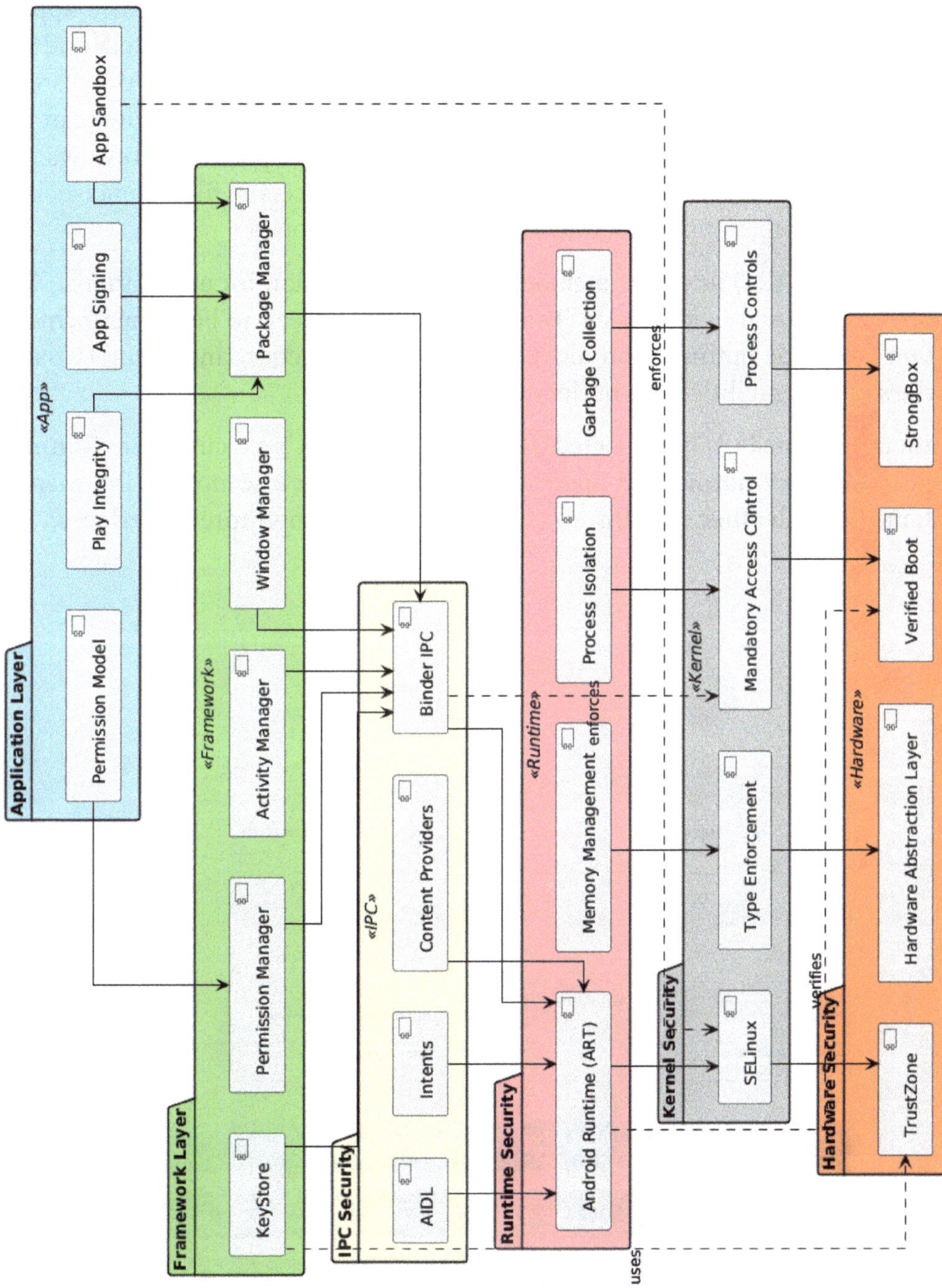

Figure 5. The big picture of Android Security Model

Let's start from the outermost layer.

Application Sandbox and Android Runtime

One of Android's foundational defenses is the application sandbox. Each installed application runs as a distinct Linux user ID (UID), isolating its processes and files at the filesystem and kernel levels. The UID helps track application activities and verify their permission to access the system resources. Besides, the isolation limits the interaction between applications. No application can read another app's data by default, ensuring that even if a malicious app slips past store reviews, its ability to harm the system or other apps is substantially limited. For instance, the filesystem isolation prevents unauthorized access to other apps' files due to sandboxed directories.

The Android Runtime (ART) manages memory and code execution for applications. ART provides just-in-time (JIT) and ahead-of-time (AOT) compilation which lead to better performance through pre-compilation and code optimization alongside garbage collection and memory safety features that reduce classic vulnerabilities like buffer overflows.

The combination of isolated UIDs, restricted filesystems, and ART's execution environment provides separated secure silos in Android that applications could run in a secure environment interacting with the system and each other only through well-defined and monitored interfaces.

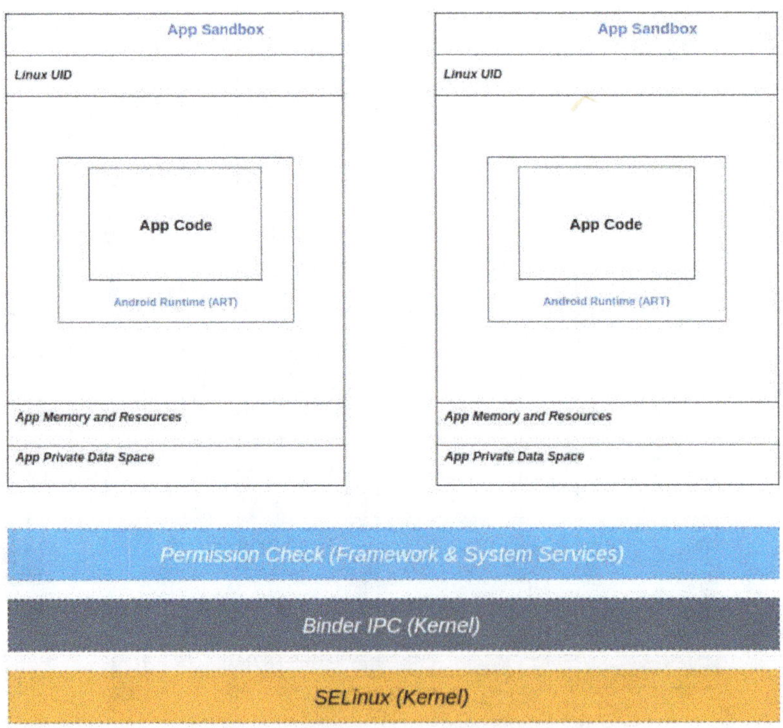

Figure 6. An overview of Android Sandbox

Application Signing

The app signing technique identifies the developer and ensures application integrity. Before an application runs, Android requires that it be cryptographically signed by the developer and stored somewhere secure. This code-signing step helps verify the author's identity and ensures that the app's code and resources have not been altered after signing. At install time, the system verifies the signature against the developer's certificate, rejecting any application that fails verification.

The Android signing solution has been improved by introducing new versions. Newer signing schemes, such as APK Signature Scheme v2 and v3, reinforce the protection by signing the entire package or using block-based signing. V2 was introduced in Android 7.0 by signing the whole app instead of the file-by-file method used in V1, while V2 provides better performance than V1. Version 3 is based on V2 and has additional metadata. Supporting key rotation in V3 makes it possible to use multiple signing keys and designate future keys that can be trusted after a specific time or version.

The newest version, V4, is supported by Android 1 and stores the signature file as a separate *.apk.idsig*. Unlike in V1, V2, and V3, the signature was stringed as a signing block in-app. V4 is officially an external companion to V2 and V3 to enable incremental installation.

This approach prevents attackers from adding or modifying files inside the APK undetected. Moreover, developers must manage their signing keys securely since compromised keys could allow attackers to impersonate and push malicious updates. The platform also supports Android App Bundles, ensuring the Google Play Store validates the final distributed package.

It is important to remember that Android employs a self-signing paradigm which means that the developer's identity is not automatically confirmed by any central authority, even though all apps must be cryptographically signed before being installed, unlike platforms where trusted third parties issue certificates, Android allows developers to generate their signing keys without external validation. As a result an app's signing certificate may contain arbitrary or misleading information, and a developer's genuine identity cannot be verified via the signature alone. The main benefits of app signing are code integrity and safe updates.

Below is a comparative overview of APK Signature Schemes v1, v2, v3, and v4:

Aspect	V1 (JAR Signing)	V2 (APK Signature Scheme)	V3 (Enhanced APK Signature Scheme)	V4 (APK Signature Scheme v4)
Introduction	Android 1.0+	Android 7.0 (Nougat)	Android 9.0 (Pie)	Android 11+

Aspect	V1 (JAR Signing)	V2 (APK Signature Scheme)	V3 (Enhanced APK Signature Scheme)	V4 (APK Signature Scheme v4)
Main Goal	Original signing method, per-file checks	Whole-APK signing for stronger integrity and speed	Builds on V2, adds metadata for key rotation & version targeting	Facilitates incremental (streaming) installs for faster verification
Signing Location	Inside META-INF (JAR-style)	Dedicated signing block within the APK	Dedicated signing block (V2 block + extra metadata)	External file (e.g., *.apk.idsig) separate from the APK
Integrity Coverage	Per-file, not fully covering all APK bytes	Whole APK integrity (except the signing block)	Whole APK integrity (same as V2) plus additional constraints	Requires pairing with V2/V3 for integrity; focuses on incremental verification rather than full APK coverage
Verification Scope	File-by-file checks (slower)	Single-block verification (faster)	Single-block verification + key rotation and platform version metadata	Incremental verification of streamed APK parts (improves install performance)
Security Strength	Vulnerable to certain ZIP-level exploits	Stronger, prevents modification attacks and ZIP-level tricks	Equal to V2 plus future-proofing via key rotation	Depends on V2/V3 for security; V4 alone doesn't provide security but enhances delivery
Key Rotation Support	Not supported	Not supported	Supported (future keys declared for long-term security)	Not directly related to key rotation; relies on V2/V3 keys

Aspect	V1 (JAR Signing)	V2 (APK Signature Scheme)	V3 (Enhanced APK Signature Scheme)	V4 (APK Signature Scheme v4)
Backward Compatibility	Works on all Android versions (legacy)	Often included alongside V1 for older devices	Typically combined with V1 and V2 for broad device support	Requires V2 or V3 inside APK; only beneficial on Android 11+
Performance Impact	Slower installs due to per-file checks	Faster verification at install time	Similar performance to V2, with extra key management features	Optimizes incremental installs, reducing time to use on devices that support streaming
Primary Use Case Today	Legacy support only; not recommended alone	Modern baseline for secure signing and verification	Long-term planning, key rotation, and flexible upgrade paths	Enhancing user experience in incremental delivery (e.g., Play Store), not a replacement for V2/V3

Permission and Package Manager

The permission model is the first line of defense against unauthorized resource access in Android. Each app must declare the required permissions in its manifest. Different permission protection levels are defined in Android. You can see here the permission protection levels:

- normal
- dangerous
- signature
- special permissions

Accessing to sensitive data like location, camera, or microphone need the user runtime approval for "dangerous" permissions. Once the permissions are granted, they remain in effect until the user explicitly revokes them, which adds a significant degree of user empowerment and transparency.

Special permissions will be defined by OEM or developer for their specific purposes. Considering different levels of protection and organizing them into various groups follows the principles of "Least privilege" and "Separation of privilege." Therefore, developers could declare the minimum required permissions in the app and request them only when needed.

Over the years, Android has introduced features like permission groups, scoped storage, and runtime permission dialogs to address user data security and privacy concerns. Scoped storage restricts how apps access external storage, preventing them from trivially browsing arbitrary files. The Package Manager enforces these rules by verifying permissions during installation and granting or revoking them based on user actions. Pre-installed systems or OEM applications often have privileged permissions by default, which are tightly controlled and monitored to prevent abuse.

For instance, an application can only request read-only access to external storage and cannot modify anything. The newer Android versions have even gone further and tried to split the permission into more specific ones.

SELinux

Android enforces Security-Enhanced Linux (SELinux) policies at the kernel level to implement Mandatory Access Control (MAC). MAC aims to prevent apps from accessing sensitive system components. SELinux is slightly customized to fit Android requirements, but the overall functionalities remain the same.

SELinux classifies processes, files, and system resources into "types" and "domains." It applies strict policies that limit how a compromised component may interact with others. In this model, the rules define what each process can do regarding accessing resources such as reading, writing, and finding; all the processes are centrally controlled and cannot be bypassed simply by gaining root privileges.

This shift from discretionary to mandatory controls means SELinux stands guard even if an attacker gains elevated privileges, preventing unfettered access to sensitive system components. Device manufacturers customize SELinux policies to fit their unique hardware and software configurations, but these policies must be robust and fail-safe/fail-secure to pass Android Compatibility Test Suites. In a word, we could imagine SELinux as a role and rule-based kernel security feature.

As mentioned, the OEMs could modify SELinux to suit a custom secure environment for the application, and the system they develop demands the right understanding and knowledge about how it works and how Google provides the base code to utilize it. There is one more thing that, as developers, we need to know that SELinux could run in two modes: *"Permissive"* and *"Enforcement"*. In the *Permissive* mod,e SELinux will only observe what is happening and won't block any activities; it will create some system logs, which could be checked through *dmesg* command. This mode might be helpful for debugging purposes to put an application, services, etc., up and running for a very limited time. On the other hand, the *Enforcement* mode observes and applies the rules defined in the system. So, any undefined access will be blocked and reported.

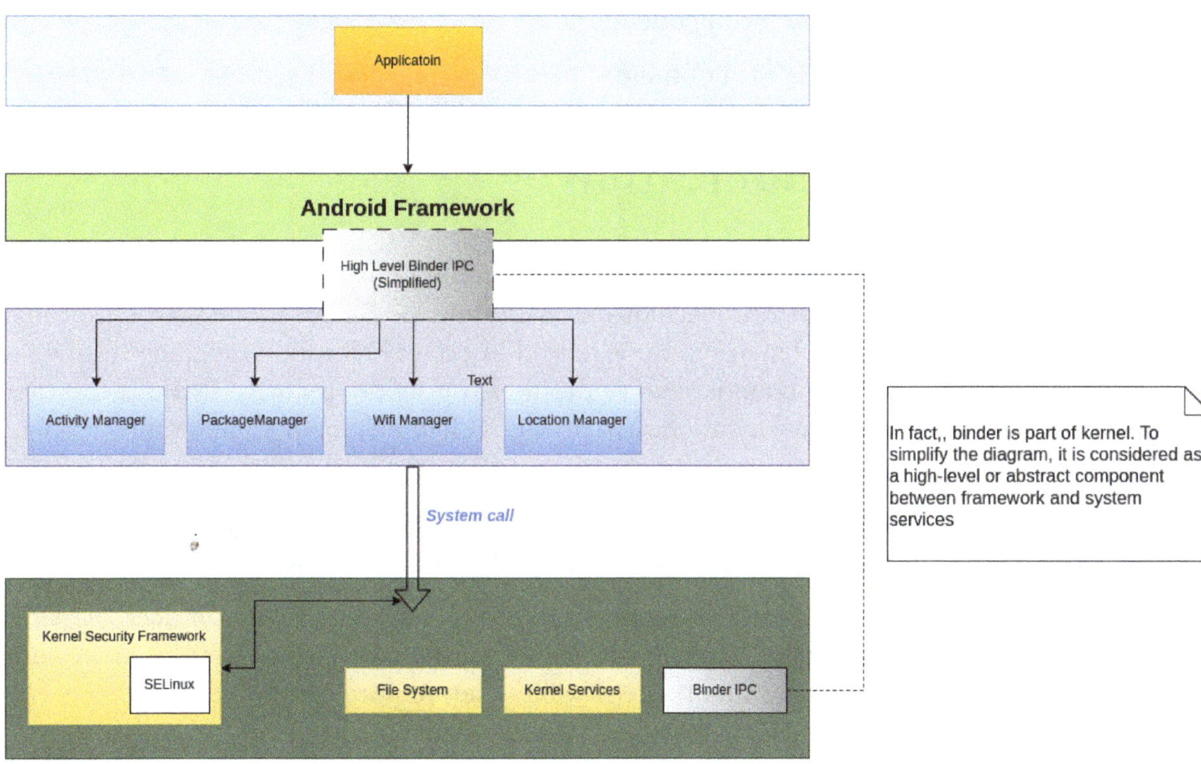

Figure 7. Simplified version of SELinux in Android Architecture

AndroidManifest and Components

An application's AndroidManifest.xml serves as a blueprint for the system, declaring its components, such as activities, services, broadcast receivers, and content providers. The manifest file also determines what permissions are required for the application. Developers specify whether other apps can access certain components in this manifest file. It gives an overview of application components and explains how Android security features are employed to protect the application.

We could consider it an entry point for Android to process the application at different times, such as installation, binding, etc. As a security feature, the components declared could be protected by the permissions added by the developer (mentioned earlier) or even blocked from being accessed if they are not exported.

For example, a Service intended only for internal use should not be accessible to every other app on the device. Similarly, Broadcast Receivers should handle incoming broadcasts carefully, checking permissions or signatures to ensure that only authorized senders can trigger them. Properly configured manifests serve as a key security gate, preventing external parties from easily manipulating or hijacking application components.

In the next sections, we will discuss each of them.

Inter-process communication

One of the basic requirements is that communication between apps and system services happen securely. Android provides multiple IPC mechanisms, including the Binder framework—its primary IPC system—Content Providers, Intents, and the Android Interface Definition Language (AIDL) for defining interfaces across process boundaries. Android also provides security features to protect the IPC mechanism. However, as we mentioned in previous chapters, input validation could play a strong role in mitigating the threats.

Binder enforces permission checks and maintains a strict reference counting system, reducing the likelihood that a malicious process can inject or intercept data without detection.

Intents, both explicit and implicit, allow components to start activities and services or deliver broadcasts. Developers should favor explicit intents whenever possible, restricting messages to known recipients. Although implicit intents are flexible, they require careful handling to prevent "intent hijacking," where a malicious app intercepts and manipulates the communication.

Broadcasts and Content Providers must validate all incoming data to avoid SQL injection or unauthorized access to protected resources. Proper URI permissions, token-based authentication, and signature-level restrictions help ensure that IPC remains a reliable and secure data exchange method.

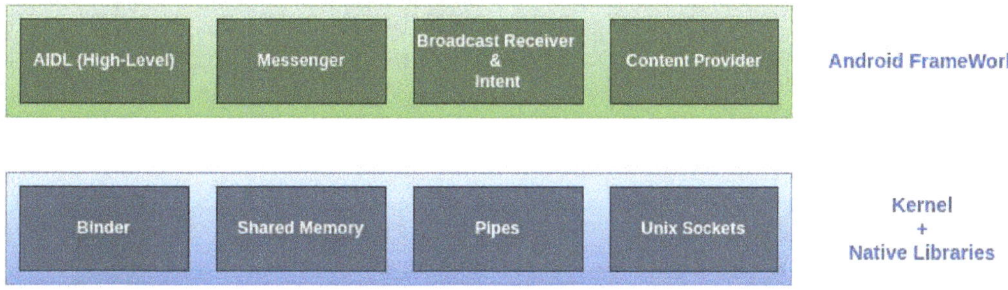

Figure 8. IPC mechanisms in Android Layers

IPC Mechanism	Implemented In	Details
AIDL (Android Interface Definition Language)	Application Framework + Kernel	High-level abstraction over Binder, used for defining service interfaces.
Messenger	Application Framework	Built on Binder; used for passing `Message` objects between processes.
Content Providers	Application Framework	Framework abstraction for shared data access, using Binder for IPC.
Broadcast Receivers	Application Framework	Framework-based system for broadcasting messages across processes, relying on Binder.
Shared Memory	Kernel + Native Libraries	Uses Linux shared memory mechanisms (e.g., `ashmem`, `mmap`) for data exchange.
Pipes	Kernel + Native Libraries	Implements Linux pipes for unidirectional IPC in native components.
Unix Sockets	Kernel + Native Libraries	Standard Linux mechanism for bidirectional IPC, used in native components.

We will briefly examine the IPCs and provide some hints on how we could secure them in our implementation.

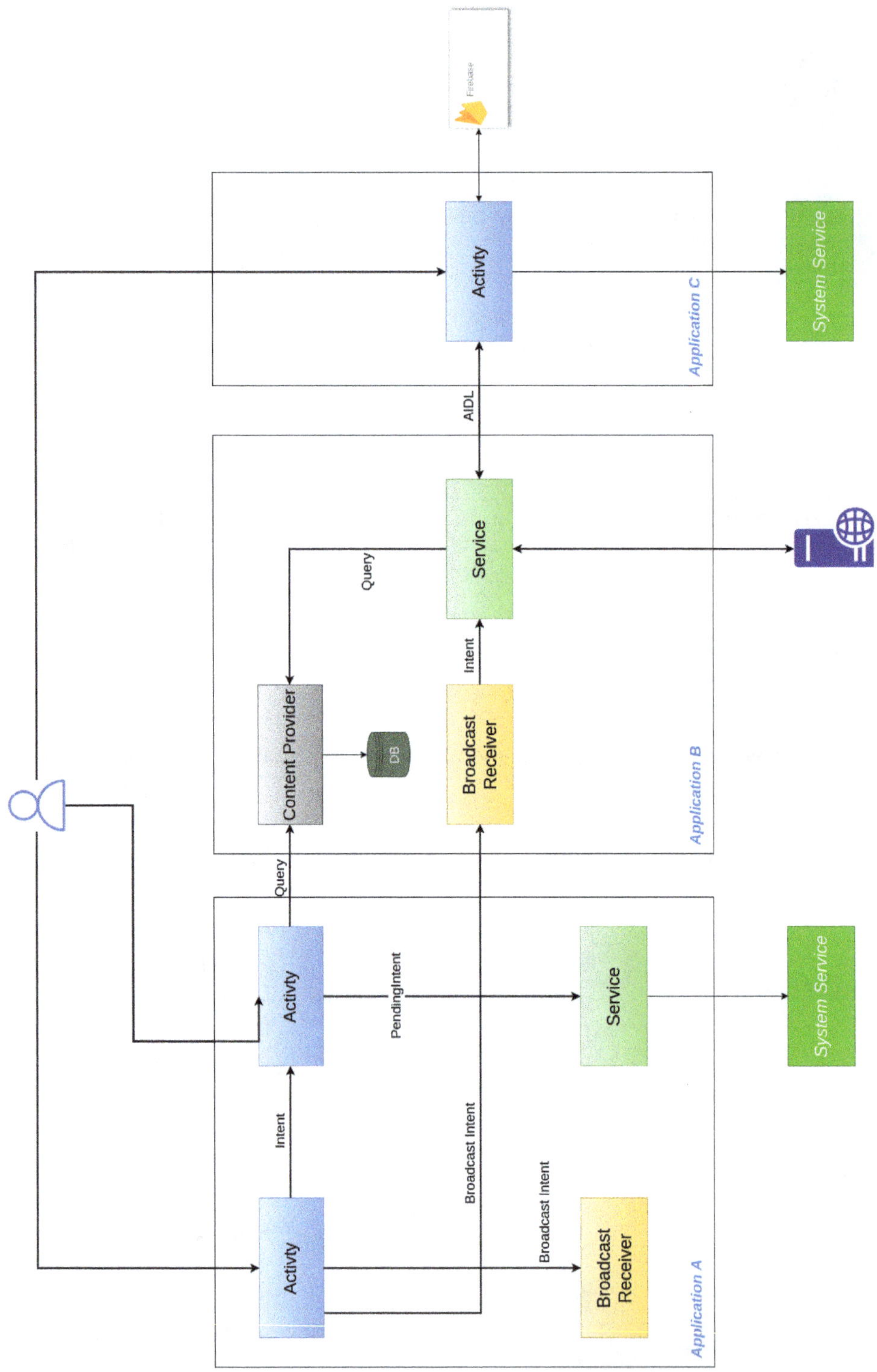

Figure 9. An overview of IPC between Applications

AIDL (application level)

Android Interface Definition Language (AIDL) is a powerful tool Android provides for facilitating communication between different processes, particularly between client and server applications. It allows developers to define the programming interface the client and service agree upon when communicating using IPC. This is especially useful for performing operations requiring interaction with background services or accessing functionalities other applications provide.

Securing AIDL involves understanding and implementing several core security concepts. Each concept outlined below integrates best practices to mitigate potential vulnerabilities and ensure that IPC remains secure and efficient. We need to cover different grounds to secure AIDL; however, that's not complicated if you know where to look and how to protect.

Service Binding

Service binding is the mechanism through which a client application binds to a service to perform IPC. Securely binding services are crucial to prevent unauthorized access and ensure that only legitimate clients can communicate with the service.

Security considerations:

- **Explicit Binding:** Use **explicit intents** when binding to services to ensure that each service is uniquely identified and that only the intended service is bound. This prevents malicious applications from binding to unintended services.

```
// Example of explicit binding in Kotlin
val intent = Intent(this, MyService::class.java)
bindService(intent, serviceConnection, Context.BIND_AUTO_CREATE)
```

- **Permission Enforcement:** Define and enforce the **permissions** required to bind to the service. By specifying permissions in the service declaration within the `AndroidManifest.xml`, you ensure that only applications with the appropriate permissions can initiate a binding.

```xml
<!-- Example in AndroidManifest.xml -->
<service
    android:name=".MyService"
    android:permission="com.example.app.BIND_MY_SERVICE">
    <intent-filter>
        <action android:name="com.example.app.MyService" />
    </intent-filter>
</service>
```

- **Secure Intent Filters**: Avoid using **implicit intents** for binding services unless necessary, and ensure that intent filters are as restrictive as possible to prevent unauthorized service discovery.

Interface Methods

Defining and restricting the methods exposed via AIDL interfaces is essential to control the functionalities accessible to client applications. Limiting the exposed methods reduces the attack surface and prevents misuse.

Security considerations:

- **Minimal Exposure**: **Expose only necessary methods** through AIDL interfaces. Avoid providing methods that are not essential for client operations to minimize potential exploitation vectors.
- **Method-Level Access Control**: Implement **access control checks** within each method to verify the identity and permissions of the calling client before performing sensitive operations.

```java
// Example of method-level access control in Java
@Override
public void sensitiveOperation() throws RemoteException {
    if (!hasRequiredPermission()) {
        throw new SecurityException("Unauthorized access");
    }
    // Proceed with the operation
}
```

- **Input Validation**: **Validate all inputs** received through AIDL methods to prevent injection attacks, buffer overflows, and other forms of malicious data exploitation.

AIDL Transaction Security

One other aspect of AIDL communication is securing data transactions to prevent unauthorized access, data tampering, and the leakage of sensitive information during IPC.

Security considerations:

- **Data Encryption: Encrypt sensitive data** transmitted between client and service to protect it from eavesdropping and interception, especially when dealing with untrusted networks or storage.
- **Transaction Validation: Validate transaction parameters** rigorously. Ensure that the data being passed adheres to expected formats, types, and ranges to prevent malformed data from causing unintended behavior.
- **Use of Parcelable Objects:** Utilize **Parcelable** objects for data transfer, which are optimized for IPC and help maintain data integrity.

Bound Services Security

Ensuring that only authorized applications can bind to services via AIDL is fundamental to maintaining the integrity and confidentiality of the service's operations and data.

Security considerations:

- **Permission-Based Binding:** As mentioned earlier, **declare permissions** must bind to the service. This ensures that only applications with the necessary permissions can establish a connection.
- **Dynamic Permission Checks:** In addition to manifest-declared permissions, perform **runtime permission checks** within the service to dynamically enforce security policies based on the application's context or state.
- **Restricting Service Exposure:** Set the `android:exported` attribute appropriately if a service is intended only for internal use, set `android:exported="false"` to prevent external applications from accessing it.

```
<!-- Example in AndroidManifest.xml -->
<service
    android:name=".MyService"
    android:exported="false"
    android:permission="com.example.app.BIND_MY_SERVICE">
    <!-- Intent filters -->
</service>
```

Cross-process Communication

Managing cross-process communication without exposing sensitive operations is essential to control unauthorized access, data breaches, and exploitation of IPC mechanisms.

Security considerations:

- **Secure IPC Channels:** Make use of **secure IPC channels** such as Binder, which have integrated authorization and authentication procedures to guarantee that only authorized clients can interact with the service.
- **Isolation of Processes: Isolate client and server processes** by running them under different UIDs or within separate security contexts. This restricts the potential effect of a compromised process.
- **Avoid Sharing Sensitive Data: Minimize the sharing of sensitive data** across processes. If necessary, ensure that data is adequately protected through encryption and access controls.
- **Logging and Monitoring:** Implement **comprehensive logging and monitoring** of IPC interactions to notice and respond to suspicious activities quickly.

Broadcasts and Intents

In the context of secure coding and Android development, securing Android broadcasts and intents is essential to preventing unauthorized access to system resources and sensitive data. Android broadcasts and intents serve as a communication mechanism between different application components, allowing data transfer and triggering specific actions within the application.

Android Broadcasts

Broadcasts are messages that Android applications can send and receive. They allow communication with other applications running on the same device. System services utilize broadcasts to convey system-wide events, such as boot completion and connectivity changes. Android applications can also send and receive custom broadcasts.

There are two types of broadcasts in Android:

1. Normal broadcasts: Asynchronous and are generally meant for system-wide communication.
2. Ordered broadcasts: Synchronous, allowing recipients to abort the broadcast, preventing it from reaching others.

Securing Android Broadcasts

To ensure the security of broadcasts, it is essential to enforce proper access controls and leverage secure coding practices. Following are some guidelines to secure Android broadcasts:

1. Do not send sensitive data through broadcasts: Broadcasting sensitive data might expose it to malicious applications, leading to data leakage. Instead, consider using appropriate IPC mechanisms, such as bound services, to exchange sensitive information.
2. Use Local Broadcasts for private in-app messaging: Use LocalBroadcastManager to prevent messages from being broadcast to other applications. This class allows you to register for and send broadcasts within your application, mitigating the risks associated with malicious eavesdropping apps.
3. Define permissions for custom broadcasts: By defining the required permissions for sending and receiving custom broadcasts, the application can ensure that only authorized components interact with it.
4. Broadcast receiver should be protected against injection attacks in different scenarios:

- Listening for system-wide broadcasts and securing receivers against broadcast injection attacks.
- Ensuring ordered broadcasts are securely handled to avoid priority inversion or manipulation.
- Safeguarding sensitive information from being exposed via sticky broadcasts.

Example

In AndroidManifest.xml, define the custom permission:

```
<permission
 android:name="com.example.app.RECEIVE_DATA"
 android:protectionLevel="dangerous" />
```

For the receiver component, set the required permission:

```
<receiver
 android:name=".MyBroadcastReceiver"
 android:permission="com.example.app.RECEIVE_DATA">
 <intent-filter>
    <action android:name="com.example.app.intent.SEND_DATA" />
 </intent-filter>
</receiver>
```

Sender application can send the broadcast with specified permission:

```
Intent intent = new Intent("com.example.app.intent.SEND_DATA");
sendBroadcast(intent, "com.example.app.RECEIVE_DATA");
```

Android Intents

Intents are messages that components, such as activities and services, use to request actions from other components or the Android system. They enable operations like starting an activity, triggering a service, launching a broadcast, or performing specific tasks within an application.

Securing Android Intents

To ensure the security of intents in Android, developers should consider the following best practices:

1. Do not send sensitive data through intents: Sending sensitive data via intents may inadvertently expose the information to other applications listening for the same intent. Instead, use secure communication channels that enforce proper access controls.
2. Use explicit intents: Implicit intents trigger components that can handle the requested action by declaring the desired action and data. However, this can lead to unintended components receiving the intent if they declare the same action. Instead, use explicit intents that specify the target component, ensuring that only the intended recipient can handle the action.

Example

```
val intent = Intent(this, TargetActivity::class.java)
intent.putExtra("key", "value")
startActivity(intent)
```

3. Validate data received through intents: Ensure that any data received from intents is validated for necessary properties, such as correctness, completeness, and formatting. Inadequate validation can lead to potential security issues, such as injection attacks and data corruption.

Note: This example only check the input validity. Based on the use case a secure validator might be needed to be implemented.

Example

```
// ReceiverActivity.kt

...

class ReceiverActivity : AppCompatActivity() {

    override fun onCreate(savedInstanceState: Bundle?) {
        super.onCreate(savedInstanceState)
        setContentView(R.layout.activity_receiver)

        val username = intent.getStringExtra("username")
        val email = intent.getStringExtra("email")

        if (InputValidator.validateIntentData(username, email)) {
            // Safe and validated input; proceed
            Toast.makeText(this, "Welcome, $username!", Toast.LENGTH_SHORT).show()
        } else {
            // Invalid input detected; handle securely
            Toast.makeText(this, "Invalid or malicious input detected!", Toast.LENGT\
H_LONG).show()
            finish() // Close activity immediately
        }
    }
}

object InputValidator {
    // Validate username: Alphanumeric, underscores, 3-15 chars
    fun isValidUsername(username: String?): Boolean {
        return !username.isNullOrBlank() && username.matches(Regex("^[a-zA-Z0-9_]{3,\
15}$"))
    }

    // Validate email format securely using Android Patterns
    fun isValidEmail(email: String?): Boolean {
        return !email.isNullOrBlank() && Patterns.EMAIL_ADDRESS.matcher(email).match\
es()
    }

    // Comprehensive security check
    fun validateIntentData(username: String?, email: String?): Boolean {
        return isValidUsername(username) && isValidEmail(email)
    }
}
```

4. Use startActivityForResult() for returning results: If the application expects a result from the called activity or service, use startActivityForResult() in combination with onActivityResult() rather than relying on sending back values via intents. This ensures that only the original calling component can retrieve the results.
5. Set permissions for activities exposed to other applications: If the activity should be accessible through intents, define the necessary permissions in the Android manifest file to restrict access to authorized applications only.
6. Securing pending intents to avoid unauthorized access or hijacking.

In AndroidManifest.xml, define the permission for the exposed activity.

Example

```
<activity
 android:name=".ExposedActivity"
 android:permission="com.example.app.ACCESS_EXPOSED_ACTIVITY"
 android:exported="true" >
 <intent-filter>
    <action android:name="com.example.app.intent.ACCESS_EXPOSED_ACTIVITY" />
 </intent-filter>
</activity>
```

Securing Android broadcasts and intents protects sensitive data and other system resources from malicious actors while providing a reliable communication mechanism between application components. By following security recommendations for broadcasts and intents, developers can prevent unauthorized access, reduce potential security risks, and improve their Android apps' overall security posture.

Content provider

ContentProviders is an Android component that enables structured data sharing between different applications or as an inter-application interface. This interface role makes it a valuable target for attackers when it is exported to be accessed by other applications. Here, we will cover the security aspects of using content providers.

AndroidManifest.xml:

Like other Android components, AndroidManifest supports security features for content providers. After declaring it in AndroidManifest as an exported component, the first step is to consider adding custom permissions. The level of protection selected for the permission will determine which application can access the content provider. Here is an example of a content provider using different permissions for read and write access. The protection level or even the permission could be changed based on the security and project requirements.

Example

```
<manifest ...>
  <permission
      android:name="com.example.app.provider.READ_DATA"
      android:protectionLevel="dangerous" />


  <permission
      android:name="com.example.app.provider.WRITE_DATA"
      android:protectionLevel="dangerous" />


  <provider
      android:name=".ExportedSecureContentProvider"
      android:authorities="com.example.app.provider"
      android:exported="true"
      android:readPermission="com.example.app.provider.READ_DATA"
      android:writePermission="com.example.app.provider.WRITE_DATA" />
</manifest>
```

Considerations on Content Provider implementation:

1. **URI Permissions:**

- ContentProviders expose data through URIs (`content://authority/path`).
- You can restrict which parts of the data are accessible to other apps by using URI permissions.
- Instead of giving broad access to the entire provider, you can grant temporary or limited access to specific URIs using `grantUriPermission()`.

2. **SQL Injection Prevention:**

- Never construct SQL statements by directly concatenating user input.
- Always use selection arguments (`selectionArgs`) to prevent injection. For example, `selection = "name=?"` and `selectionArgs = new String[] {"Alice"}`.
- Use parameterized queries and rely on the built-in query mechanism of `SQLiteDatabase` or `SupportSQLiteDatabase`.

3. **Granting Access (grantUriPermission):**

- You can dynamically grant permissions to access a particular data subset.
- This allows you to implement least-privilege principles: apps get access only to the specific data they need and only for the time they need it.

4. **Row-Level Security:**

- Implement logic so that even if an app can access the provider, it only gets the subset of rows it is authorized for.
- For example, if your provider stores user-specific data, ensure that a calling app only accesses rows that belong to that user.
- Before returning data, perform runtime checks (e.g., verify the caller's identity or match a user ID column).

5. **ContentResolver Validation:**

- When external apps query the ContentProvider via `ContentResolver`, carefully validate all incoming parameters (selection, sort order, etc.).
- Confirm that the caller holds the required permissions.
- Confirm that the requested columns, tables, or URIs are allowed.

Example Implementation

Note: This example includes only part of the solution not a complete code

```
    ...

class ExportedSecureContentProvider : ContentProvider() {

  companion object {
      const val AUTHORITY = "com.example.app.provider"
      const val PATH_USERS = "users"
      val CONTENT_URI: Uri = Uri.parse("content://$AUTHORITY/$PATH_USERS")

      private const val USERS = 1
      private const val USER_ID = 2

      private val uriMatcher = UriMatcher(UriMatcher.NO_MATCH).apply {
          addURI(AUTHORITY, PATH_USERS, USERS)
          addURI(AUTHORITY, "$PATH_USERS/#", USER_ID)
      }
  }

  private lateinit var dbHelper: SupportSQLiteOpenHelper

  override fun onCreate(): Boolean {
```

```
      val config = SupportSQLiteOpenHelper.Configuration.builder(context!!)
          .name("appdata.db")
          .callback(object : SupportSQLiteOpenHelper.Callback(1) {
              override fun onCreate(db: SupportSQLiteDatabase) {
                  // Example table: users with a "owner_id" to support row-level sec\
urity.
                  db.execSQL("CREATE TABLE users (_id INTEGER PRIMARY KEY AUTOINCREM\
ENT, owner_id TEXT, name TEXT, email TEXT)")
              }

              override fun onUpgrade(db: SupportSQLiteDatabase, oldVersion: Int, new\
Version: Int) {
                  // Handle DB upgrades as needed.
              }
          })
          .build()

      dbHelper = FrameworkSQLiteOpenHelperFactory().create(config)
      return true
  }

  /**
   * Row-level Security Example:
   * Let's say each row in the 'users' table has an 'owner_id' that identifies which\
 user/client owns it.
   * You could associate the calling identity with an owner and only return rows tha\
t match that owner_id.
   * For demonstration, we will assume the callingPackage can be mapped to a particu\
lar owner_id.
   * In a real scenario, this might rely on authenticated sessions, tokens, or other\
 logic.
   */
  private fun getOwnerIdForCaller(): String? {
      val callingPkg = callingPackage
      // Map calling package to a known owner_id. Here we just log and return a stat\
ic value or null.
      // In a real scenario, you might have a map of authorized package -> owner_id
      // or perform an additional authentication step.
      Log.d("ExportedSecureContentProvider", "Request from package: $callingPkg")
      return if (callingPkg == "com.example.trustedclient") "trusted_owner_id" else \
null
  }
```

```
    override fun query(
        uri: Uri,
        projection: Array<out String>?,
        selection: String?,
        selectionArgs: Array<out String>?,
        sortOrder: String?
    ): Cursor? {
        // Check row-level permissions before querying.
        val ownerId = getOwnerIdForCaller() ?: return null // If caller not recognized\
, return no data.

        val db = dbHelper.readableDatabase

        return when (uriMatcher.match(uri)) {
            USERS -> {
                // Restrict to rows that match the caller's owner_id
                val finalSelection = addOwnerIdRestriction(selection, "owner_id=?")
                val finalSelectionArgs = addOwnerIdArg(selectionArgs, ownerId)

                db.query("users", projection, finalSelection, finalSelectionArgs, null\
, null, sortOrder)
            }
            USER_ID -> {
                val id = uri.lastPathSegment ?: return null
                // Also enforce owner_id check for a single row
                val finalSelection = addOwnerIdRestriction(selection, "_id=? AND owner\
_id=?")
                val finalSelectionArgs = addOwnerIdArg(selectionArgs, ownerId, id)

                db.query("users", projection, finalSelection, finalSelectionArgs, null\
, null, sortOrder)
            }
            else -> throw IllegalArgumentException("Unknown URI: $uri")
        }
    }

    override fun getType(uri: Uri): String? {
        return when (uriMatcher.match(uri)) {
            USERS -> "vnd.android.cursor.dir/vnd.$AUTHORITY.$PATH_USERS"
            USER_ID -> "vnd.android.cursor.item/vnd.$AUTHORITY.$PATH_USERS"
            else -> null
        }
    }
```

```

  /**
   * Utility functions to enforce row-level filtering using owner_id and to prevent \
SQL injection:
   */

  // Add the owner_id restriction to an existing selection
  private fun addOwnerIdRestriction(existingSelection: String?, ownerClause: String)\
: String {
      return if (existingSelection.isNullOrEmpty()) {
          ownerClause
      } else {
          "($existingSelection) AND $ownerClause"
      }
  }

  // Append owner_id and optionally an additional argument (like a row ID) to select\
ionArgs safely
  private fun addOwnerIdArg(existingArgs: Array<out String>?, ownerId: String, varar\
g additionalArgs: String): Array<String> {
      val newArgsList = mutableListOf<String>()
      if (existingArgs != null) {
          newArgsList.addAll(existingArgs)
      }
      // Add row-specific arguments first (if provided) to maintain order correspond\
ing to the selection
      newArgsList.addAll(additionalArgs)
      // Add owner_id last or in correct position depending on how the selection was\
 constructed
      newArgsList.add(ownerId)
      return newArgsList.toTypedArray()
  }

    ...

}
```

HAL Layer

The **Hardware Abstraction Layer (HAL)** provides a standard interface for the Android framework and the system services to communicate with hardware drivers implemented by device manufacturers (OEMs). By decoupling the Android system from the hardware, HAL allows OEMs to supply functionality through a well-defined contract. This means the Android framework can interact with hardware (e.g., sensors, cameras, and audio devices) consistently and reliably without delving into vendor-specific implementation details.

System Daemon Isolation

System daemons are native applications running as separate pfacilitatingacilitate communication between the Android system services and hardware components. They are integral to the core platform and must be isolated to prevent unauthorized access, lateral movement by attackers, or data leakage. Daemons could be developed in C,C++, or Rust, and they will be compiled by native system libraries. They might be a system or vendor daemon which in both cases, the security should be considered seriously.

- **Strong Access Control with SELinux**: Implement strict **SELinux (Security-Enhanced Linux)** policies to enforce **Mandatory Access Control (MAC)**. Label system daemons with appropriate SELinux contexts to restrict their interactions with other processes and system resources. Similar to system daemons, enforce strict SELinux policies for vendor-native daemons. Assign unique SELinux contexts and domains to each vendor daemon to limit their access to only the resources they require
- **Least Privilege Principle**: Run system or vendor daemons under dedicated, non-privileged **User IDs (UIDs)** and **Group IDs (GIDs)**. Grant only the minimal set of permissions necessary for their operation, reducing the potential impact if a daemon is compromised.
- **Dedicated SELinux Domains**: Assign each system daemon to its own SELinux domain, ensuring that even if one daemon is compromised, it cannot easily interact with or escalate privileges within other domains.
- **Secure IPC Mechanisms**: Utilize secure Inter-Process Communication (IPC) mechanisms like **Binder** to facilitate communication between vendor daemons and the Android framework. Avoid exposing raw sockets or unsecured file interfaces that could be exploited.

Hardware Abstraction Security

At the HAL boundary, strict controls on communication between the Android framework and hardware must be enforced. This includes validating requests, ensuring data integrity, and preventing unauthorized access to low-level hardware interfaces.

- **Robust Input Validation in HAL Code**: Thoroughly validate all incoming requests from the framework. Check parameter ranges and data types and ensure that inputs conform to expected formats to prevent malformed data from causing unintended behavior.
- **Memory Safety and Safe Programming Practices**: Implement memory-safe coding practices within HAL implementations. Use modern programming languages and constructs that minimize the risk of buffer overflows, memory leaks, and other vulnerabilities.
- **Avoid Direct Pointer Passing**: Prevent the use of direct memory pointers across the HAL boundary. Instead, data can be handled using structured data types and managed objects to reduce the risk of memory corruption.

Vendor HAL and Secure Implementation

Since OEMs are responsible for implementing their HAL modules, they should follow the best practices to secure their implementations.

- **Enforce Strict HAL Interface Contracts with HIDL/AIDL**: Define clear and versioned interfaces using **HIDL (HAL Interface Definition Language)** or **AIDL (Android Interface Definition Language)**. This ensures that HAL implementations adhere to expected contracts, reducing the likelihood of undefined behavior.
- **Least Privilege Principle**: Design HAL implementations to perform only the necessary operations required for their functionality. Avoid granting excessive permissions or exposing unnecessary interfaces.
- **Robust Error Handling**: Implement comprehensive error checking and handling within HAL code to gracefully manage unexpected conditions without exposing vulnerabilities.
- **Code Auditing and Testing**: Audit HAL code regularly for security vulnerabilities. Use static analysis tools and memory sanitizers, and perform rigorous testing (including fuzz testing) to identify and mitigate potential security issues.

Binderized HAL

Modern HALs utilize the **Binder IPC mechanism**, which provides a stable and secure means of communication between the Android framework and hardware components.

- **Secure Binder Transactions**: Validate all Binder transaction codes and parThe process. Pro-crecognizesecognexpects expected transactions, rejecting unknown or malformed transactions.
- **Permission Checks**: Leverage Binder's capability-based security to enforce permissions on IPC calls. Ensure that only authorized components can initiate transactions with the HAL.
- **Controlled Data Flow**: Use Binder to manage data exchanges, preventing unauthorized memory access or data leakage between the framework and HAL implementations.

HIDL (HAL Interface Definition Language)

HIDL defines stable, versioned interfaces between the HAL and the Android framework, promoting compatibility and reducing the risk of memory corruption through well-defined contracts.

- **Strict Typing and Method Definitions**: Utilize HIDL's strict typing to define clear data structures and method signatures. This minimizes the chances of type-related errors and undefined behavior.
- **Versioning and Backwards Compatibility**: Implement versioned HIDL interfaces to ensure that updates to the HAL do not break existing framework integrations. Maintain backward compatibility where possible to facilitate seamless updates.
- **Memory Safety**: HIDL reduces the risk of memory corruption by avoiding direct pointer exchanges and relying on structured, typed data. All data passed through HIDL interfaces must be validated and sanitized to ensure this.

Direct Memory Access (DMA)

Direct Memory Access (DMA) allows hardware components to read from and write to system memory directly.

- **Use of IOMMU (I/O Memory Management Unit)**: Implement IOMMUs to isolate DMA operations. This ensures that hardware components can only access designated memory regions, preventing a compromised HAL from overwriting arbitrary system memory.
- **SELinux and Device Node Protections**: Protect device nodes (e.g., `/dev/something`) with SELinux policies, ensuring only authorized HAL daemons or their SELinux domains can access them.
- **Buffer Validation**: Rigorously validate DMA buffer sizes, offsets, and alignment before passing them to hardware interfaces. Never trust buffer sizes provided by the framework without verification to prevent buffer overflows and memory corruption.
- **Controlled DMA Access**: Restrict DMA operations to trusted components and enforce strict access controls to ensure only authorized processes can initiate DMA transfers.

Play Integrity

The Play Integrity API offers a robust solution for safeguarding Android applications against potential risks and fraudulent activities, such as cheating and unauthorized access. We will look at the advantages of employing the Play Integrity API and explore effective integration strategies for your Android app development process.

Play Integrity API: A Comprehensive Solution

The Play Integrity API furnishes numerous benefits for Android developers:

- Shields apps from threats like cheating and unauthorized access
- Enables developers to take appropriate protective measures against attacks and abuse
- is compatible with Android 4.4 and later devices

The API's responses encompass crucial information such as:

- The integrity of the app (binary files)
- The user/account licensing status
- The authenticity of the Android device powered by Google Play services

While the Play Integrity API significantly enhances app security, it should be utilized with other security mechanisms to ensure comprehensive protection.

Key Considerations for Play Integrity API Implementation

Generating an integrity token using the Play Integrity API can be resource-intensive, potentially increasing battery usage and processing time. Moreover, the number of API calls is limited daily. Developers should reserve the API for the most critical app activities to optimize usage. Generating Nonces and Thwarting PITM Attacks To produce nonces and guard against person-in-the-middle (PITM) tampering attacks, developers should: Implement nonce generation within a secure server environment Employ diverse responses to hinder imitation attempts

Play Integrity API Integration

The Play Integrity API integration process entails multiple roles and actors:

- Device: Requests a unique value from the app's server and subsequently generates a token via the Integrity API

- Server: Produces a unique value upon the app's request and forwards the received token from the device to Play's server
- Play's server: Decrypts, verifies the token's validity and communicates the result to the app's server

Upon receiving Play's server response, the app's server evaluates the app's request and integrity level received from the device to make informed decisions.

Platform Compatibility

The Play Integrity API currently supports Java, Kotlin, Unity, and native libraries.

The Play Integrity API is a resource for fortifying Android applications against potential threats and fraudulent actions. By integrating the API into a well-rounded security strategy and adhering to these best practices and limitations, developers can establish a secure user environment and effectively safeguard their applications from potential attacks.

- Play Protect: Google's built-in malware protection service.
- Play Integrity API: A mechanism to ensure app integrity and prevent tampering or unauthorized modifications.

9.1 Play Integrity API: A Comprehensive Solution

- Device Integrity Checks: Verifying the integrity of the device environment.
- Attestation Tokens: Authenticating devices and apps to verify integrity.
- SafetyNet Integration: Collaboration between SafetyNet and Play Integrity.

9.2 Key Considerations for Play Integrity API Implementation

- App Behavior Validation: Verifying that apps behave as expected.
- User Authentication: Ensuring users interact with a genuine app.
- Geo and Device Restrictions: Limiting access based on device compliance and geography.

9.3 Play Integrity API Integration

- Server-Side Validation: Using server-side APIs to verify integrity tokens.
- Token Expiry and Rotation: Managing token life cycles for security.
- App Integrity in Multi-Layer Systems: Ensuring Play Integrity works in complex app architectures.

9.4 Platform Compatibility

- Backward Compatibility: Supporting older versions of Android.
- Device Fragmentation: Addressing compatibility issues across different devices and manufacturers.

Jetpack libraries

Jetpack libraries have been around for quite a long time to be one of the Android developers' valuable development resources. They provide lots of functionalities and facilities that we could use directly. Besides, we don't need to consider compatibility and security since Google continually develops and fixes issues. Since Google is developing Android and Jetpack, we don't need to worry about known or unknown issues. Google receives lots of reports yearly from partners and developers regarding bugs, security flaws, etc., which helps improve the code. I recommend utilizing Jetpack wherever you can instead of using third-party libraries. But, we might need some time to choose a 3rd party SDK/library over Jetpack for strong reasons.

Protecting Data

Data life-cycle

I would prefer to categorize data based on their life-cycle since strategy could be changed and also the protection mechanisms. There are different ways to categories storage in Android. For instance we are able to look at them them based on the type of them or even the location they are being stored.

- Internal Storage
- External Storage
- Cache Storage
- Media Storage
- In-Memory
- In-Transit
- etc.

There are some overlaps in these categories. For instance, a media file could be stored internally or externally. The main idea is to explain how to keep them safe and secure in our projects.So, we will discuss them in 4 categories:

- In-Memory
- In-Transit
- Temporary
- Persistive

In-Transit

Covers security measures for data while being transmitted over a network.

- Network Communication – Restricted TLS Versions (Android 15) enforce stronger encryption by deprecating outdated TLS 1.0 and 1.1.
- API Requests & Responses – No new direct enhancements, but TLS enforcement and certificate validation remain best practices.
- Cookies & Tokens in Transit – Secure flags (`Secure`, `HttpOnly`) should still be used to protect sensitive cookies.

Protect sensitive data exchanged between the client and server using Transport Layer Security (TLS), such as API requests and responses containing personally identifiable information (PII) or sensitive user data.

Encrypt important information on the device to prevent theft, tampering, or unwanted access. Android has built-in encryption tools, such as shared preferences encryption, room database encryption, and the Android Keystore system, for storing cryptographic keys.

You can reduce the amount of private information kept in memory by safely erasing or overwriting it after use. To produce random values, avoid mutable data structures like arrays. Instead, consider using Java's SecureRandom.

We discuss the network and Bluetooth communication later.

In-Memory

Protects sensitive data that exists temporarily in application memory.

- Runtime Variables & Session Tokens – Scoped Storage (Android 10+) prevents unauthorized access but does not manage transient memory directly.
- Activity State & View Models – Protected App Directories (Android 14/15) prevent unauthorized file access but do not encrypt memory contents.
- Clipboard Data – No new changes in Android 14/15, requiring us to manually clear clipboard-sensitive data.
  There's no in-system security option to protect clipboard. If you need to secure the clipboard content you need to implement a custom encryption class/wrapper for yourself.
- Stack Traces & Logs – Play Integrity API (Android 14) helps detect and block apps that log sensitive information improperly.
- JNI Memory – Best practices for secure memory handling (e.g., explicit wiping) remain necessary, with no new system-level updates.

Temporary

Covers data that exists for a short time and must be properly managed and removed.

- Ephemeral Files – Scoped Storage (Android 10+) continues enforcing app-specific storage policies.
- Cache Data – File Integrity Verification (Android 14) ensures cache files are protected from unauthorized modifications.
- Downloaded Media – App Archiving (Android 15) helps reduce stored media by preserving apps while removing unnecessary data.
- Crash Logs – Google Play Protect (Android 14/15) enhances detection of apps improperly storing or sharing sensitive logs.

- Debug Information – Secured Background Activity Launches (Android 15) prevents unauthorized app actions that could expose sensitive debug data.
- File Integrity Verification (Android 14) – Strengthens Temporary Data Protection

Persistent (Long-Term)

Covers long-term data storage that requires strict security and encryption.

- SharedPreferences – EncryptedSharedPreferences (General Android Security) remains the best method for securing sensitive key-value pairs.
- Local Databases (SQLite/Room) – SQLCipher & Keystore Integration (General Android Security) are still recommended for encrypting databases.
- Key/Secret Management – Android Keystore (General Android Security) remains the secure method for managing cryptographic keys.
- External Storage (SD Cards) – Scoped Storage (Android 10+) restricts app access to shared storage, preventing unauthorized reads.
- Backup Data – Google Drive Encrypted Backups (Android 14/15) ensure that only the user's device can decrypt stored backups.
- Application Assets – Private Space (Android 15) provides a hidden, secure location for storing sensitive app assets.
- Document & Configuration Files – Private Space (Android 15) and Encrypted Storage Policies (General Android Security) apply to protect sensitive documents.
- Biometric Templates – Android's Biometric API (General Android Security) ensures biometric data is securely stored within system-managed storage.
- Private Space (Android 15) – Enhances Long-Term Storage Protection
- Dynamic Code Loading Restrictions (Android 14) – Prevents unauthorized modifications to app code but does not impact long-term storage.
- 2G Connectivity Controls (Android 14) – A security enhancement but unrelated to storage.

Insecure storage could lead to unauthorized access to a sensitive data, such as user credentials, personal information, or API keys, that are stored without proper protection on an Android device. Accessing these data could let attackers modify or steal them. Common insecure storage methods include plaintext files, shared preferences, SQLite databases, and external storage.

What Google has done to address insecure storage

Encrypted Shared Preferences: Google introduced Encrypted Shared Preferences, part of the AndroidX Security library, which allows us to store key-value pairs with encryption. This feature makes data unreadable without the right key, which we consider an extra layer of security in Android, especially for sensitive data.

- Encrypted File Storage: The AndroidX Security library also includes EncryptedFile, a class that helps store files securely by encrypting their contents. We can use this class to save sensitive data in encrypted files, guaranteeing that unauthorized users cannot read or tamper with it.

Key Chain and Key Store Provider: The key store provider eliminates the possibility of extracting the key from the app process by removing it from the process. By enforcing restrictions outside the app, the key chain protects the keys from unauthorized access. On the other hand, the key chain allows the keys to be shared/used through the system with user authorization.

Recent Android security improvements

The recent Android versions 15,14,13 and 12 have introduces new feature to improve data protection within Android. Private space in Android 15, File Integrity in Android 14 with the other new security features could be considered as big and effective steps toward more user security and privacy.

We can mention separate permissions to access images, photos, videos, and audio files in Android 13 that keeps the entire media gallery safe by the photo keeper and blocks not matching Intent and dynamically registered broadcast receivers are other new features in the app's security domain.

In Android 12, Google introduced numerous security enhancements, including more robust encryption and improved sandboxing. These improvements make it more difficult for attackers to access sensitive data stored on Android devices.

Despite what Google has done, insecure storage can be a significant security concern for Android applications if we store data in external storage without any encryption, though employing the new libraries, mechanisms, and techniques can help manage this issue effectively. By looking at Android development, we can see the way it has come to make a more reliable, stable, and secure ecosystem. So, we can expect more facilities in the future to tackle security threats.

Scoped Storage

While in Android 10, applications could access out-of-scoped storage, in Android 11 and higher, they are restricted to Scoped Storage, limiting their ability to read or write data outside of their sandbox. This feature significantly reduces the risks associated with insecure storage, preventing unauthorized access to sensitive data. Different access levels are introduced by Scoped Storage, improving user data privacy.

- App-specific storage
- Media store access
- Shared storage restrictions

Secure File Storage

Sensitive user information may be accessible to third parties through insecure data storage. The use of world-readable file permissions, which allow any application on the device to access the file, frequently illustrates this issue in Android applications.

Using private file permissions, which restrict access to the file to the application only, would be a safe substitute:

```
public void saveToFileUnsafe(String fileName, String data)
        throws FileNotFoundException {
    FileOutputStream outputStream = openFileOutput(fileName, Context.MODE_PRIVATE);
    try {
        outputStream.write(data.getBytes());
    } catch (IOException e) {
        e.printStackTrace();
    } finally {
        try {
            outputStream.flush();
            outputStream.close();
        } catch (IOException e) {
                e.printStackTrace();
        }
    }
}
```

Encrypting file's content

```
import android.content.Context
import androidx.security.crypto.EncryptedFile
import androidx.security.crypto.MasterKeys
import java.io.File

class SecureFileStorage(private val context: Context) {

    private val masterKeyAlias = MasterKeys.getOrCreate(MasterKeys.AES256_GCM_SPEC)

    // Securely store file in app's private space with encryption
```

```
    fun saveToPrivateFile(fileName: String, data: String) {
        val file = File(context.filesDir, fileName) // Private internal storage

        val encryptedFile = EncryptedFile.Builder(
            file,
            context,
            masterKeyAlias,
            EncryptedFile.FileEncryptionScheme.AES256_GCM_HKDF_4KB
        ).build()

        encryptedFile.openFileOutput().use { outputStream ->
            outputStream.write(data.toByteArray())
        }
    }

    // Securely retrieve file content from private encrypted storage
    fun readFromPrivateFile(fileName: String): String {
        val file = File(context.filesDir, fileName)

        val encryptedFile = EncryptedFile.Builder(
            file,
            context,
            masterKeyAlias,
            EncryptedFile.FileEncryptionScheme.AES256_GCM_HKDF_4KB
        ).build()

        encryptedFile.openFileInput().use { inputStream ->
            return inputStream.readBytes().decodeToString()
        }
    }
}
```

Android Keychain and KeyStore for Secure Credential Storage

Security is of utmost importance in Android development. This is especially true when it comes to storing sensitive information, such as user credentials, encryption keys, or other private data. The Android operating system provides us with two essential components to help ensure the secure storage of this information: the Keychain and the KeyStore.

Since Android is a multi-user operating system, providing different levels of security is necessary. Its architecture requires careful management of security components so that users can confidently store sensitive information on their devices.

Keychain and KeyStore: A Brief Overview

Android provides a secure and centralized system-level feature called Keychain, which is as a repository for credentials like certificates, private keys, and other sensitive data. It is designed to provide a unified storage solution that is accessible to different apps without putting user data at risk.

The Android KeyStore, on the other hand, is a key management system specifically designed to store cryptographic keys in a container protected by the device's hardware-backed security features. The KeyStore enforces policies like encryption and access control and is available for devices running Android 4.3 (API level 18) and higher.

Using the Android Keychain for Secure Credential Storage

For developers who want to use the Keychain for secure credential storage, the Android developer guide provides detailed documentation on how to go about this process. Android manages a KeyChain API to save and retrieve client certificates and private keys. Apps can use this API to manage their credentials securely.

When creating an application utilizing the Keychain API, we must request the `USE_CREDENTIALS` permission in their AndroidManifest.xml file, as shown here:

```
<manifest xmlns:android="http://schemas.android.com/apk/res/android"
   package="com.example.myapp">
   ...
   <uses-permission android:name="android.permission.USE_CREDENTIALS" />
   ...
</manifest>
```

Once the appropriate permissions have been granted, an app can request access to a stored certificate by calling the `KeyChain.choosePrivateKeyAlias` method, as shown in the below example:

```
import android.app.Activity
import android.content.Context
import android.security.KeyChain
import android.security.KeyChainAliasCallback
import java.security.PrivateKey
import java.security.cert.X509Certificate
import android.util.Log

class SecureKeyChainManager(private val context: Context) {

    private var keyAlias: String? = null

```

```
    // Step 1: Request user to choose a private key alias
    fun choosePrivateKeyAlias(activity: Activity, callback: (String?) -> Unit) {
        KeyChain.choosePrivateKeyAlias(
            activity,
            object : KeyChainAliasCallback {
                override fun alias(alias: String?) {
                    keyAlias = alias
                    callback(alias)
                }
            },
            null,  // Accept any key type
            null,  // Accept any certificate issuer
            null,  // No specific hostname restriction
            -1,    // No port restriction
            null   // No pre-selected alias
        )
    }

    // Step 2: Retrieve the private key and certificate chain (Must run on a backgro\
und thread)
    fun getPrivateKeyAndCertificate(callback: (PrivateKey?, Array<X509Certificate>?)\
 -> Unit) {
        if (keyAlias == null) {
            Log.e("SecureKeyChainManager", "No key alias selected")
            callback(null, null)
            return
        }

        Thread {
            try {
                val privateKey = KeyChain.getPrivateKey(context, keyAlias)
                val certChain = KeyChain.getCertificateChain(context, keyAlias)
                callback(privateKey, certChain)
            } catch (e: Exception) {
                Log.e("SecureKeyChainManager", "Error retrieving key/certificate: ${\
e.message}")
                callback(null, null)
            }
        }.start()
    }
}
```

How to use

```
...

 secureKeyChainManager = SecureKeyChainManager(this)

        // Step 1: Ask the user to select a private key
        secureKeyChainManager.choosePrivateKeyAlias(this) { alias ->
            if (alias != null) {
                Log.d("MainActivity", "Selected Key Alias: $alias")

                // Step 2: Retrieve the private key and certificate chain
                secureKeyChainManager.getPrivateKeyAndCertificate { privateKey, cert\
Chain ->
                    if (privateKey != null && certChain != null) {
                        Log.d("MainActivity", "Private Key Retrieved: $privateKey")
                        Log.d("MainActivity", "Certificate Chain Size: ${certChain.s\
ize}")
                    } else {
                        Log.e("MainActivity", "Failed to retrieve key/certificates")
                    }
                }
            } else {
                Log.e("MainActivity", "No key alias selected")
            }
        }
...
```

Using the Android KeyStore for Secure Key Storage

For developers who want to use the Android KeyStore to store cryptographic keys securely, the system provides the `android.security.KeyStore` class, which functions as a wrapper around the Android KeyStore system.

Here's an example in Kotlin to generate an RSA key pair and store it securely in the Android KeyStore:

Keystore & RSA example

```
import android.security.keystore.KeyGenParameterSpec
import android.security.keystore.KeyProperties
import java.security.KeyPairGenerator
import java.security.KeyStore
import java.security.PrivateKey
import java.security.PublicKey
import javax.crypto.Cipher
import android.util.Base64

class SecureKeystoreRSA(private val keyAlias: String = "secure_rsa_key") {

    private val keystore: KeyStore = KeyStore.getInstance("AndroidKeyStore").apply {\
 load(null) }

    init {
        generateKeyPairIfNeeded()
    }

    private fun generateKeyPairIfNeeded() {
        if (!keystore.containsAlias(keyAlias)) {
            val keyPairGenerator = KeyPairGenerator.getInstance(KeyProperties.KEY_AL\
GORITHM_RSA, "AndroidKeyStore")
            val parameterSpec = KeyGenParameterSpec.Builder(
                keyAlias,
                KeyProperties.PURPOSE_ENCRYPT or KeyProperties.PURPOSE_DECRYPT
            )
                .setEncryptionPaddings(KeyProperties.ENCRYPTION_PADDING_RSA_PKCS1)
                .setKeySize(2048) // Secure key size
                .setUserAuthenticationRequired(false) // Set to true for biometric/P\
IN authentication
                .build()

            keyPairGenerator.initialize(parameterSpec)
            keyPairGenerator.generateKeyPair()
        }
    }

    private fun getPublicKey(): PublicKey {
        val entry = keystore.getEntry(keyAlias, null) as KeyStore.PrivateKeyEntry
        return entry.certificate.publicKey
    }

    private fun getPrivateKey(): PrivateKey {
```

```
        val entry = keystore.getEntry(keyAlias, null) as KeyStore.PrivateKeyEntry
        return entry.privateKey
    }

    fun encrypt(data: String): String {
        val publicKey = getPublicKey()
        val cipher = Cipher.getInstance("RSA/ECB/PKCS1Padding")
        cipher.init(Cipher.ENCRYPT_MODE, publicKey)
        val encryptedBytes = cipher.doFinal(data.toByteArray())
        return Base64.encodeToString(encryptedBytes, Base64.DEFAULT)
    }

    fun decrypt(encryptedData: String): String {
        val privateKey = getPrivateKey()
        val cipher = Cipher.getInstance("RSA/ECB/PKCS1Padding")
        cipher.init(Cipher.DECRYPT_MODE, privateKey)
        val decryptedBytes = cipher.doFinal(Base64.decode(encryptedData, Base64.DEFA\
ULT))
        return String(decryptedBytes)
    }
}
```

How to use

```
val secureRSA = SecureKeystoreRSA()

// Encrypt data
val encrypted = secureRSA.encrypt("Sensitive Data")
println("Encrypted: $encrypted")

// Decrypt data
val decrypted = secureRSA.decrypt(encrypted)
println("Decrypted: $decrypted")
```

When to use

- If you need public-key encryption where only the private key can decrypt data.
- If you need encryption without sharing the private key (e.g., sending encrypted data securely).

Keystore & AES example

```
import android.security.keystore.KeyGenParameterSpec
import android.security.keystore.KeyProperties
import java.security.KeyStore
import javax.crypto.Cipher
import javax.crypto.KeyGenerator
import javax.crypto.SecretKey
import javax.crypto.spec.GCMParameterSpec
import android.util.Base64

class SecureKeyStore {
    private val keyAlias = "secure_key"
    private val keystoreType = "AndroidKeyStore"
    private val cipherAlgorithm = "AES/GCM/NoPadding"
    private val ivSize = 12 // 12-byte IV for AES-GCM

    init {
        generateKey()
    }

    // Generate AES Key if not already present
    private fun generateKey() {
        val keyStore = KeyStore.getInstance(keystoreType).apply { load(null) }
        if (!keyStore.containsAlias(keyAlias)) {
            val keyGen = KeyGenerator.getInstance(KeyProperties.KEY_ALGORITHM_AES, k\
eystoreType)
            val keyGenParamSpec = KeyGenParameterSpec.Builder(
                keyAlias,
                KeyProperties.PURPOSE_ENCRYPT or KeyProperties.PURPOSE_DECRYPT
            )
                .setBlockModes(KeyProperties.BLOCK_MODE_GCM)
                .setEncryptionPaddings(KeyProperties.ENCRYPTION_PADDING_NONE)
                .setKeySize(256) // AES-256 bit encryption
                .build()

            keyGen.init(keyGenParamSpec)
            keyGen.generateKey()
        }
    }

    // Retrieve AES Key from Android Keystore
    private fun getKey(): SecretKey? {
        val keyStore = KeyStore.getInstance(keystoreType).apply { load(null) }
        return keyStore.getKey(keyAlias, null) as? SecretKey
```

```
    }

    // Encrypt Data
    fun encrypt(data: String): String {
        val cipher = Cipher.getInstance(cipherAlgorithm)
        cipher.init(Cipher.ENCRYPT_MODE, getKey())
        val iv = cipher.iv // Initialization vector
        val encryptedBytes = cipher.doFinal(data.toByteArray())

        // Combine IV and encrypted data for decryption
        val combined = iv + encryptedBytes
        return Base64.encodeToString(combined, Base64.DEFAULT)
    }

    // Decrypt Data
    fun decrypt(encryptedData: String): String {
        val decodedData = Base64.decode(encryptedData, Base64.DEFAULT)

        // Extract IV and encrypted data
        val iv = decodedData.sliceArray(0 until ivSize)
        val encryptedBytes = decodedData.sliceArray(ivSize until decodedData.size)

        val cipher = Cipher.getInstance(cipherAlgorithm)
        val spec = GCMParameterSpec(128, iv) // 128-bit authentication tag
        cipher.init(Cipher.DECRYPT_MODE, getKey(), spec)

        val decryptedBytes = cipher.doFinal(encryptedBytes)
        return String(decryptedBytes)
    }
}
```

```
val secureKeyStore = SecureKeyStore()

// Encrypt Data
val encryptedText = secureKeyStore.encrypt("Sensitive Data")
println("Encrypted: $encryptedText")

// Decrypt Data
val decryptedText = secureKeyStore.decrypt(encryptedText)
println("Decrypted: $decryptedText")
```

When to use

- If you need fast encryption for large files, databases, or bulk data.
- If you can securely store and retrieve the AES key

Using Hardware-Backed Keys for Added Security

We can also use the Android KeyStore to generate hardware-backed cryptographic keys for added security. These keys are stored and operated on within the secure environment of the device's Trusted Execution Environment (TEE) or Secure Element (SE). This provides better protection against potential attacks like key extraction or key misuse.

The following is an example of creating a hardware-backed key using the `KeyGenParameterSpec.Builder` class:

```
KeyGenParameterSpec.Builder keyGenParameterSpecBuilder = new KeyGenParameterSpec.Bui\
lder(
        "my_alias",
        KeyProperties.PURPOSE_ENCRYPT | KeyProperties.PURPOSE_DECRYPT)
        .setKeySize(256)
        .setBlockModes(KeyProperties.BLOCK_MODE_CBC)
        .setEncryptionPaddings(KeyProperties.ENCRYPTION_PADDING_PKCS7)
        .setIsStrongBoxBacked(true);
```

SharedPreference - Securely storing

Storing and transmitting data securely is necessary to prevent data leakage or tampering. For instance, using encryption can protect the stored data in SharedPreferences. The following is an example of encrypting data using AndroidX's EncryptedSharedPreferences library:

```
val context = requireContext()
val encryptedSharedPreferences = EncryptedSharedPreferences.create(
   context,
   "secure_prefs",
   MasterKeys.getOrCreate(MasterKeys.AES256_GCM_SPEC),
   EncryptedSharedPreferences.PrefKeyEncryptionScheme.AES256_SIV,
   EncryptedSharedPreferences.PrefValueEncryptionScheme.AES256_GCM
)


// Save encrypted data
val editor = encryptedSharedPreferences.edit()
editor.putString("key", "untrustedData")
```

```
editor.apply()


// Read encrypted data
val untrustedData = encryptedSharedPreferences.getString("key", "")
```

Encrypt SQLite Database (SQLCipher + Room)

Add Dependency

```
dependencies {
    implementation "net.zetetic:android-database-sqlcipher:4.5.0"
    implementation "androidx.sqlite:sqlite:2.1.0"
}
```

Secure Room Database with SQLCipher

```
import android.content.Context
import androidx.room.Room
import net.sqlcipher.database.SQLiteDatabase
import net.sqlcipher.database.SupportFactory

class SecureDatabase(context: Context) {
    private val passphrase: ByteArray = SQLiteDatabase.getBytes("secure_password".to\
CharArray())
    private val factory = SupportFactory(passphrase)

    val database = Room.databaseBuilder(
        context,
        AppDatabase::class.java,
        "secure_db"
    )
        .openHelperFactory(factory)
        .build()
}
```

Dynamic Code Loading Restrictions (Android 14)

Though the recommendation is to not having any dynamically-loaded code, there are some recommendation to prevent an unauthorized change alongside Android security features. The dynamically loaded code stored in a files which is not part of the APK. These files could be targeted by other applications. That means we need to get the file's content over a secure connection and store them in a protected space.A new feature from Android 14 enforces all dynamically-loaded files to be marked as read-only to prevents unauthorized modifications to app code. Therefore the files that is not marked to read-only leads to throwing an exception. This new feature helps to identify and prevents any changes to .jar or .dex files by enforcing stricter runtime class loading.

File Integrity Verification

FileIntegrityManager API is a new feature in Android 14 to verify files integrity through digital signatures. For instance before using any files stored in external storage or the download folder we could check verify the file authenticity with the new APIs to ensure that they have not changes in between or after downloading with another actor.

Example

```
val fileIntegrityManager = context.getSystemService(FileIntegrityManager::class.java)
val integrityCheckResult = fileIntegrityManager?.verify(file, expectedHash)
if (integrityCheckResult == FileIntegrityManager.STATUS_OK) {
    // Safe to use
} else {
    // Possible tampering detected
}
```

Private Space

"Private Space" is a hidden, encrypted storage area where sensitive apps & data introduced in Android 15 could to stored separately from the main user profile. The applications inside this area is fully isolated from other apps. Also they are secured with another layer since the storage is encrypted to prevent any unauthorized access. This private space works like a secure vault to store credential documents, private applications, etc. which might be ideal for corporate profiles.

We can check if their app is in Private Space by using:

```
val privateSpaceManager = context.getSystemService(PrivateSpaceManager::class.java)
val isInPrivateSpace = privateSpaceManager?.isAppInPrivateSpace()
```

Authentication, Network, and Protocols

Android AccountManager for Access Control

Secure coding is a crucial aspect of the Android development process. Proper access control helps ensure that sensitive data is protected from unauthorized access, and Android's AccountManager is one of the essential tools developers can use for this purpose.

AccountManager is a central repository that stores and manages account credentials across various Android applications. It allows developers to share authentication tokens across multiple applications, enabling single sign-on (SSO) and other access control features that provide a seamless user experience.

2. Why use AccountManager?

AccountManager provides several advantages over traditional authentication methods, including:

Shared authentication mechanism: AccountManager offers an abstract layer and eases code reuse, allowing third-party applications to manage accounts.

- Secure storage: AccountManager stores sensitive user data, such as usernames and passwords, in an encrypted form to protect it from unauthorized access.
- Single sign-on (SSO) and token management: Account managers can request and manage authentication tokens, enabling SSO and efficient token caching.
- Centralized account management: Users can configure and manage their accounts from a single place in device settings.
- Versioning support: AccountManager provides an update mechanism to notify apps of changes in user account information.

3. Components of AccountManager

AccountManager comprises four primary components:

- Account: Represents a single user account and consists of the account's name and the type of service it is linked to (e.g., Google, Facebook, etc.) Account Authenticator: This is a background process responsible for handling the authentication mechanism, such as verifying usernames and passwords or generating authentication tokens.

- Account Manager Service (AMS): A system-level process that manages Account objects and communicates with Account Authenticators. Authenticator API: This is a set of interfaces and methods for interacting with AccountManager. Developers use it to create, modify, and retrieve accounts and tokens.

4. Integrating AccountManager

To integrate AccountManager in an Android application, you must follow three main steps: create an authenticator, register the authenticator with the system, and implement the authentication API in your app.

4.1 Creating an Authenticator

To create an authenticator, you must extend the AbstractAccountAuthenticator class and implement its various methods.

Example

```
import android.accounts.AbstractAccountAuthenticator;
import android.accounts.Account;
import android.accounts.AccountAuthenticatorResponse;
import android.content.Context;
import android.os.Bundle;


public class MyAccountAuthenticator extends AbstractAccountAuthenticator {
 private final Context context;


 public MyAccountAuthenticator(Context context) {
     super(context);
     this.context = context;
 }


 @Override
 public Bundle editProperties(AccountAuthenticatorResponse response, String accountT\
ype) {
     // Custom properties editor will be implemented later
     throw new UnsupportedOperationException();
 }


 @Override
```

```
 public Bundle addAccount(AccountAuthenticatorResponse response, String accountType,
                          String authTokenType, String[] requiredFeatures, Bundle op\
tions) {
     // Adding account functionality will be implemented later
     throw new UnsupportedOperationException();
 }


 // Implement other abstract methods as needed
}
```

4.2 Registering the Authenticator

After creating the authenticator, register it with the system by declaring it in the AndroidManifest.xml file.

Example

```
<manifest>
 <!-- ... -->


 <application>
     <!-- ... -->


     <service
         android:name=".authenticator.MyAccountAuthenticatorService"
         android:exported="false">
         <intent-filter>
             <action android:name="android.accounts.AccountAuthenticator" />
         </intent-filter>
         <meta-data
             android:name="android.accounts.AccountAuthenticator"
             android:resource="@xml/authenticator" />
     </service>
 </application>
</manifest>
```

4.3 Implementing the Authentication API

Finally, implement the authentication API in your app to interact with AccountManager using the Authenticator API.

Example

```java
import android.accounts.Account;
import android.accounts.AccountManager;
import android.os.Bundle;


public class MainActivity extends AppCompatActivity {
 private static final String ACCOUNT_TYPE = "com.example.myapp";
 private static final String AUTH_TOKEN_TYPE = "my_token_type";


 @Override
 protected void onCreate(Bundle savedInstanceState) {
     super.onCreate(savedInstanceState);
     setContentView(R.layout.activity_main);


     AccountManager accountManager = AccountManager.get(this);


     // Create account
     Account account = new Account("user@example.com", ACCOUNT_TYPE);
     accountManager.addAccountExplicitly(account, "password", null);


     // Request auth token for the account
     accountManager.getAuthToken(account, AUTH_TOKEN_TYPE, null, this,
         future -> {
             try {
                 Bundle result = future.getResult();
                 String authToken = result.getString(AccountManager.KEY_AUTHTOKEN);
             } catch (Exception e) {
                 // Handle error
             }
         }, null);
  }
}
```

- User Authentication: Centralized management of accounts and credentials.
- OAuth Integration: Use of OAuth 2.0 for securing third-party API access.
- Access Tokens: Handling of access and refresh tokens for user sessions.
- Multi-account Support: Managing multiple user accounts within a single app.
- Secure Credential Storage: Ensuring sensitive credentials are stored securely.
- Revocation of Access: Handling account disconnections and token revocations.

Credential Manager

A new feature introduced in Android 15 enables linking a specific view with Credential Manager request. ThisThis link leads to displays an autofill UIs once the user focuses on one these views.

Example

```
import android.app.Activity
import android.content.Context
import android.util.Log
import androidx.biometric.BiometricPrompt
import androidx.credentials.*
import kotlinx.coroutines.*
import java.util.concurrent.Executor
import java.util.concurrent.Executors

class CredentialManagerHelper(private val context: Context) {

    private val credentialManager = CredentialManager.create(context)
    private val executor: Executor = Executors.newSingleThreadExecutor()

    // Step 1: Authenticate user using biometric prompt
    fun authenticateWithPasskey(
        activity: Activity,
        onSuccess: (String) -> Unit,
        onFailure: (String) -> Unit
    ) {
        val biometricPrompt = createBiometricPrompt(activity, onSuccess, onFailure)
        val promptInfo = createBiometricPromptInfo()

        biometricPrompt.authenticate(promptInfo)
    }

    // Step 2: Create a biometric prompt
    private fun createBiometricPrompt(
        activity: Activity,
        onSuccess: (String) -> Unit,
        onFailure: (String) -> Unit
    ): BiometricPrompt {
        return BiometricPrompt(activity, executor, object : BiometricPrompt.Authenti\
cationCallback() {
            override fun onAuthenticationSucceeded(result: BiometricPrompt.Authentic\
ationResult) {
```

```
                super.onAuthenticationSucceeded(result)
                CoroutineScope(Dispatchers.Main).launch {
                    try {
                        val credentialResponse = requestCredential()
                        onSuccess(credentialResponse)
                    } catch (e: Exception) {
                        onFailure("Credential Manager Error: ${e.message}")
                    }
                }
            }

            override fun onAuthenticationFailed() {
                super.onAuthenticationFailed()
                onFailure("Biometric authentication failed")
            }
        })
    }

    // Step 3: Create a biometric prompt info dialog
    private fun createBiometricPromptInfo(): BiometricPrompt.PromptInfo {
        return BiometricPrompt.PromptInfo.Builder()
            .setTitle("Sign in with Passkey")
            .setSubtitle("Use biometric authentication to continue")
            .setNegativeButtonText("Cancel")
            .build()
    }

    // Step 4: Request a stored passkey using Credential Manager (THIS IS THE LINK)
    private suspend fun requestCredential(): String {
        return withContext(Dispatchers.IO) {
            try {
                Log.d("CredentialManagerHelper", "Requesting passkey...")

                val credentialRequest = GetCredentialRequest.Builder()
                    .addCredentialOption(
                        PublicKeyCredentialOption(
                            """
                            {
                                "challenge": "random-string-from-server",
                                "timeout": 60000,
                                "requestType": "webauthn.get"
                            }
                            """.trimIndent()
```

```
                        )
                    )
                    .build()

                val credentialResponse: GetCredentialResponse = credentialManager.ge\
tCredential(credentialRequest)
                val passkeyData = credentialResponse.credential.data

                Log.d("CredentialManagerHelper", "Passkey retrieved: $passkeyData")
                passkeyData
            } catch (e: Exception) {
                Log.e("CredentialManagerHelper", "Credential Manager Error: ${e.mess\
age}")
                throw e
            }
        }
    }
}
```

How to use

```
    credentialHelper = CredentialManagerHelper(this)

    // Trigger biometric authentication & credential request
    credentialHelper.authenticateWithPasskey(
        this,
        onSuccess = { credentialData ->
            Toast.makeText(this, "Authenticated Successfully: $credentialData", Toas\
t.LENGTH_LONG).show()
        },
        onFailure = { error ->
            Toast.makeText(this, "Error: $error", Toast.LENGTH_LONG).show()
        }
    )
```

Android Biometric Authentication

With the rapid growth of technology, the security of personal data is more critical than ever. Android biometric authentication is a security feature that enables users to verify their identity through unique biological characteristics, such as facial recognition, fingerprints, or iris scanning technology. This type of authentication offers a more convenient and secure confirmation method than traditional PINs or passwords.

We will discuss low-level and high-level solutions and provide code examples using C, C++, Java, or Kotlin.

History of Biometric Authentication

Biometric authentication has been around in various forms since ancient times. One of the earliest examples dates back to 14th-century China, where fingerprinting was used to authenticate legal documents. However, modern biometric systems gained popularity in the late 20th century, and with the introduction of various smartphone technologies, biometric authentication has since become an integral part of mobile security.

Apple was the first major company to implement biometric authentication in its devices by introducing the Touch ID fingerprint sensor in the iPhone 5s in 2013. The success of Touch ID paved the way for fingerprint sensors in other smartphones, including Android devices.

Virtually all major Android smartphone manufacturers have implemented biometric authentication since then. Google also introduced native biometric APIs, starting from Android 6.0 Marshmallow, allowing developers to leverage biometric authentication in their apps.

Advantages of Biometric Authentication

1. Convenience: Biometric authentication uses the unique biological characteristics of the user, so there is no need to remember passwords or PINs.
2. Security: Biological traits are much harder to steal or duplicate than traditional authentication methods.
3. Multi-factor Authentication: Biometric authentication can be combined with other authentication methods, like passwords, for increased security.
4. Faster Authentication: Biometric authentication is usually faster than entering long passwords or PINs.

Integrating Android Biometric Authentication

In Android development, fingerprint authentication was introduced in Android 6.0 Marshmallow through the FingerprintManager API. However, Android 9.0 (Pie) deprecated the FingerprintManager API and introduced the BiometricPrompt API, which manages fingerprint authentication, face recognition, and iris scanning (if the device supports them).

To implement biometric authentication in your Android application, you must adhere to the following steps:

1. Add biometric authentication dependencies.

For Java and Kotlin applications, add the following dependency to the app-level build.gradle file:

```
dependencies {
 implementation 'androidx.biometric:biometric:1.1.0'
}
```

2. Ensure biometric hardware is available.

Check if the device has hardware that supports biometric authentication using the BiometricManager class:

```
BiometricManager biometricManager = BiometricManager.from(context);
switch (biometricManager.canAuthenticate()) {
 case BiometricManager.BIOMETRIC_SUCCESS:
     // The device has biometric hardware and the user has biometric data available
     break;
 case BiometricManager.BIOMETRIC_ERROR_NO_HARDWARE:
     // The device does not have biometric hardware
     break;
 case BiometricManager.BIOMETRIC_ERROR_HW_UNAVAILABLE:
     // The biometric hardware is temporarily unavailable
     break;
 case BiometricManager.BIOMETRIC_ERROR_NONE_ENROLLED:
     // The device has biometric hardware, but the user has not yet set up biometric\
 data
     break;
}
```

3. Implement biometric authentication using the BiometricPrompt API.

The BiometricPrompt class handles the process of presenting a dialog to the user and requesting biometric authentication:

```
// Create a prompt info object to show a custom description in the prompt
BiometricPrompt.PromptInfo promptInfo = new BiometricPrompt.PromptInfo.Builder()
     .setTitle("Biometric Authentication")
     .setSubtitle("Use your biometric data to authenticate")
     .setDescription("This app uses biometric authentication to protect your data")
     .setNegativeButtonText("Cancel")
     .build();


Executor executor = ContextCompat.getMainExecutor(context);
BiometricPrompt biometricPrompt = new BiometricPrompt(this, executor, new BiometricP\
rompt.AuthenticationCallback() {
 @Override
 public void onAuthenticationError(int errorCode, CharSequence errString) {
     super.onAuthenticationError(errorCode, errString);
     // Handle authentication errors
 }


 @Override
 public void onAuthenticationSucceeded(BiometricPrompt.AuthenticationResult result) {
     super.onAuthenticationSucceeded(result);
     // Authentication succeeded
 }


 @Override
 public void onAuthenticationFailed() {
     super.onAuthenticationFailed();
     // Handle failed authentication attempts
 }
});


// Show the biometric prompt to the user
biometricPrompt.authenticate(promptInfo);
```

Potential Risks

Biometric authentication, albeit very secure, is partially foolproof. There have been instances where fingerprint and face recognition technologies have been deceived or bypassed. Additionally, biometric data is considered sensitive personally identifiable information (PII), which, if compromised, can cause severe privacy issues for users.

For these reasons, developers should ensure that biometric data is securely stored and that the overall implementation of biometric authentication is thoroughly tested. Moreover, developers should provide users with an alternative authentication method, such as passwords or PINs, to ensure accessibility and compatibility with various devices.

Android Network Security Configuration

With the increasing number of users and applications on Android devices, security has become a significant concern for developers and users. One of the most critical aspects of security in Android is securing network communications between the application and the server. Network Security Configuration is a feature introduced in Android 6.0 (API level 23) that provides a straightforward and flexible way to enforce security and application-specific networking policies such as trust anchors, VPNs, SSL pinning, etc.

Overview

Network Security Configuration is an XML file that Android applications can include to specify the network security policies for the app. The Android operating system, through the contents of this file, determines rules to allow or block network traffic and provides additional security features. Using Network Security Configuration, developers can modify the app's secure communication settings without needing code change or recompilation.

Components

The Network Security Configuration mainly consists of the following components:

1. Trust anchors: These are the Certificate Authorities (CAs) that the application trusts to provide SSL certificates. By default, Android trusts all the CAs that are part of the Android system. However, with Network Security Configuration, developers can override this default behavior and restrict the CAs that the application trusts.
2. Debug-only overrides: These settings apply only when the application is built with the debug build type. They allow developers to change certain security configurations during development without affecting the end users.
3. Domain configurations: These configurations apply to specific domains and can override the default settings. They can be used to provide domain-specific policies, such as certificate pinning or custom trust anchors.
4. Cleartext traffic: By default, Android blocks all cleartext (HTTP) traffic for applications targeting API level 28 or higher. However, Network Security Configuration can permit cleartext traffic for specific safe domains.

Examples

1. Trust Anchors

Consider a scenario where an Android application communicates only with servers that use SSL certificates signed by a particular CA. In this case, developers can create a custom trust anchor set that includes only the desired CA. Here's an example of Network Security Configuration that trusts only a specific CA:

```
<network-security-config>
 <base-config>
     <trust-anchors>
         <certificates src="@raw/my_ca"/>
     </trust-anchors>
 </base-config>
</network-security-config>
```

This configuration file instructs the app to trust only the specified CA, which should be stored as a raw resource in the `res/raw` directory named `my_ca.crt`.

2. Debug-only Overrides

Debug-only overrides can allow developers to access servers with self-signed certificates during development. Here's an example of a Network Security Configuration file that trusts self-signed certificates only during development:

```
<network-security-config>
 <debug-overrides>
     <trust-anchors>
         <certificates src="user"/>
     </trust-anchors>
 </debug-overrides>
</network-security-config>
```

3. Domain Configurations

If an application requires SSL pinning for a specific domain, domain configurations can be used. For example, the following Network Security Configuration file enforces SSL pinning for `www.example.com` using a specified public key:

```
<network-security-config>
 <domain-config>
     <domain includeSubdomains="true">www.example.com</domain>
     <pin-set>
         <pin digest="SHA-256">7HIpactkIAq2Y49orFOOQKurWxmmSFZhBCoQYcRhJ3Y=</pin>
     </pin-set>
 </domain-config>
</network-security-config>
```

4. Cleartext Traffic

To allow cleartext traffic for specific domains, use the following Network Security Configuration:

```
<network-security-config>
 <domain-config cleartextTrafficPermitted="true">
     <domain includeSubdomains="true">example.com</domain>
 </domain-config>
</network-security-config>
```

Implementation

Once the Network Security Configuration file is created, it should be stored in the application's `res/xml` directory. The file should be named `network_security_config.xml`. Next, add a reference to the Network Security Configuration file in the `AndroidManifest.xml` file as shown below:

```
<application android:networkSecurityConfig="@xml/network_security_config" ...>
 ...
</application>
```

- Cleartext Traffic Control: Enforcing policies to block cleartext HTTP traffic requires HTTPS.
- Custom Trust Anchors: Specifying trusted certificate authorities (CAs) for secure communication.
- Domain-specific Policies: Defining security settings for specific domains or IP addresses.
- Certificate Pinning: Ensuring the correct server certificate is used to prevent man-in-the-middle attacks.
- TLS Handshake: Customize and enforce security parameters during the TLS handshake process.
- Key Encryption Algorithms: Enforcing stronger algorithms like AES-256 or RSA-2048.
- SSL Bypass Prevention: Preventing bypass of SSL certificates in debugging and production environments.

Sniffing

An attack known as sniffing happens when a hacker intercepts and monitors network communication in order to obtain private data. Android provides several security features, such as SSL/TLS encryption and certificate pinning, to prevent sniffing attacks.

```
class NetworkSecurityExample {
 private fun setupSecureConnection() {
     val url = URL("https://api.example.com")
     val connection = url.openConnection() as HttpsURLConnection

     connection.apply {
         // Set timeouts
         connectTimeout = 10000
         readTimeout = 10000

         // Enable hostname verification
         hostnameVerifier = HostnameVerifier { hostname, session ->
             HttpsURLConnection.getDefaultHostnameVerifier().verify(hostname, sessio\
n)
         }

         // Configure SSL context
         SSLContext.getInstance("TLS").apply {
             init(null, getTrustedCertificates(), SecureRandom())
             sslSocketFactory = socketFactory
         }
     }
 }

 private fun getTrustedCertificates(): Array<TrustManager> {
     val trustManagerFactory = TrustManagerFactory.getInstance(
         TrustManagerFactory.getDefaultAlgorithm()
     )
     trustManagerFactory.init(null as KeyStore?)
     return trustManagerFactory.trustManagers
 }
}
```

Security Considerations:

- Use SSL/TLS encryption to protect network traffic from sniffing attacks.

- Implement certificate pinning to prevent man-in-the-middle (MITM) attacks.
- To protect private information, use a secure communication protocol such as HTTPS.

Known Vulnerabilities CVE: CVE-2019-5767 (Android sniffing vulnerability) CVE-2020-8913: Local MITM vulnerability CWE-300: Channel Accessible by Non-Endpoint CWE-319: Cleartext Transmission of Sensitive Information

Best Practices

Traffic Protection

- Use HTTPS for all network communications
- Implement certificate pinning
- Enable strict transport security

Data Handling

- Encrypt sensitive data before transmission
- Implement proper session management
- Man-in-the-Middle (MITM) Attacks: Defending against MITM attacks on network traffic.
- Packet Sniffing: Protecting app communications from being intercepted by network sniffers.
- Wi-Fi Security: Risks associated with public or untrusted Wi-Fi networks.
- Encrypted Communications: Using end-to-end encryption in network traffic is important to prevent sniffing.
- VPN Protection: Securing communications over Virtual Private Networks (VPN).

Certificate Pinning in Android Applications

Secure communication over public networks has become essential for modern mobile applications. One of the methods used to achieve this is establishing a secure connection over SSL/TLS protocols, which are responsible for encrypting the data transmitted between the client (mobile application) and the server. Digital certificates serve to establish a connection between a user and a network server for the purpose of encryption. However, there are certain risks involved in this approach, such as potential Man-in-the-Middle (MITM) attacks carried out by hackers. To address this risk, Android applications utilize a method known as Certificate Pinning.

What Is Certificate Pinning?

Certificate pinning is associating a host with its certificate or public key. This process replaces The server certificate with a known, verified certificate or public key. By doing this, attackers cannot easily impersonate the server, as they need to have the private key associated with the pinned public key. The main goal of certificate pinning is to prevent MITM attacks, where an attacker intercepts and potentially alters the data transmitted between the client and server.

The process of pinning can be accomplished in two ways:

1. Pinning the Leaf Certificate: The leaf certificate, or the end-user certificate, is directly added to the host. This provides maximum protection against MITM attacks but lacks flexibility, as the certificate needs to be replaced if it expires or is revoked.
2. Pinning the CA Certificate: The certificate of the Certificate Authority (CA) that issued the leaf certificate is added to the host. This provides less protection than pinning the leaf certificate, but it is more flexible as it only needs to be replaced if the entire CA is compromised.

Implementing Certificate Pinning in Android Applications

Various libraries and approaches can be used to implement certificate pinning in Android. We will focus on two popular libraries: OkHttp and TrustKit.

1. Implementing Certificate Pinning using OkHttp:

OkHttp is a widely used HTTP library for Android that offers built-in support for certificate pinning. The following steps outline how to implement certificate pinning using OkHttp in Android applications:

Step 1: Add the OkHttp library to the project. In the build.gradle (module: app) file, add the following dependency:

```
implementation 'com.squareup.okhttp3:okhttp:4.9.1'
```

Step 2: Create an OkHttpClient instance with pinned certificates. The following code snippet demonstrates how to pin the leaf certificate using OkHttp:

```
import okhttp3.CertificatePinner
import okhttp3.OkHttpClient

val certificatePinner = CertificatePinner.Builder()
    .add("example.com", "sha256/AAAAAAAAAAAAAAAAAAAAAAAAAAAAAAAAAAAAAAAAAAA=")
    .build()
val client = OkHttpClient.Builder()
    .certificatePinner(certificatePinner)
    .build()
```

Replace "example.com" with the target domain you want to pin and "sha256/AAAAAAAAAAAAAAAAAAAA with the actual SHA-256 hash of the certificate in Base64 encoding.

Step 3: Use the OkHttpClient instance for secure network requests. Whenever you make an HTTP request using OkHttp, use the client instance created in Step 2 to ensure that the network call is made with pinned certificates.

2. Implementing Certificate Pinning using TrustKit:

TrustKit is a comprehensive security library for Android that offers a reliable certificate pinning implementation. The following steps outline how to implement certificate pinning using TrustKit in Android applications:

Step 1: Add the TrustKit library to the project. In the build.gradle (module: app) file, add the following dependency:

```
implementation 'com.datatheorem.android.trustkit:trustkit:1.1.3'
```

Step 2: Configure TrustKit in the AndroidManifest.xml file. Add the following metadata configuration:

```
<application>
    <!-- ... -->
    <meta-data android:name="com.datatheorem.android.trustkit.config.domain"
               android:resource="@string/domain" />
    <!-- ... -->
</application>
```

Step 3: Create an XML file called "domain.xml" in the "res/values" folder. Add the following content to the file:

```
<resources>
 <string-array name="domain">
     <item>@string/high_level_domain</item>
     <item>enforcePinning</item>
     <item>@array/certificates</item>
 </string-array>
 <string name="high_level_domain">example.com</string>
 <array name="certificates">
     <item>sha256/AAAAAAAAAAAAAAAAAAAAAAAAAAAAAAAAAAAAAAAAAAA=</item>
 </array>
</resources>
```

Replace "example.com" with the target domain you want to pin and "sha256/AAAAAAAAAAAAAAAAAA with the actual SHA-256 hash of the certificate in Base64 encoding.

Step 4: Initialize TrustKit in your Application class:

```
import android.app.Application
import com.datatheorem.android.trustkit.TrustKit

class MyApplication : Application() {
 override fun onCreate() {
     super.onCreate()
     TrustKit.initializeWithNetworkSecurityConfiguration(this)
 }
}
```

This will initialize TrustKit with your Android application's default network security configuration, allowing it to enforce certificate pinning whenever a network request is made.

Implementing Certificate Pinning in C, C++, Java, and Kotlin

Since Android applications are developed primarily in Java and Kotlin, and the NDK allows for native development using C and C++, the following examples demonstrate how to implement certificate pinning in these languages.

Java example

```
import java.security.cert.X509Certificate;
import javax.net.ssl.HostnameVerifier;
import javax.net.ssl.HttpsURLConnection;
import javax.net.ssl.SSLContext;
import javax.net.ssl.SSLPeerUnverifiedException;
import javax.net.ssl.TrustManager;
import javax.net.ssl.X509TrustManager;

public class CertificatePinning {
 public static void main(String[] args) throws Exception {
     TrustManager tm = new X509TrustManager() {
         public void checkClientTrusted(X509Certificate[] chain,
                                        String authType) {
         }

         public void checkServerTrusted(X509Certificate[] chain,
                                        String authType) throws CertificateException\
 {
             if (chain == null || chain.length == 0
                     || authType == null || authType.length() == 0) {
                 throw new IllegalArgumentException("Error: checkServerTrusted metho\
d parameters");
             }
             try {
                 chain[0].checkValidity();
             } catch (Exception e) {
                 throw new CertificateException("Certificate not valid or trusted");
             }
             String fingerprint = getFingerprint(chain[0]);
             String pinnedFingerprint = "sha1/AAAAAAAAAAAAAAAAAAAAAAAAAAAAAAAAAAAAA\
AAAAA=";
             if (!fingerprint.equals(pinnedFingerprint)) {
                 throw new CertificateException("Certificate not trusted because the\
 fingerprint doesn't match");
             }
         }

         public X509Certificate[] getAcceptedIssuers() {
             return new X509Certificate[0];
         }
     };

     SSLContext sslContext = SSLContext.getInstance("TLS");
```

```
     sslContext.init(null, new TrustManager[]{tm}, null);
     HttpsURLConnection.setDefaultSSLSocketFactory(sslContext.getSocketFactory());

     HostnameVerifier hostnameVerifier = (hostname, session) -> {
         X509Certificate cert;
         try {
             cert = (X509Certificate) session.getPeerCertificates()[0];
         } catch (SSLPeerUnverifiedException e1) {
             return false;
         }
         return hostname.equals(cert.getSubjectDN().getName());
     };

     HttpsURLConnection.setDefaultHostnameVerifier(hostnameVerifier);

     // Make network request using HttpsURLConnection ...
 }
}
```

Kotlin example

```
import java.security.cert.X509Certificate
import javax.net.ssl.HttpsURLConnection
import javax.net.ssl.SSLContext
import javax.net.ssl.X509TrustManager

fun main() {
 val trustManager = object : X509TrustManager {
     override fun checkClientTrusted(chain: Array<out X509Certificate>?, authType: S\
tring?) {
         // Don't do anything
     }

     override fun checkServerTrusted(chain: Array<out X509Certificate>?, authType: S\
tring?) {
         if (chain == null || authType == null || chain.isEmpty() || authType.isEmpt\
y()) {
             throw IllegalArgumentException("Error: checkServerTrusted method parame\
ters")
         }
         try {
             chain[0].checkValidity()
         } catch (e: Exception) {
```

```
             throw CertificateException("Certificate not valid or trusted")
         }
         val fingerprint = getFingerprint(chain[0])
         val pinnedFingerprint = "sha1/AAAAAAAAAAAAAAAAAAAAAAAAAAAAAAAAAAAAAAAA="
         if (fingerprint != pinnedFingerprint) {
             throw CertificateException("Certificate not trusted because the fingerp\
rint doesn't match")
         }
     }

     override fun getAcceptedIssuers(): Array<X509Certificate> {
         return arrayOf()
     }
 }

 val sslContext = SSLContext.getInstance("TLS")
 sslContext.init(null, arrayOf(trustManager), null)
 HttpsURLConnection.setDefaultSSLSocketFactory(sslContext.socketFactory)

 val hostnameVerifier = HostnameVerifier { hostname, session ->
     val cert = session.peerCertificates[0] as? X509Certificate
     hostname == cert?.subjectDN?.name
 }

 HttpsURLConnection.setDefaultHostnameVerifier(hostnameVerifier)

 // Make network request using HttpsURLConnection ...
}
```

Another example for OkHttp

```
val certificates = listOf(CertificatePinner.Pin.fromCertificatePemResource("<PEM_res\
ource>"))
val pin = CertificatePinner.Builder()
 .add("example.com", *certificates.toTypedArray())
 .build()
val client = OkHttpClient.Builder()
 .certificatePinner(pin)
 .build()
```

Network Security Configuration

Use the Android Network Security Configuration feature to establish rules and policies for your application's network connections, such as requiring TLS and pinning certificates.

Example

```
<!-- res/xml/network_security_config.xml -->
<network-security-config>
 <domain-config>
     <domain includeSubdomains="true">example.com</domain>
     <pin-set>
         <pin digest="SHA-256">7HIpactkIAq2Y49orFO62ou0jxCAH9CWuRxXLkIXELM=</pin>
     </pin-set>
 </domain-config>
</network-security-config>
```

Examples in C and C++ are beyond the scope of this chapter. Implementing certificate pinning in these languages requires a different approach, which involves customizing the SSL/TLS library, such as OpenSSL, to validate certificates.

- Static vs Dynamic Pinning: Differences and use cases for hardcoded certificates vs dynamic certificate pinning.
- Security Benefits: Preventing MITM attacks even when a trusted certificate authority is compromised.
- Implementation Best Practices: Ensuring proper pinning implementation to avoid breaking connections with legitimate servers.
- Pinning with Android Network Security Configuration: Combining pinning with Android's Network Security Configuration for comprehensive protection.
- Handling Certificate Expiration: Manage certificate expiry and update pins without disrupting app functionality.
- Fallback Mechanisms: Creating a secure fallback in case of pinning failures.
- Pinning Validation Errors: How to handle validation errors without exposing vulnerabilities.

Implementing SSL/TLS for Android Network Communications

Transport Layer Security (TLS) and Secure Socket Layer (SSL) are standard Internet security protocols that encrypt and authenticate network connections. These technologies became widely adopted due to the increasing need for data privacy and secure data communications. In Android, SSL/TLS is typically used for network communications involving sensitive data, such as user login credentials, personal information, or financial transaction data.

1. SSL/TLS Overview

SSL and TLS are cryptographic protocols being used to secure communication between parties over a public network. Netscape initially developed SSL, while the Internet Engineering Task Force (IETF) designed TLS as its successor. TLS 1.3 is currently the latest version of the protocol, whereas SSL 2.0 and 3.0 are considered deprecated and should not be used in new applications due to security vulnerabilities.

Both SSL and TLS use certificates to authenticate the entities involved in a communication process and guarantee the integrity and confidentiality of data transmission.

2. Android Network Security Configuration

Android provides a network security configuration feature to customize the application's secure network connections. This feature allows app developers to specify trusted SSL/TLS certification authorities (CAs), enforce specific cipher suites, restrict cleartext traffic, and enable Certificate Transparency (CT) checks.

To implement SSL/TLS in Android applications, follow these steps:

1. Create a 'res/xml' folder in your Android project if it doesn't already exist.
2. Create a new XML file called 'network_security_config.xml' in the 'res/xml' folder.
3. Edit the 'network_security_config.xml' file with specific network security settings.
4. Update the 'AndroidManifest.xml' file to reference your security configuration.

For example, the following 'network_security_config.xml' enables the use of a custom certificate authority (CA):

```xml
<?xml version="1.0" encoding="utf-8"?>
<network-security-config>
 <base-config>
     <trust-anchors>
         <certificates src="@raw/custom_ca"/>
         <certificates src="system"/>
     </trust-anchors>
 </base-config>
</network-security-config>
```

Update the 'AndroidManifest.xml' file to include the following attribute in the `<application>` tag:

```
android:networkSecurityConfig="@xml/network_security_config"
```

3. SSL/TLS Implementation in Android Applications

When implementing SSL/TLS for network communications in Android applications, developers should follow these best practices:

1. Use HTTPS for all network connections.
2. Use the latest supported TLS version for increased security and performance.
3. Enable hostname verification to prevent man-in-the-middle (MITM) attacks.
4. Avoid hard-coding SSL/TLS settings in the source code.
5. Use public key pinning to minimize the risk of MITM attacks.

For instance, here is a Java example of using an `HttpsURLConnection`:

```java
import java.io.InputStream;
import java.net.HttpURLConnection;
import java.net.URL;

public void fetchData() throws IOException {
 URL url = new URL("https://secure.example.com/data");
 HttpURLConnection connection = (HttpURLConnection) url.openConnection();
 connection.setConnectTimeout(5000);
 connection.setReadTimeout(5000);

 if (connection.getResponseCode() != HttpURLConnection.HTTP_OK) {
     throw new IOException();
 }

 InputStream in = connection.getInputStream();
 // Process the input stream as required.
}
```

In Kotlin, the example becomes:

```
import java.io.InputStream
import java.net.HttpURLConnection
import java.net.URL

fun fetchData() {
 val url = URL("https://secure.example.com/data")
 val connection = url.openConnection() as HttpURLConnection
 connection.connectTimeout = 5000
 connection.readTimeout = 5000
 if (connection.responseCode != HttpURLConnection.HTTP_OK) {
     throw IOException()
 }

 val `in`: InputStream = connection.inputStream
 // Process the input stream as required.
}
```

A third-party library like OkHttp can simplify and optimize SSL/TLS-based connections implementation. In Java:

```
import okhttp3.OkHttpClient;
import okhttp3.Request;
import okhttp3.Response;

public void fetchData() throws IOException {
 OkHttpClient client = new OkHttpClient();
 Request request = new Request.Builder()
         .url("https://secure.example.com/data")
         .build();

 try (Response response = client.newCall(request).execute()) {
     if (!response.isSuccessful()) {
         throw new IOException();
     }

     String data = response.body().string();
     // Process the received data.
 }
}
```

And in Kotlin:

```
import okhttp3.OkHttpClient
import okhttp3.Request
import okhttp3.Response

fun fetchData() {
 val client = OkHttpClient()
 val request = Request.Builder()
     .url("https://secure.example.com/data")
     .build()

 client.newCall(request).execute().use { response ->
     if (!response.isSuccessful) {
         throw IOException()
     }

     val data = response.body()?.string()
     // Process the received data.
 }
}
```

4. Example in C/C++

Due to the low-level nature of C and C++, implementing SSL/TLS typically requires the use of third-party libraries such as OpenSSL. Here's an example for a simple HTTPS GET request using OpenSSL in C:

```
#include <stdio.h>
#include <unistd.h>
#include <openssl/ssl.h>
#include <openssl/bio.h>

int main() {
 SSL_library_init();
 OpenSSL_add_all_algorithms();
 SSL_load_error_strings();
 SSL_CTX *ctx = SSL_CTX_new(SSLv23_client_method());
 BIO *bio = BIO_new_ssl_connect(ctx);
 BIO_set_conn_hostname(bio, "secure.example.com:443");
 BIO_set_ssl(bio, NULL, BIO_CLOSE);
 BIO_set_nbio(bio, 1);
  char buf[1024];
 snprintf(buf, sizeof(buf),
```

```
            "GET /data HTTP/1.1\r\n"
            "Host: secure.example.com\r\n"
            "User-Agent: test\r\n"
            "Accept: */*\r\n"
            "Connection: close\r\n"
            "\r\n");
    BIO_write(bio, buf, strlen(buf));

    while (1) {
        int r = BIO_read(bio, buf, sizeof(buf) - 1);
        if (r <= 0) break;
        buf[r] = 0;
        printf("%s", buf);
    }

    BIO_free_all(bio);
    SSL_CTX_free(ctx);
    return 0;
}
```

In this example, the SSL_CTX and BIO structures from OpenSSL manage SSL/TLS connections and process I/O.

- TLS Versions: Enforcing TLS 1.2 or higher for stronger encryption.
- SSL Deprecation: Avoid using deprecated SSL protocols due to known vulnerabilities.
- Cipher Suites: Enforcing secure cipher suites for network communications.
- TLS Handshake Optimization: Reducing latency while maintaining security during the handshake process.
- SSL Certificates: Proper usage of SSL certificates issued by trusted CAs for HTTPS communication.
- Secure Socket Layer: Using SSLSocket and SSLEngine to manage secure network connections in Android.
- TrustManager and KeyManager: Customizing SSL trust handling via TrustManager and KeyManager implementations.
- Session Resumption: Improving performance in secure communications by leveraging TLS session tickets.

OAuth and OpenID Connect for Android Applications

Proper security measures are crucial when developing Android applications requiring user logins or authentication. Two open-standard protocols, OAuth and OpenID Connect, can provide safe access to resources in Android applications. They were designed to provide decentralized and delegated authorization by authenticating users and allowing them to access specific resources from another application without sharing their credentials (such as usernames and passwords).

OAuth

OAuth (Open Authorization) is an open-standard protocol used for delegated authorization. Through user authentication and permission acquisition (in the form of access tokens), third-party applications can access users' resources from a different application (resource server). This eliminates the need for users to share their credentials with third-party applications.

OAuth 2.0 is the latest version of this protocol, which is widely used in many applications and services, including Android applications.

OAuth works through interactions between the client application, resource server, and authorization server. The key components of the OAuth 2.0 flow are:

1. Client Application: The third-party application that wants to access the user's resources.
2. Resource Server: The server hosting the user's resources (e.g., user profile, photos, etc.).
3. Authorization Server: It authenticates the user and issues access tokens to the client application.

OAuth 2.0 defines four grant types (authorization flows) to acquire an access token:

1. Authorization Code Grant: Used by server-side web applications.
2. Implicit Grant: Suitable for browser-based applications (e.g., Single Page Applications).
3. Resource Owner Password Credentials Grant: Used when the client application is highly trusted by the user (not recommended for third-party applications).
4. Client Credentials Grant: Abstaining from user involvement, the application requests an access token for its resources.

The client application can acquire an access token from the authorization server using the appropriate grant type. The access token represents the user's permission to access their resources from the resource server.

OpenID Connect

OpenID Connect (OIDC) is an identity layer built on OAuth 2.0. It allows developers to authenticate users and obtain basic profile information about them in a standardized, interoperable way. OIDC introduced a new token type called the "ID token," which carries user authentication information.

OIDC extends OAuth by providing additional features like:

1. User Authentication: OIDC enables applications to verify the user's identity and obtain basic user profile information.
2. ID Tokens: An additional token that carries user authentication information (e.g., user's unique identifier, issuer, expiration time, etc.).
3. UserInfo Endpoint: A standardized API to access more detailed user profile information, if required and if the user allows this.

OIDC uses the same components as OAuth 2.0, besides adding UserInfo Endpoint. The typical OIDC flow includes:

1. The client application requests an access token and an ID token from the authorization server.
2. The user is redirected to authenticate with the authorization server.
3. The authorization server authenticates the user and, if successful, sends the access and ID tokens to the client application.
4. The client can now access the user's resources using the access token and verify the user's identity using the ID token.

Implementing OAuth and OIDC in Android Applications

Multiple libraries are available to implement OAuth and OIDC in Android applications. One popular library is the AppAuth-Android library, developed by the OpenID Foundation.

AppAuth-Android is a client SDK for OAuth 2.0 and OIDC authentication and authorization for Android applications. It implements OAuth 2.0 authorization flows, supports OIDC ID token validation, and consumes the UserInfo Endpoint. It also has built-in support for PKCE (Proof Key for Code Exchange), a significant security enhancement for public clients (as described in OAuth 2.0 best practices).

Example: Implementing OAuth 2.0 and OIDC in Java (Android Studio)

First, add the AppAuth-Android library to your app-level 'build.gradle' file:

```
dependencies {
 implementation 'net.openid:appauth:0.8.1'
}
```

Next, create a configuration object for your OAuth2/OIDC provider in the 'strings.xml' file:

```
<string name="oauth_authorization_endpoint">https://example.com/authorize</string>
<string name="oauth_token_endpoint">https://example.com/token</string>
<string name="oauth_client_id">YourClientId</string>
<string name="oauth_redirect_uri">YourRedirectUri</string>
<string name="oauth_scope">openid profile email</string>
```

Below is an example implementation of the OAuth 2.0 and OIDC in Java using the AppAuth-Android library:

```
import android.content.Intent;
import android.net.Uri;
import android.support.annotation.NonNull;
import android.support.annotation.Nullable;
import android.support.v7.app.AppCompatActivity;
import net.openid.appauth.AuthState;
import net.openid.appauth.AuthorizationException;
import net.openid.appauth.AuthorizationRequest;
import net.openid.appauth.AuthorizationService;
import net.openid.appauth.AuthorizationServiceConfiguration;

public class LoginActivity extends AppCompatActivity {
 private static final int RC_AUTH = 100;
 private AuthorizationService authService;

 @Override
 protected void onCreate(Bundle savedInstanceState) {
     super.onCreate(savedInstanceState);
     setContentView(R.layout.activity_login);
     AuthState authState = new AuthState();
     authService = new AuthorizationService(this);

     // Create an authorization request
     AuthorizationRequest.Builder authRequestBuilder = new AuthorizationRequest.Buil\
der(
             new AuthorizationServiceConfiguration(
                     Uri.parse(getString(R.string.oauth_authorization_endpoint)),
```

```
                        Uri.parse(getString(R.string.oauth_token_endpoint))),
                getString(R.string.oauth_client_id),
                AuthorizationRequest.RESPONSE_TYPE_CODE,
                Uri.parse(getString(R.string.oauth_redirect_uri)))
                .setScope(getString(R.string.oauth_scope));

        AuthorizationRequest authRequest = authRequestBuilder.build();

        // Start the authorization flow
        Intent authIntent = authService.getAuthorizationRequestIntent(authRequest);
        startActivityForResult(authIntent, RC_AUTH);
    }

    @Override
    protected void onActivityResult(int requestCode, int resultCode, @Nullable Intent d\
ata) {
        if (requestCode == RC_AUTH && resultCode == RESULT_OK) {
            AuthorizationResponse authResponse = AuthorizationResponse.fromIntent(data);
            AuthorizationException authException = AuthorizationException.fromIntent(da\
ta);
            if (authResponse != null) {
                // Handle successful authorization
            } else {
                // Handle error
            }
        } else {
            super.onActivityResult(requestCode, resultCode, data);
        }
    }

    @Override
    protected void onDestroy() {
        super.onDestroy();
        authService.dispose();
    }
}
```

Example: Implementing OAuth 2.0 and OIDC in Kotlin (Android Studio)

First, add the AppAuth-Android library to your app-level 'build.gradle' file:

```
dependencies {
 implementation 'net.openid:appauth:0.8.1'
}
```

Next, create a configuration object for your OAuth2/OIDC provider in the 'strings.xml' file:

```
<string name="oauth_authorization_endpoint">https://example.com/authorize</string>
<string name="oauth_token_endpoint">https://example.com/token</string>
<string name="oauth_client_id">YourClientId</string>
<string name="oauth_redirect_uri">YourRedirectUri</string>
<string name="oauth_scope">openid profile email</string>
```

Below is an example implementation of the OAuth 2.0 and OIDC in Kotlin using the AppAuth-Android library:

```
import android.content.Intent
import android.net.Uri
import android.os.Bundle
import android.support.v7.app.AppCompatActivity
import net.openid.appauth.AuthState
import net.openid.appauth.AuthorizationService
import net.openid.appauth.AuthorizationServiceConfiguration
import net.openid.appauth.AuthorizationException
import net.openid.appauth.AuthorizationRequest

class LoginActivity : AppCompatActivity() {
 private val RC_AUTH = 100
 private lateinit var authService: AuthorizationService

 override fun onCreate(savedInstanceState: Bundle?) {
     super.onCreate(savedInstanceState)
     setContentView(R.layout.activity_login)

     val authState = AuthState()
     authService = AuthorizationService(this)

     // Create an authorization request
     val authRequestBuilder = AuthorizationRequest.Builder(
             AuthorizationServiceConfiguration(
                     Uri.parse(getString(R.string.oauth_authorization_endpoint)),
                     Uri.parse(getString(R.string.oauth_token_endpoint))),
             getString(R.string.oauth_client_id),
```

```
            AuthorizationRequest.RESPONSE_TYPE_CODE,
            Uri.parse(getString(R.string.oauth_redirect_uri)))
            .setScope(getString(R.string.oauth_scope))

        val authRequest = authRequestBuilder.build()

        // Start the authorization flow
        val authIntent = authService.getAuthorizationRequestIntent(authRequest)
        startActivityForResult(authIntent, RC_AUTH)
    }

    override fun onActivityResult(requestCode: Int, resultCode: Int, data: Intent?) {
        if (requestCode == RC_AUTH && resultCode == RESULT_OK) {
            val authResponse = AuthorizationResponse.fromIntent(data!!)
            val authException = AuthorizationException.fromIntent(data)
            if (authResponse != null) {
                // Handle successful authorization
            } else {
                // Handle error
            }
        } else {
            super.onActivityResult(requestCode, resultCode, data)
        }
    }

    override fun onDestroy() {
        super.onDestroy()
        authService.dispose()
    }
}
```

Bluetooth

Modern Android devices are built with Bluetooth technology, which allows for smooth wireless communication with various peripherals and Internet of Things devices. However, Bluetooth's adaptability has serious security issues. Several security procedures and guidelines have been provided in Android to protect the confidentiality and integrity of data sent over Bluetooth connections.

Bluetooth Security Protocols

Android protects Bluetooth data sharing using strong security mechanisms, including AES encryption, Low Energy (LE) Secure Connections, and Secure Simple Pairing (SSP). AES encryption protects data from tampering and eavesdropping, while SSP authenticates devices using a combination of passkey entry and public key cryptography. Thus, Bluetooth communication is kept private and secure from unwanted access.

Classic Bluetooth vs. Bluetooth Low Energy (BLE)

Classic Bluetooth and BLE differ not only in their use cases but also in their security requirements. BLE, designed for low-power devices, incorporates advanced encryption techniques and authentication mechanisms tailored for short bursts of data transfer. Classic Bluetooth, commonly used for audio and continuous data streams, employs secure pairing but has distinct security profiles. Understanding these differences allows Android developers to implement a proper secure communication.

Pairing Modes

Android supports multiple pairing modes—Just Works, Numeric Comparison, and Passkey Entry—each offering different levels of security. Just Works provides convenience but is vulnerable to man-in-the-middle (MITM) attacks, while Numeric Comparison and Passkey Entry provide more substantial protection by requiring user verification. An appropriate pairing mode based on the device's security requirements could help to maintain a secure connection.

Man-in-the-Middle (MITM) Protection

MITM attacks pose a significant threat during the Bluetooth pairing process. Android mitigates this risk by implementing secure pairing protocols that verify the identity of connected devices. Numeric Comparison and Passkey Entry modes, for instance, ensure that users confirm device authenticity, reducing the likelihood of an attacker intercepting the connection.

Bluetooth Profiles and Associated Risks

Bluetooth profiles define the functionality of Bluetooth-enabled devices, such as hands-free communication (HFP) or audio streaming (A2DP). Each profile carries unique security risks, as vulnerabilities in specific profiles could expose sensitive data. Android has provided secure implementation and updates of Bluetooth profiles to address known threats and prevent exploitation.

Securing BLE Advertising and GATT Communications

BLE advertising allows devices to broadcast information, making it a potential vector for security risks. Android incorporates mechanisms to secure BLE advertising data and protect Generic Attribute Profile (GATT) communications.

Nearby Permissions

Efficient management of Bluetooth permissions is a key component of Android's security architecture. To ensure user awareness and consent, applications that request Bluetooth access must provide essential permissions, such as location or background access. The runtime permission mechanism provides additional security by enabling users to grant or remove permissions as necessary which users could revoke them at their will.

Preventing Bluetooth Sniffing

Bluetooth sniffing is a significant risk in which hackers intercept transferred data. Android, through protections like encryption, frequency hopping, and random address creation, makes it harder for hackers to listen in on conversations.

Practical Scenarios

Below is each scenario presented in a consistent structure:

1. **Project Description**
2. **Architecture**
3. **Shostack's Four Question Framework**[1]

    - (1) What are we building?
    - (2) What can go wrong? (followed by the Threat Table)
    - (3) What are we going to do about it? (includes relevant code)
    - (4) Did we do a good job?

Note Any scenario defined in this chapter could be a big project that requires extensive technical discussion and analysis beyond the scope of this book. The main goal of this chapter is to provide some basic examples to practice some of the concepts we have discussed.

Financial Android Application

Project Description

> "This is a financial Android application where users can log in with their username and password. The application can check the current balance and transaction history, and transfer money to other accounts. To be enabled, it must scan a one-time QRCode with credentials. The user may configure the app to store some financial information (e.g., transaction history) locally and keep them synchronized. It can also notify users (via push notifications) of critical events such as withdrawals, receiving e-invoices, etc."

Architecture

- **Mobile App** (Android)

    - Handles user login (username/password).
    - Scans a **one-time QR code** for initial credential setup.
    - Optionally stores financial data locally.
    - Receives/sends data to the **Bank Server** over **TLS** (HTTPS).

[1] Shostack, Adam. Threat Modeling: Designing For Security. John Wiley & Sons, 2014

- Receives push notifications (e.g., FCM).

- **Bank Server**
  - Holds user account info, processes transactions.
  - Issues or validates QR code credentials.

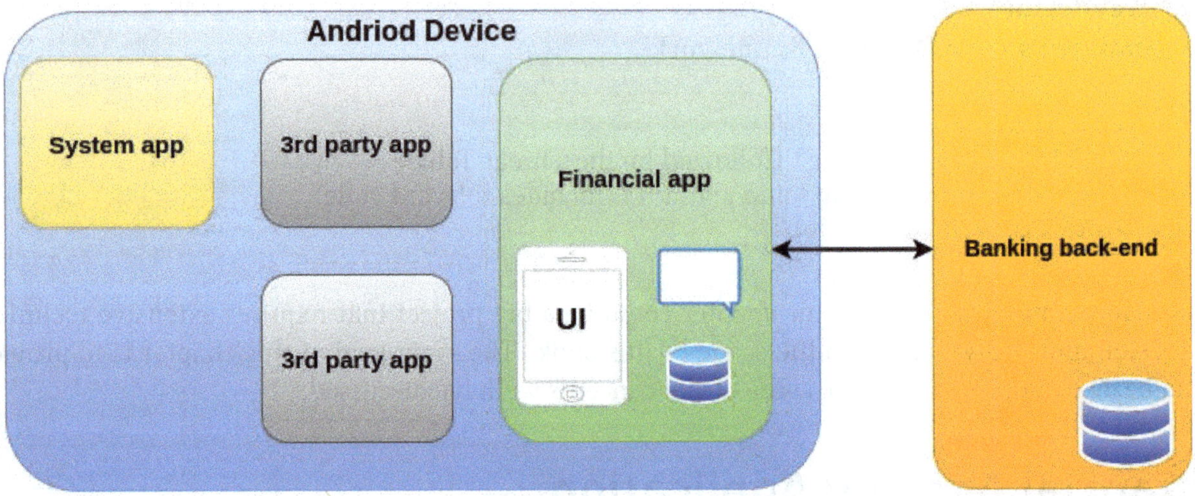

Figure 10. The app functionalities

1) What are we building?

- An **Android app** that allows:
  - Username/password **authentication.**
  - Viewing **account balances** and **transaction history**.
  - **Transferring** money to other accounts.
  - One-time **QR code**–based initialization.
  - **Optional** local storage of financial data.
  - **Push notifications** for critical events.

2) What can go wrong?

- **Potential Threats (Bullet List)**
  - Credential interception or theft (e.g., via keyloggers, insecure communication).

- Local data extraction (unprotected credentials or transaction history).
- Unauthorized account access with stolen credentials.
- Malicious or phishing QR codes compromising the initialization flow.
- Man-in-the-Middle (MITM) attacks intercepting or modifying requests.
- Replay or injection attacks on transaction endpoints.
- Configuration tampering (changing app settings to compromise security).
- Push notification spoofing or interception.
- Data leakage in logs or app cache.

Threats, Severity, and Risk (Table)

#	Threat	Severity	Risk
1.	Credential Interception	High	High
2.	Local Data Extraction (creds, financial info)	High	High
3.	Unauthorized Access via Stolen Credentials	Critical	High
4.	Malicious/Phishing QRCodes	High	Medium
5.	Man-in-the-Middle (MITM) Attacks	Critical	High
6.	Replay/Injection Attacks (transactions)	High	Medium
7.	Configuration Tampering	Medium	Medium
8.	Push Notification Spoofing	Medium	Low
9.	Data Leakage via Logs/Cache	Medium	Low

3) What are we going to do about it?

Protect Stored Data

1. **Hardware-backed Keystore**

   - Store cryptographic keys so they remain inaccessible even with root privileges.
   - For example:

```
    KeyGenParameterSpec keySpec = new KeyGenParameterSpec.Builder(
            "FinanceKey",
            KeyProperties.PURPOSE_ENCRYPT | KeyProperties.PURPOSE_DECRYPT)
            .setBlockModes(KeyProperties.BLOCK_MODE_GCM)
            .setEncryptionPaddings(KeyProperties.ENCRYPTION_PADDING_NONE)
            .setUserAuthenticationRequired(true)
            .build();

KeyGenerator keyGenerator = KeyGenerator.getInstance(KeyProperties.KEY_ALGORITHM_AES
, "AndroidKeyStore");
keyGenerator.init(keySpec);
SecretKey secretKey = keyGenerator.generateKey();
```

2. **File/Database Encryption**

   - Use **AES-256-GCM** to encrypt local transaction history.
   - Regularly sanitize or **truncate** sensitive data that's no longer needed.

Network Security & Anti-MITM

1. **TLS (HTTPS)**

   - Enforce **TLS 1.2+** or **TLS 1.3** for all client–server communication.
   - Use **certificate pinning** in your Network Security Configuration:

```
<network-security-config>
  <domain-config cleartextTrafficPermitted="false">
    <domain includeSubdomains="true">api.example.com</domain>
    <pin-set expiration="2026-12-31">
      <pin digest="SHA-256">Base64EncodedPin==</pin>
    </pin-set>
  </domain-config>
</network-security-config>
```

Credential & QR Security

1. **FLAG_SECURE**

   - Prevent screenshots in sensitive activities:

```
getWindow().setFlags(WindowManager.LayoutParams.FLAG_SECURE,
                     WindowManager.LayoutParams.FLAG_SECURE);
```

2. **Username/Password + 2FA/Biometrics**

   - Enforce strong passwords, short session tokens, auto-logout.

3. **QR Code Encryption & Validation**

   - Encrypt the QR payload; sign server-side.
   - Validate on the server as soon as scanned.

Push Notification Safety

- Avoid embedding **sensitive data** directly in notifications.
- If needed, store critical info server-side and only show a generic alert until the user opens the app (which then retrieves details securely).

Logging & Cache Protections

- Avoid logging **PII** or financial info.
- Clear caches or ephemeral data (e.g., transaction history previews) after the session ends.

4) Did we do a good job?

- **Validation & Testing**
  - Test for MITM with proxy tools (confirm certificate pinning works).
  - Attempt replay attacks on the transaction API with old tokens.
  - Conduct local storage checks to confirm data is encrypted.
- **Ongoing Maintenance**
  - Keep cryptographic libraries updated.
  - Monitor logs for suspicious activities.
  - Provide user education on scanning only **trusted** QR codes.

Key Provider Service

Project Description

> "We need an Android system service that provides API keys to authorized applications. This service is part of the system image, ensuring it can be updated via OTA or a company-specific package manager. Client apps communicate through an Android IPC (e.g., AIDL). Because these API keys control critical backend resources, we must prevent unauthorized usage or extraction of the keys."

Architecture

- **System Service (KeyProviderService)**:
  - Runs as a privileged or system app.
  - Provides an AIDL interface to distribute API keys.
  - Stores keys securely (hardware-backed or file-based encryption).
- **Authorized Client Apps**:
  - Bind via `bindService()`.
  - Must pass permission/signature checks.

As it is clear, the primary responsibilities of the service are: *Providing the API keys to the authorized applications*

The service should have access to the API keys, either stored as a hard-coded value or fetching them from a server. In either case, the service should store the fetched keys and the other data locally. It means that *the stored keys should be protected.* Upon an authorized application, the service will hand over the appropriate API key to the app. There are only two considerable interfaces:

- AIDL
- Content Provider

I think that is obvious why I didn't consider other solutions such as Intent!

Each one has it is own Pros & Cons. Let's consider whether we should implement an AIDL interface to communicate with the service. So, each application needs to get its API key and use the same AIDL interface to bind and fetch it. The next point has just been revealed: *The AIDL interface must be protected.*

Now, we can list out the points we have extracted from the project definition:

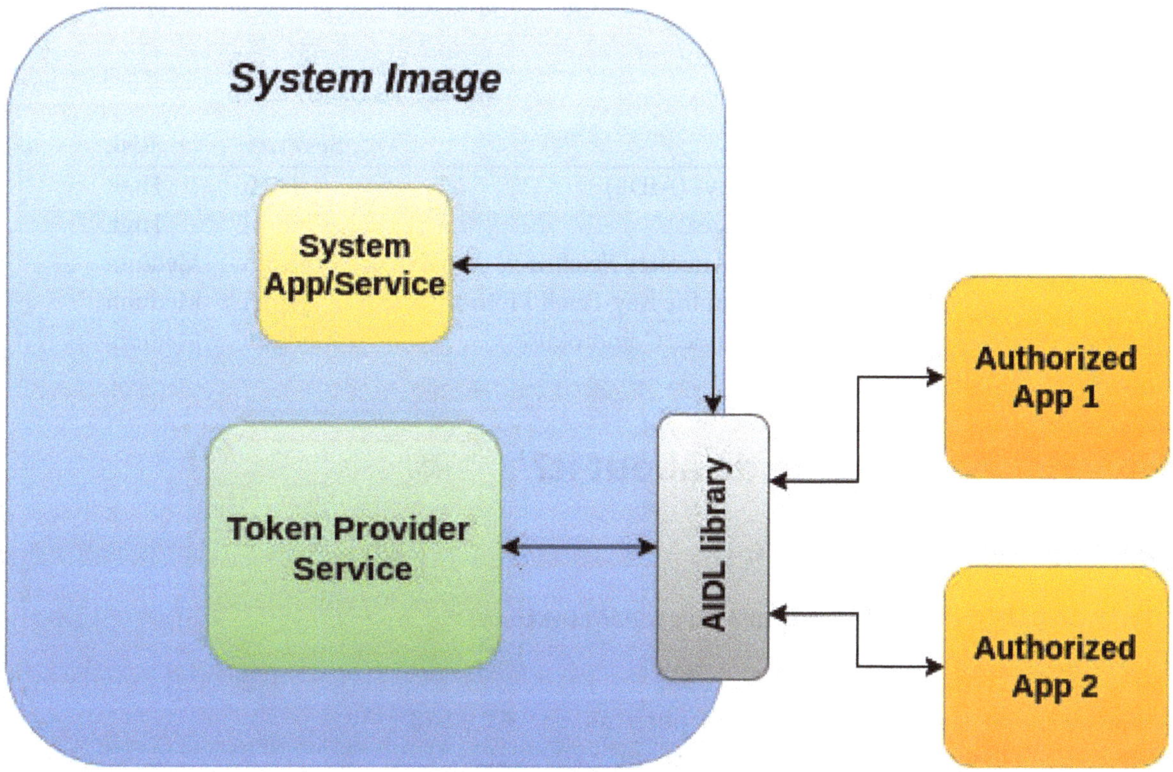

Figure 11. The architecture of the app

1) What are we building?

- A **system-level Android service** that:
  - Safely **stores** or fetches **API keys**.
  - Exposes a **secure AIDL interface** so only trusted apps can get those keys.
  - Uses minimal privileges and can be updated via OTA.

2) What can go wrong?

- **Potential Threats (Bullet List)**
  - Unauthorized apps binding to the service to obtain keys.
  - Extraction of keys from local storage (e.g., unencrypted on disk).
  - Man-in-the-middle (MITM) if keys are fetched from a remote server.

  - Replay attacks on remote key-fetch protocols.
  - Privilege escalation if the service is over-privileged or misconfigured.

Threats, Severity, and Risk (Table)

#	Threat	Severity	Risk
1.	Unauthorized Access to Keys (AIDL)	High	High
2.	Key Extraction from Storage	Critical	High
3.	MITM Attack if Keys are Remotely Fetched	High	Medium
4.	Replay/Injection Attacks on the Key-Fetch Protocol	High	Medium
5.	Privilege Escalation via Service Compromise	Medium	Medium

3) What are we going to do about it?

Restricting the AIDL Interface

1. **Signature-Level Permission** in `AndroidManifest.xml`:

```
<permission
    android:name="com.example.permission.GET_KEYS"
    android:protectionLevel="signatureOrSystem" />

<service
    android:name=".KeyProviderService"
    android:exported="true"
    android:permission="com.example.permission.GET_KEYS"/>
```

2. **Caller Checks** in `onBind()`:

```
@Override
public IBinder onBind(Intent intent) {
    if (!isCallerAuthorized(getCallingUid())) {
        return null; // Reject
    }
    return keyProviderBinder;
}
```

Secure Key Storage

- **Android Keystore** for hardware-backed key protection.
- Alternatively, store encrypted keys with file-based encryption (AES-256).
- Example code to generate an AES key:

```
KeyGenParameterSpec keySpec = new KeyGenParameterSpec.Builder(
        "MySecureKey",
        KeyProperties.PURPOSE_ENCRYPT | KeyProperties.PURPOSE_DECRYPT)
        .setBlockModes(KeyProperties.BLOCK_MODE_GCM)
        .setEncryptionPaddings(KeyProperties.ENCRYPTION_PADDING_NONE)
        .setUserAuthenticationRequired(true)
        .build();

KeyGenerator keyGenerator = KeyGenerator.getInstance(KeyProperties.KEY_ALGORITHM_AES\
, "AndroidKeyStore");
keyGenerator.init(keySpec);
SecretKey secretKey = keyGenerator.generateKey();
```

Secure Remote Fetch (If Applicable)

- **TLS** with **certificate pinning**.
- Validate the server's identity before accepting new/updated keys.
- Use nonces/timestamps to prevent replay attacks.

Minimal Privileges & SELinux

- Run the service in a **restricted SELinux domain** with only the required permissions.

4) Did we do a good job?

- **Validation & Testing**
  - Attempt to bind from an unauthorized/malicious app.
  - Check if keys can be extracted from local storage on a rooted device.
- **Ongoing Maintenance**
  - Rotate keys if possible.
  - Patch the system image with new security updates.

Sensor HAL Layer Daemon

Project Description

"A new sensor was added to the vehicle cabin to check the oxygen level and detect poisonous gases. It has an MCU connected to the Infotainment system through SOME/IP. The sensor sends data every minute and alarm messages when needed. Other devices can subscribe to these events. The info is then displayed in the Infotainment system. The architecture team decided not to define VHAL properties."

Architecture

- **Sensor MCU**
  - Measures oxygen/poison gas levels.
  - Sends data via **SOME/IP** every minute or on alarms.
- **Sensor HAL Daemon**
  - Receives data from the sensor over SOME/IP.
  - Allows **subscriptions** from other vehicle/Infotainment components.
- **Subscribers**
  - Infotainment apps or processes that display sensor info or act on alarms.

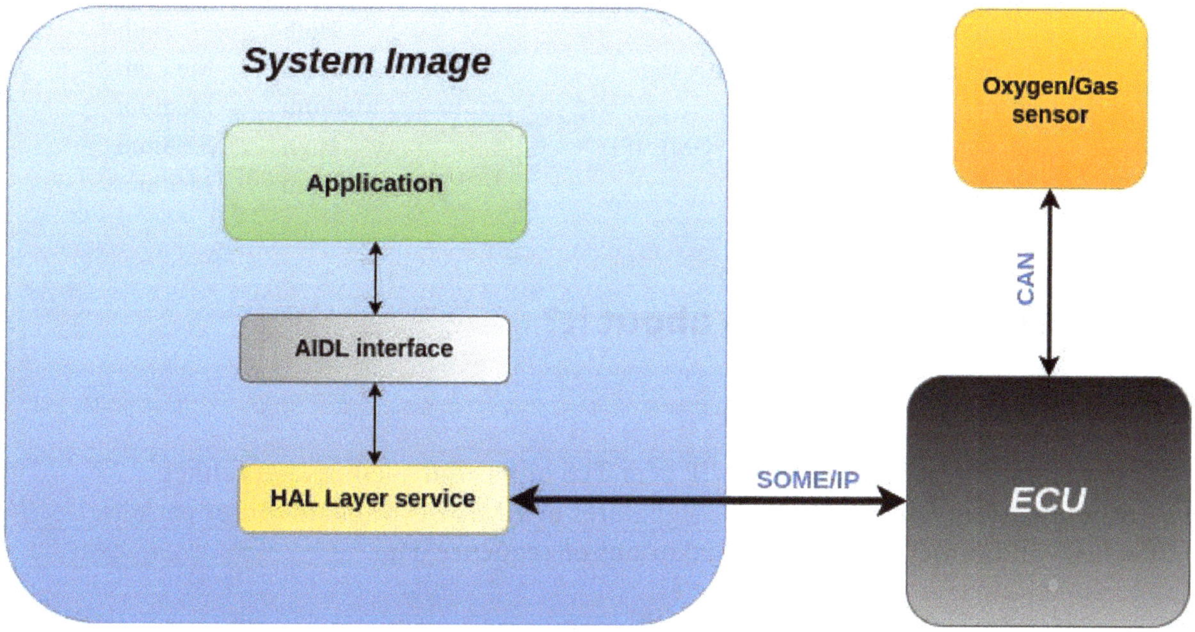

Figure 12. The architecture of the app

1) What are we building?

- A **daemon** (or HAL service) that:
  - Collects sensor data from the cabin sensor.
  - Publishes periodic updates or alarm events.
  - Lets other system components subscribe for real-time data.

2) What can go wrong?

- **Potential Threats (Bullet List)**
  - Tampering with sensor data (injecting false readings).
  - Unauthorized subscriptions (apps with no permission can get data).
  - Denial of Service (spamming subscription requests or sending malformed packets).
  - Insecure communication (SOME/IP with no encryption/auth).
  - Privilege escalation if the daemon is compromised.

Threats, Severity, and Risk (Table)

#	Threat	Severity	Risk
1.	Tampering with Sensor Data	High	High
2.	Unauthorized Subscriptions	High	Medium
3.	Denial of Service	Medium	Medium
4.	Insecure Communication (SOME/IP)	High	Medium
5.	Privilege Escalation	Medium	Medium

3) What are we going to do about it?

Secure SOME/IP

- **Encryption**: If feasible, run SOME/IP over TLS or an equivalent secure tunnel.
- **Authentication**: Use cryptographic signatures or HMAC to validate sensor packets.
- **Packet Validation**: Reject malformed or out-of-sequence data.

Subscription Access Control

- Implement a signature-level permission or allowlisting approach:

```
<permission android:name="com.example.permission.SENSOR_EVENTS"
            android:protectionLevel="signature" />

<service android:name=".SensorService"
         android:exported="true"
         android:permission="com.example.permission.SENSOR_EVENTS"/>
```

- **Caller Checks** in `onBind()`:

```
@Override
public IBinder onBind(Intent intent) {
    if (!isCallerAuthorized(getCallingUid())) {
        return null; // Reject
    }
    return sensorBinder;
}
```

DoS Mitigation

- **Rate-limit** subscription requests.
- Drop packets that exceed expected frequency or size.

Privilege Separation

- Run daemon under a minimal-privilege user.
- SELinux rules confining the daemon's operations.

4) Did we do a good job?

- **Validation & Testing**

  - Attempt MITM or replay on SOME/IP to see if the system detects anomalies.
  - Try subscribing from an unauthorized app.

- **Ongoing Monitoring**

  - Keep logs for suspicious or malformed packets.
  - Patch system updates for the Infotainment OS and SOME/IP library vulnerabilities.

Vehicle Data Logger Application

Project Description

"A vehicle company provides a logger application (installed through the Play Store on the Infotainment system) that stores the vehicle's path by accessing location data. The data can be shared with the user via Bluetooth to a paired phone app, which explores the history and displays it on a map. The app can also record other vehicle data (like fuel level) with user consent."

Architecture

- **Infotainment Logger App**
  - Records location data (and optional fuel level).
  - Stores logs locally (possibly encrypted).
  - Shares logs via **Bluetooth** with a paired phone app.
- **Phone App**
  - Receives data from the Infotainment system.
  - Visualizes the data (e.g., map).
  - Stores data locally (again, possibly encrypted).

1) What are we building?

- An **Infotainment-based** app that logs vehicle location and possibly other data (fuel, usage).
- A **paired phone app** that displays and manages these logs.

2) What can go wrong?

- **Potential Threats (Bullet List)**
  - Unauthorized access to location data on Infotainment.
  - Unauthorized access to vehicle data (fuel level) if user consent is bypassed.
  - Bluetooth MITM or eavesdropping.
  - Rogue or malicious pairing with the Infotainment system.
  - Extraction of encryption keys from either device.
  - Physical theft of the vehicle/phone to access stored data.
  - Data leakage via logs or caches.

Threats, Severity, and Risk (Table)

#	Threat	Severity	Risk
1.	Unauthorized Access to Stored Location Data	High	High
2.	Unauthorized Access to Vehicle Data	Medium	Medium
3.	Bluetooth MITM Attacks	High	High
4.	Unauthorized Pairing (malicious device)	High	High
5.	Extraction of Encryption Keys	Critical	High
6.	Device Spoofing (fake trusted device)	High	Medium
7.	Physical Device Theft (vehicle/phone)	High	Medium
8.	Replay Attacks (Bluetooth transmission)	Medium	Medium
9.	Weak Data Sync (phone app)	Medium	Medium
10.	Data Leakage via Logs/Cache	Medium	Low

3) What are we going to do about it?

Encrypt Data at Rest

- **Hardware-backed Keystore** for storing encryption keys on both Infotainment and phone.
- Use **AES-256-GCM** for location/fuel logs.
- Example code (phone side) for generating an AES key:

```
KeyGenParameterSpec keySpec = new KeyGenParameterSpec.Builder(
        "VehicleLoggerKey",
        KeyProperties.PURPOSE_ENCRYPT | KeyProperties.PURPOSE_DECRYPT)
        .setBlockModes(KeyProperties.BLOCK_MODE_GCM)
        .setEncryptionPaddings(KeyProperties.ENCRYPTION_PADDING_NONE)
        .setUserAuthenticationRequired(true)
        .build();

KeyGenerator keyGenerator = KeyGenerator.getInstance(KeyProperties.KEY_ALGORITHM_AES\
, "AndroidKeyStore");
keyGenerator.init(keySpec);
SecretKey secretKey = keyGenerator.generateKey();
```

Secure Bluetooth Pairing & Transfer

- **Secure Simple Pairing** (SSP) with numeric comparison or out-of-band.
- Use **Bluetooth Secure Connections** (LE Security Mode 1 Level 4 or classic Secure Connections).
- Maintain a **trusted device list** (cryptographic identity checks) to prevent spoofing.

Physical Security & Consent

- Encourage users to enable **device lock screen** on phone & Infotainment.
- Prompt explicit **user consent** for logging additional data (fuel, usage).
- Provide a way to **delete** or **revoke** stored data/pairings if the vehicle is sold or phone is lost.

Logs/Cache Management

- Do **not** log actual GPS coordinates or fuel data in plain text.
- Clear ephemeral caches or temporary files after use.

4) Did we do a good job?

- **Validation & Testing**
  - Attempt Bluetooth MITM with known hacking tools to confirm encryption.
  - Try pairing from an untrusted device and confirm it's blocked.
  - Check that locally stored logs are indeed encrypted.
- **Ongoing Maintenance**
  - Patch Infotainment OS and phone app regularly.
  - Consider **key rotation** or re-pairing after certain intervals.

Compilers and Tools

The techniques and principles explained in the previous chapters could be strengthened using other tools, such as compiler security features and obfuscators. The principles work like a lighthouse in the development process's darkness; you face many unknowns. Android's internal knowledge helps you apply the principles and use the available facilities provided by the OS. The common techniques could help you avoid the known pitfalls. After utilizing them, the compiler options and obfuscators could work as a fence, adding obstacles to decompiling the code.

We will explore how compiler features, obfuscators, and analysis tools contribute to the security of Android applications. Specifically, we will examine:

- The role of Clang/GCC security features in preventing vulnerabilities during code compilation.
- The importance of obfuscation tools like ProGuard and R8 in protecting your application from reverse engineering.
- The value of static and dynamic analysis tools in identifying and addressing security flaws.

Clang and GCC Security Features

When generating an executable from the code, we can maximize the application's safety potential by understanding and enabling the security and protection features. These features could include activating specific types of warnings or adding procedures to the executable file to manage unexpected situations that may arise due to flaws or vulnerabilities being exploited. In the following sections, we will examine some characteristics, how they work, and the role of compilers in secure code.

Compiler Warnings

Each compiler supports different levels of warnings that can be used to identify probable problems, issues, or vulnerabilities. It's critical to enable, check, and try to fix these warnings since any of them might indicate a flaw in the code that causes a hole.

Example – Wall Flag in Clang/GCC: The "-Wall" flag enables warnings about various issues in the source code. Some of these warnings are related to potential security vulnerabilities.

Example

```
// Compile with Clang: clang -Wall warning_example.c -o output
// Compile with GCC: gcc -Wall warning_example.c -o output


#include <stdio.h>
#include <stdlib.h>


int main() {
  char *str = malloc(50);
  printf("This code might generate some compiler warnings related to security.\n");
  return 0;
}
```

The "-Wall" flag enables compiler warnings related to security vulnerabilities in the code, such as memory leaks or unsafe functions.

Other features could be enabled by using the flags to highlight unsafe practices, incorrect logic, or non-portable code:

Flag	Description
`-Wall`	Enables a broad set of commonly useful warnings.
`-Wextra`	Adds additional warnings not included in `-Wall`.
`-Werror`	Treats all warnings as errors, stopping compilation until resolved.
`-Wpedantic`	Enforces strict compliance with the C/C++ standard.
`-Wshadow`	Warns about variable shadowing (hiding outer scope variables).
`-Wformat`	Checks format string mismatches in functions like `printf` and `scanf`.
`-Wunused`	Warns about unused variables, functions, and parameters.
`-Wuninitialized`	Warns about uninitialized variables being used.
`-Wconversion`	Warns about implicit type conversions that may cause precision loss or unexpected results.
`-Wnull-dereference`	Warns about potential null pointer dereferences.

Stack Protection

One of the most common vulnerabilities is buffer overflow, which occurs when a program writes data beyond the bounds of allocated memory, typically on the stack. Compilers have built-in protections to mitigate stack buffer overflows, also known as stack protection or stack smashing protection. These protections provide checks to ensure the stack is not tampered with or mark stack memory as non-executable.

Example – Stack Protector in Clang/GCC: They implement the “-fstack-protector” and “-fstack-protector-strong” flags to enable stack protection. When these flags are used, the compiler inserts code to check the integrity of the stack at runtime.

Example

```
// Compile with Clang: clang -fstack-protector stack_protection.c -o smashing
// Compile with GCC: gcc -fstack-protector stack_protection.c -o smashing
// Run: ./smashing TryToAccessOutOfBoundary
#include <stdio.h>
#include <stdlib.h>
#include <string.h>
    #include <unistd.h>


void *__stack_chk_guard = (void *)0xdeadbeef;


void __stack_chk_fail(void)
{
  fprintf(stderr, "Stack smashing detected!!!\n");
  exit(1);
}


void copyInputData(char *input_data);


int main(int argc, char **argv)
{
  if (argc > 1) {
      printf("Usage: %s <input_string>\n", argv[1]);
      copyInputData(argv[1]);
  }
  printf("\nTerminated normally!\n");
  return 0;
}


void copyInputData(char *input_data)
{
```

```
  char buffer[8];
  strcpy(buffer, input_data);
}
```

Flag	Clang Support	Description
`-fpie, -fPIC, -fpic`	Fully supported	Generates position-independent executables/code necessary for ASLR.
`-fstack-protector-strong`	Fully supported	Protects against stack buffer overflow attacks by inserting stack canaries.
`-fstack-check`	Limited support (GCC feature)	Inserts explicit stack boundary checks (primarily supported by GCC, limited in Clang).
`-fstack-clash-protection`	Supported since Clang 11	Protects against stack clash attacks by guarding stack allocations.
`-Wl,-z,relro,-z,now`	Fully supported	Enhances memory protection through RELRO (Read-Only Relocations) and immediate binding (NOW).
`-fsanitize=address`	Fully supported	Detects address-related errors (memory corruption, leaks, buffer overflows).

The "-fstack-protector" flag can be used to protect the code against stack buffer overflows.

Address Space Layout Randomization (ASLR)

Another security option available in GCC and Clang is randomizing the application's memory address, which makes it difficult for attackers to find their target address. This option protects programs from being easy and straightforward targets for hackers by randomizing the memory addresses of Stack, Heap, and Shared libraries.

Example: To enable ASLR using GCC/Clang for your program, you must compile it as a Position-Independent Executable (PIE). You can use the "-pie" and "-fPIE" flags.

The first implementation of ASLR was added to the kernel in 2001 as a patch.h From Android 5.0, the non-PIE has been dropped, and all the dynamically linked libraries must support position independence.

Example

```
// Compile with Clang: clang -fPIE -pie stack_protection.c -o smashing_nx
// Compile with GCC: gcc -fPIE -pie stack_protection.c -o smashing_nx
#include <stdio.h>


void vulnerable_function() {
  printf("This function could be vulnerable to buffer overflows or other memory corr\
uption attacks.\n");
}


int main() {
  vulnerable_function();
  return 0;
}
```

In this example, ASLR is enabled by compiling the code with the "-fPIE" and "-pie" flags.

Library order randomization

In November 2003, OpenBSD 3.4 introduced a new feature that randomized the order of loading libraries. A long time later, in August 2016, it was added to Android Nougat. However, it was not a significant feature; it was a slight improvement over ASLR.

Data Execution Prevention (DEP)

NX or Non-Excutable is a CPU option reducing the attack surface and protect software from code injection/ overflow techniques. This feature in most CPUs helps prevent code from running from non-executable memory regions. Then, by marking the pages as non-executable, the operating system prevents running any code from the data, including stack and heap. This feature can be emulated if it does not exist in hardware. From Android 2.3, it accessible for any architecture supporting it. Since May 2010, the NX has been enabled by default in Android to lock many overflow attacks.

GNU compiler = -z noexecstack prelink package s= –noexecstack

Example – DEP in Clang/GCC: To enable DEP , you can use the commands below:

Compile with:

GCC

```
gcc -z execstack stack_protection.c -o smashing


gcc -z noexecstack stack_protection.c -o smashing_nx
```

Clang

```
clang -Wl,-z,execstack file.c -o smashing


clang -Wl,-z,noexecstack file.c -o smashing
```

Compare the result of the commands below:

```
readelf -l smashing | grep GNU_STACK -B1


GNU_STACK      0x0000000000000000 0x0000000000000000 0x0000000000000000
               0x0000000000000000 0x0000000000000000  RWE    0x10
```

```
readelf -l smashing_nx | grep GNU_STACK -B1


GNU_STACK      0x0000000000000000 0x0000000000000000 0x0000000000000000
               0x0000000000000000 0x0000000000000000  RW     0x10
```

As you can see the second one “smashing_nx” marked as “RW” while the first one is “RWE”

Control Flow Integrity (CFI)

Control Flow Integrity (CFI) ensures the application’s execution flow adheres to the intended program logic. It helps prevent attacks like **Return-Oriented Programming (ROP)** and **Jump-Oriented Programming (JOP)**, which exploit vulnerabilities to execute arbitrary code paths.

- CFI validates the legitimacy of indirect control transfers, such as function pointers and return addresses.
- It inserts runtime checks to ensure control flow transitions are valid according to the program’s control flow graph.

CFI can be enabled by using `-fcf-protection` option.

```
gcc -fcf-protection -o cfi_example cfi_example.c
```

or

```
clang -fcf-protection -o cfi_example cfi_example.c
```

Example

```
#include <stdio.h>


void secure_function() {
  printf("Secure function executed.\n");
}


void (*func_ptr)();


int main() {
  func_ptr = secure_function; // Valid control flow
  func_ptr();
  return 0;
}
```

Compiling with `-fcf-protection` ensures that only valid targets can be called through function pointers, mitigating potential exploitation.

Fortify Source

The `Fortify Source` feature enhances the security of commonly used C library functions by detecting and preventing buffer overflows and other vulnerabilities at compile time or runtime.

- `Fortify Source` replaces standard library functions with safer versions that include bounds checking.
- If a potentially unsafe operation is detected, the program aborts execution or logs a warning.

The `Fortify Source` feature is controlled through the `-D_FORTIFY_SOURCE` option and works only with optimization enabled (`-O` or higher).

- `-D_FORTIFY_SOURCE=1`: Provides basic protection.
- `-D_FORTIFY_SOURCE=2`: Provides stricter checks (recommended).

```
gcc -D_FORTIFY_SOURCE=2 -O2 -o fortify_example fortify_example.c
```

or

```
clang -D_FORTIFY_SOURCE=2 -O2 -o fortify_example fortify_example.c
```

Example

```
#include <string.h>
#include <stdio.h>


int main() {
  char buffer[10];
  strcpy(buffer, "This is too long for the buffer!"); // Unsafe
  printf("Buffer contains: %s\n", buffer);
  return 0;
}
```

Compiling with:

```
gcc -D_FORTIFY_SOURCE=2 -O2 -o fortify_example fortify_example.c
```

or

```
clang -D_FORTIFY_SOURCE=2 -O2 -o fortify_example fortify_example.c
```

Android Sanitizer

In 2012, Google introduced a class of tools called code sanitizers to detect program bugs. The first tool was the address sanitizer, which enabled memory corruption detection using shadow memory. Though some sanitizers are available outside the Android scope, our focus will be on Android sanitizers. In this section, I will cover the available sanitizers in Android and give you a big picture of what they do.

Address Sanitizer (ASan)

ASan is a compile-based tool introduced with Android O (API level 27) running on both ARM and X86 architecture (32-bit & 64-bit) to detect memory bugs such as:

- Stack and heap buffer overflow/underflow
- Heap use after free

- Stack use outside scope
- Double free/wild free

It does not support Java/Kotlin applications but can be enabled in the JNI libraries. However, this will incur an overhead and prevent it from working on devices with only 2GB memory.

Enabling ASan leads to an overhead in code size, memory usage, and performance. The code size can be increased between 50% to 2X, the CPU overhead will be about 2X, and memory usage is at least 2X based on your memory allocation pattern.

Android.bp

```
cc_binary{
   sanitize: ["address"],
}
```

Android.mk

```
LOCAL_SANITIZE := address
```

There some parameters can be sent to Android Adress Sanitizer through sanitize_extra_flags :

- detect_leaks
- halt_on_error
- alloc_dealloc_mismatch
- check_initialization_order
- coverage
- fast_unwind_on_fatal

example

```
cc_binary {
   sanitize: ["address"],
   sanitize_extra_flags: [
       "detect_leaks=1",
       "fast_unwind_on_fatal=1",
   ],
}
```

HWAddress Sanitizer (HWASan)

HWAsan is introduced in Android 10 (API 29) and NDKr21 which only supports ARM 64-bit. In favour of that ASan os is deprecated for ARM 64-bit in Android 11. HWAsan supports similar detection tools/features with some exceptions:

Much smaller memory overhead (10% – 35%) compared to ASan. Stack use after return. (The extra detection)

Android.bp

```
cc_binary {
   sanitize: ["hwaddress"],
}
```

or

```
cc_binary {
   sanitize: {
       hwaddress: true,
   },
}
```

Android.mk

```
LOCAL_SANITIZE := hwaddress
```

Some flags can be used with HWAsan:

- detect_container_overflow
- detect_stack_use_after_return
- fast_unwind_on_fatal
- log_path
- max_history_size
- report_globals
- verbosity

example

```
sanitize: {
     hwaddress: true,
     extra_flags: [
         "detect_container_overflow=0",
         "detect_stack_use_after_return=1",
     ],
 },
```

Sanitizer	Description
`-fsanitize=address`	Detects memory errors like buffer overflows.
`-fsanitize=undefined`	Identifies undefined behavior.
`-fsanitize=leak`	Detects memory leaks.
`-fsanitize=thread`	Detects threading issues.
`-fsanitize=memory`	Detects uninitialized memory reads.
`-fsanitize=cfi`	Enforces control-flow integrity.

As I've already indicated, various compiler options and parameters can help provide more reports, such as warnings or errors. In addition, turning on ASLR, DEP, etc., can make our code more difficult to attack. Although imperfect, new tools and compilers offer more effective ways to safeguard our software. We must remain updated if we want to use the most recent ones. It is progress.

Obfuscation

As the number of Android-based mobiles has increased, the threats and malware targeting Android more than before. It means that we need to employ more techniques to protect the applications. Some malware tries to exploit the application by analyzing the code or memory. One of the techniques we can use to make it harder is utilizing some tools such as ProGuard. ProGuard has been known as an open-source obfuscator for Java code. However, it can shrink and optimize the Java code as well. But Let's talk about obfuscation and why it's important first. There is another reason to use the obfuscator tools other than extracting the sensitive information or changing the behavior. All the companies are interested in protecting their intellectual properties. This is important enough to consider obfuscation before publishing an application or a library.

What is Obfuscation?

Obfuscation is a software development technique used to deter reverse engineering or tampering with an application. By transforming the code into an equivalent but harder-to-understand version, obfuscation makes it more difficult for an attacker to understand and manipulate the code. The obfuscated code retains the same functionality as the original, but the variable names, class names, and method names are typically replaced with nonsensical and nondescriptive alternatives.

The obfuscation process could employ different techniques to make the code more complicated for an attacker to debug, understand, and change. Renaming the classes, variables, methods, etc., will reduce the chance of understanding the code at a glance. While encrypting resources such as strings puts some obstacles in finding the embedded keys, etc., to be discovered through skimming or searching. Another technique, like control flow obfuscation, changes the conditional, branching, and iterative parts to distort the logic in the code in a way that turns it into spaghetti-like code after de-compilation. Some obfuscators might inject dummy code to distract the attacker, but that might not run, be reached, or even be true all the time as a condition. In some cases, obfuscation might affect performance, but you will find the security more valuable compared to some percentage of dropped performance.

Minifying or shrinking is not obfuscation!

One of the standard functionalities that the obfuscators usually provide is minifying the code. They remove unused code, comments, dead code, etc, to reduce the size of the code. Removing the comments could lead to a hard moment when we want to read a de-compiled code, but it won't make the code as complicated as a real obfuscation does. I need to highlight here that obfuscation aims to generate an application or a code that will be less reversible and understandable after de-compiling. However, reducing the code's size is the main target of minifying and shrinking.

ProGuard and its Role in Obfuscation

ProGuard is an open-source tool for obfuscating Java and Kotlin code. It's integrated into the Android build system. ProGuard not only obfuscates the code but also shrinks and optimizes it, resulting in a smaller and potentially more efficient application. By removing unused code and renaming classes, methods, and fields with short, meaningless names, ProGuard makes it difficult for a person or a program to reverse-engineer the application.

The minifyEnabled flag enables or disables ProGuard. The proguardFiles line specifies the ProGuard configuration files. The first file, proguard-android-optimize.txt, is the default configuration file provided by the Android SDK. The second file, proguard-rules.pro, is where you can add project-specific rules.

An Example of ProGuard's Obfuscation

Let's consider an example to understand the effect of ProGuard's obfuscation better. Suppose you have a simple Person class like this:

```
public class Person {
  private String name;
  private int age;


  public Person(String name, int age) {
      this.name = name;
      this.age = age;
  }


  public String getName() {
      return name;
  }


  public int getAge() {
      return age;
  }
}
```

After obfuscation with ProGuard, the Person class might look something like this:

```java
public class a {
  private String a;
  private int b;


  public a(String a, int b) {
      this.a = a;
      this.b = b;
  }


  public String a() {
      return a;
  }


  public int b() {
      return b;
  }
}
```

The most important features of ProGuard

Code Shrinking:

ProGuard identifies and removes unused code from your application, including unused classes, methods, and fields. This reduces the size of your application, making it quicker to download and taking up less space on the user's device.

Code Obfuscation:

ProGuard renames classes, methods, and fields with short, meaningless names. This makes your code harder to understand if someone tries to decompile your APK, adding a layer of protection against reverse engineering.

Code Optimization:

ProGuard optimizes your bytecode, potentially making your app run faster. It performs inlining methods, removing unused fields, and optimizing loops.

Pre-verification:

ProGuard also verifies your processed code for Java Micro Edition (JME) and Java 6 and higher, which have a stack map format.

Here's how you can enable and use these features in Gradle in Android Studio:

Firstly, make sure the ProGuard settings are included in your build.gradle file:

```
android {

  ...

  buildTypes {
      release {
          minifyEnabled true
          proguardFiles getDefaultProguardFile('proguard-android-optimize.txt'), 'pr\
oguard-rules.pro'
      }
  }

  ...

}
```

In the example above, minifyEnabled true enables code shrinking and obfuscation. The proguardFiles line specifies the ProGuard configuration files that should be used.

The getDefaultProguardFile('proguard-android-optimize.txt') line gets the default ProGuard settings from the Android SDK. There are two main default files:

proguard-android.txt:

This is the base configuration file. It provides general shrinking and optimization options.

proguard-android-optimize.txt:

This extends the base file with additional optimization configurations. The 'proguard-rules.pro' file is where you can add any custom ProGuard rules for your project.

The rules in ProGuard are extensive and flexible, allowing you to define how your code should be obfuscated and shrunk. Here's an example of what some rules might look like in your proguard-rules.pro file:

```
# Keep - don't obfuscate any class that extends android.app.Activity
-keep public class * extends android.app.Activity


# Don't obfuscate or remove any members or methods that are being used in XML layouts
-keepclassmembers class * {
@android.view.View$* <methods>;
}


# Don't obfuscate or remove any native method
-keepclassmembers class * {
native <methods>;
}
```

Pros and Cons of Using ProGuard

Pros:

- Code Protection:

ProGuard's obfuscation makes your code more difficult to reverse engineer, helping to protect your intellectual property and sensitive information.

- Application Size Reduction:

ProGuard removes unused code and renames the remaining code with shorter names, which can significantly reduce the size of your application.

- Performance Optimization:

ProGuard can inline methods, remove unused fields, and perform other optimizations to make your code run faster.

Cons:

- Troubleshooting

Debugging an issue in obfuscated code can be challenging due to the changed names and structure. This is why ProGuard is typically only used in release builds.

- Configuration Complexity

ProGuard can be complex and challenging to configure correctly, especially for large projects. You should add specific rules to prevent particular code from being obfuscated or shrunk.

- Runtime Reflection

If your application uses reflection, you must carefully configure ProGuard to avoid breaking your code. Because ProGuard doesn't know about reflection calls, it might remove or rename a field or method used through reflection.

- 3rd party libraries Enabling Proguard might impact the imported libraries in the project. To avoid unforeseen issues at build or even runtime, you need to check the recommended Proguard configurations. Here are some examples of the most widely used libraries.

Example

Retrofit

Retrofit relies heavily on reflection, so you must add rules to keep your model classes from being obfuscated.

```
-keepclassmembers class * {
  @retrofit2.http.* <methods>;
}
```

Gson

Gson uses reflection to serialize/deserialize JSON, so your model classes need to be preserved:

```
-keep class com.example.models.** { *; }
```

Room

Room's annotations and reflection-based operations also require specific rules:

```
-keepclassmembers class androidx.room.* { *; }
-keepclassmembers interface androidx.room.* { *; }
```

In Android development, ProGuard is a valuable tool for protecting your application against reverse engineering, reducing its size, and optimizing its performance. However, it does have some challenges, such as making debugging harder and requiring careful configuration. Understanding how to use and configure ProGuard can help you build secure and efficient applications.

R8

R8 is not truly an obfuscator; instead, we could call it a minifier and shrinker. Its result in reducing the code size is comparable to ProGuard, which could be used instead of ProGuard. Using R8 is easy and straightforward, especially since Google has integrated it into Android Studio. Based on the information provided by Google and some test results, R8 is working well in optimizing the code. It can integrate the classes or resources and remove the unused ones, which leads to reducing the code size. Also, it can optimize the conditional statements by removing the not-reachable conditions or even turning them from a switch-case to an if-else statement. Like the other advanced tools, R8 replaces a function call with an inline function in such a case that the function is not used in many places. The overall R8 looks good in the sense of optimization. So, we can use it alongside ProGuard to take advantage of optimization and obfuscation together.

Setting up R8 is straightforward since it is part of the Android Gradle Plugin. To enable R8, you must ensure that `minifyEnabled` is set to `true` in the `build.gradle` file. Another option to enable is `isShrinkResources`, which shrinks the resources and will be handled by the Android Gradle plugin.

```
android {

  ...

  buildTypes {
      getByName("release") {
          isShrinkResources = true
          isMinifyEnabled = true
          proguardFiles(
              getDefaultProguardFile("proguard-android.txt"),
              "proguard-rules.pro"
          )
      }
  }

  ...

}
```

To explore the many options R8 supports, you can check the documents provided by Google.

The good news is that R8 uses the same rules as ProGuard, so you won't need to convert the rules from ProGuard to R8.

As a heads-up, we need to know that we can only achieve maximum security in our applications by using more than one technique or tool. Therefore, we must consider employing a combination of tools and techniques to provide protection.

Notes on hiding keys, secrets and credentials

Storing keys and secrets inside the applications has been always a hot topic. Whatever solution we use to store the date there will be a way to extract it. It could happen through de-compilation, debugging or even manipulating the application by injecting *smali code*, etc. The main difference between different solutions is the amount of effort a hacker needs to put to extract a key. Obviously there will be a huge difference between an advance obfuscator and a regular one which some of them make the code more complicated to be understood after de-compilation.

Here is some of the non-functional solutions to hide the keys:

1. **String Constants in Code**
2. **Base64 or Simple Encoding**
3. **Bit/XOR/etc manipulation**
4. **Splitting the Key**
5. **Encrypting through a native code**
6. **String Obfuscation**
7. **Reflection or Dynamic Loading**

None of them could stop a determined hacker to extract the key.

The best solution could be fetching a token through a login process and not storing an API-key/etc. inside the code. It might not possible for all the applications to take this approach. Based on the importance and sensitivity of the functionality of the app and the type of user's data we have access to we can select one of them. I don't need to mention that not all the applications are worth to extract their keys. There would be a value for the hacker to choose your application as a target. But whatever you choose, don't publish you app without with a key stored in as a plain string and not having enabled ProGuard.

There is another commercial option from *Guardsquare* known as DexGuard which I haven't used it. It claims that through lots of tempting features such as control flow obfuscation, data encryption, hook detection, tamper detection, malware protection, etc. makes applications and SDKs more secure.

Static and Dynamic Analysis Tools

What is static and dynamic code analysis?

The software has become more complicated in the last few years and has many functionalities. These functionalities demand an enormous architecture and complexity, including many modules and interactions. Usually, we work on a project from a few developers to a couple of teams. This means that the probability of having bugs increases. We must rely on something other than a single-onetime activity to find them. We must employ different approaches, such as tools, processes, etc. One of the easiest ways to find potential flaws is by using static and dynamic code analyzers. By setting them up in a CI environment, we ensure that our code is automatically and continually checked against some known problems. In continue we look into them.

Static Code Analysis

Nowadays, some IDEs include code analysis tools such as static, dynamic, and dependency analyzers. Each tool can inspect the code to find probable flaws or vulnerabilities, from stack overflow to more advanced ones. Though they can not discover all the problems, utilizing them is a big step toward more secure software. A better solution can be a mix of commercial and open-source analyzers locally or in CI/CD.

Some of the features are included in the static code analysis listed below:

- Control Flow Graph
- Code complexity
- Code style
- Dead Code Detection
- Error Detection (buffer overflow, dereference null pointer, etc)
- Resource leakage
- Type checking
- etc

Lint or linter is a static analysis tool that can discover potential flaws, bugs, etc. We can find a lint for most programming languages. Some of them are listed below:

C/C++

- CppCheck
- Clang-Tidy
- cpplint

Java

- SonarQube
- CheckStyle
- FindBugs
- Detekt

Kotlin

- Android Lint
- IntelliJ IDE
- Detekt

Python

- Flake8
- Pylint
- PyCharm IDE

These tools check for patterns or well-known bugs in the code that could result in security issues like buffer overflows, SQL injection, or command injection vulnerabilities. Static code analysis is frequently more effective than dynamic analysis. It can cover a wide range of code in a short period because it does not require the execution of the code.

There is a considerable chance of introducing vulnerabilities into the code because of the numerous third-party libraries, the handling of dependencies, and the handling of user input. Static code analysis tools ought to be in every Android developer's toolbox to reduce the known issues.

Example

```
public Connection getUserInfo(String username) {
  try {
      String url = "jdbc:mysql://localhost:3306/mydb?user=" + username ;
      Connection connection = DriverManager.getConnection(url);
      return connection;
  } catch(SQLException e) {
      e.printStackTrace();
      return null;
  }
}
```

The above example shows a potential security vulnerability for SQL injection since the user-supplied username strings are directly concatenated into the connection URL. As you can see, using the input parameter can lead to SQL-injection, and the static code analyzer will warn it.

Example – Android Studio Static Code Analysis for Java/Kotlin: Android Studio, the official IDE for Android development, includes a static code analysis tool called Lint. Lint checks the code for potential problems related to performance, security, and other aspects of Android apps.

Example

```
// main.c


#include <stdio.h>
#include <stdlib.h>
#include <string.h>
#include <unistd.h>


int main()
{
  char argc;
  char argv[20][40];
  char buffer[8];
  if (argc > 1) {
      printf("Usage: %s <input_string>\n", argv[1]);
      strcpy(buffer, argv[1]);
  }
  printf("\nTerminated normally!\n");
  return 0;
}


//cpplint lint_example.c
```

CppCheck output

```
cppcheck  --enable=all lint_example.c
```

Output

```
Checking lint_example.c …
lint_example.c:13:10: style: The scope of the variable 'argv' can be reduced. [varia\
bleScope]
char argv[20][40];
^
lint_example.c:14:10: style: The variable 'buffer' scope can be reduced. [variableSc\
ope]
char buffer[8];
^
lint_example.c:15:9: error: Uninitialized variable: argc [uninitvar]
if (argc > 1) {
^
lint_example.c:12:10: style: Variable 'argc' is not assigned a value. [unassignedVar\
iable]
char argc;
^
nofile:0:0: information: Cppcheck cannot find all the include files (use --check-con\
fig for details) [missingIncludeSystem]
```

cpplint output

```
cpplint lint_example.c
```

Output

```
lint_example.c:0:  No copyright message found.  You should have a line: "Copyright [\
year] <Copyright Owner>"  [legal/copyright] [5]
lint_example.c:11:  { should almost always be at the end of the previous line  [whit\
espace/braces] [4]
lint_example.c:17:  Almost always, snprintf is better than strcpy  [runtime/printf] \
[4]
lint_example.c:23:  Should have a space between // and comment  [whitespace/comments\
] [4]
lint_example.c:23:  Could not find a newline character at the end of the file.  [whi\
tespace/ending_newline] [5]
Done processing lint_example.c
Total errors found: 5
```

checkstyle

Example

```
public class SqlInjection {
  public Connection getUserInfo(String username) {
    try {
          String url = "jdbc:mysql://localhost:3306/mydb?user=" + username ;
          Connection connection = DriverManager.getConnection(url);
          return connection;
    } catch(SQLException e) {
          e.printStackTrace();
          return null;
    }
  }
}
```

```
java -jar checkstyle-10.10.0-all.jar -c google_checks.xml SqlInjections.java
```

Output

```
SqlInjections.java:2:1: The name of the outer type and the file do not match. [Outer\
TypeFilename]
SqlInjections.java:2:1: Missing a Javadoc comment. [MissingJavadocType]
SqlInjections.java:3:1: Line contains a tab character. [FileTabCharacter]
SqlInjections.java:3:9: 'method def modifier' has incorrect indentation level 8, exp\
ected level should be 2. [Indentation]
SqlInjections.java:3:9: Missing a Javadoc comment. [MissingJavadocMethod]
SqlInjections.java:4:1: Line contains a tab character. [FileTabCharacter]
SqlInjections.java:4:11: 'try' has incorrect indentation level 10, expected level sh\
ould be 4. [Indentation]
SqlInjections.java:5:1: Line contains a tab character. [FileTabCharacter]
SqlInjections.java:5:21: 'try' child has incorrect indentation level 20, expected le\
vel should be 6. [Indentation]
SqlInjections.java:5:86: ';' is preceded with whitespace. [NoWhitespaceBefore]
SqlInjections.java:6:1: Line contains a tab character. [FileTabCharacter]
SqlInjections.java:6:21: 'try' child has incorrect indentation level 20, expected le\
vel should be 6. [Indentation]
SqlInjections.java:7:1: Line contains a tab character. [FileTabCharacter]
SqlInjections.java:7:21: 'try' child has incorrect indentation level 20, expected le\
vel should be 6. [Indentation]
SqlInjections.java:8:1: Line contains a tab character. [FileTabCharacter]
SqlInjections.java:8:11: 'try rcurly' has incorrect indentation level 10, expected l\
evel should be 4. [Indentation]
SqlInjections.java:8:13: 'catch' is not followed by whitespace. [WhitespaceAfter]
SqlInjections.java:8:13: WhitespaceAround: 'catch' is not followed by whitespace. Em\
```

```
pty blocks                may only be represented as {} when not part of a multi-blo
ck statement (4.1.3) [WhitespaceAround]
SqlInjections.java:9:1: Line contains a tab character. [FileTabCharacter]
SqlInjections.java:9:21: 'catch' child has incorrect indentation level 20, expected \
level should be 6. [Indentation]
SqlInjections.java:10:1: Line contains a tab character. [FileTabCharacter]
SqlInjections.java:10:21: 'catch' child has incorrect indentation level 20, expected\
 level should be 6. [Indentation]
SqlInjections.java:11:1: Line contains a tab character. [FileTabCharacter]
SqlInjections.java:11:11: 'catch rcurly' has incorrect indentation level 10, expecte\
d level should be 4. [Indentation]
SqlInjections.java:12:1: Line contains a tab character. [FileTabCharacter]
SqlInjections.java:12:9: 'method def rcurly' has incorrect indentation level 8, expe\
cted level should be 2. [Indentation]
```

Dynamic Code Analysis

Dynamic code analysis, sometimes called dynamic program analysis or runtime analysis, examines an application's behavior as it is used or executed. Static code analysis may miss security holes, performance problems, or memory leaks that dynamic analysis can find.

Dynamic analysis tools execute the application in a controlled environment to track its behavior and data flow. They also attempt to modify user input or other external causes to test an application's reaction to unforeseen circumstances.

Dynamic analysis is more effective compared to static analysis. It can infer the application's behavior during execution and identify vulnerabilities that are not obvious in static code. However, dynamic analysis might take longer and require more resources.

Some of the features are included in the dynamic code analysis listed below:

- Runtime error detection
- Input validation and fuzz testing:
- Performance profiling
- Memory profiling
- Race condition detection
- Security vulnerability detection
- API monitoring and testing
- Load testing and stress testing
- User experience testing
- etc

C/C++

- LDRA
- Valgrind

Java

- JRat

Kotlin

- Android Studio

Android

- Drozer

Python

- DynaPyt

Hints on Static Analyzer tools

Running a static analyzer tool againt a project could lead to a reports with a long list of issues in different levels and priorities. To make it efficient we could use tqo approaches:

- Restricting the area to be analyzed
- Adjust the rules, etc. via the configuration file

Most of the static analyzers mentioned here support the two option. For instance you can easily select the scope of the project and the type of the analysis you want to be analyzed by AndroidStudio throug the UI. Other tools such as CppCheck, Detekt, etc.provide it through some configuration files which you can add to your project.

I recommend to use static analyzers from the very beginning of the development process to not be surprised with a long list of issues. But in case of facing this situation, you can simply start from where you are still developing and gradually covering the other part of the projects with an step by step approach to not be overwhelmed.

Example of Dynamic Code Analysis in Android:

Assume a scenario where an Android app stores sensitive user information, such as login tokens, in SharedPreferences:

```
SharedPreferences sharedPreferences = getSharedPreferences("MyApp", Context.MODE_PRI\
VATE);
sharedPreferences.edit().putString("user_token", loginToken).apply();
```

This code might not cause any issues to be discovered during static code analysis. Dynamic analysis, however, may show that attackers with physical access to the device or even other programs can access the information that has been stored. This event serves as a reminder of the need to securely store sensitive information using encryption techniques like the Android Keystore system.

Static and dynamic code analysis ensures secure coding methods, especially in Android development. While dynamic code analysis assesses the application's behavior during runtime to find security flaws that may not be obvious in the static code, static code analysis aids in detecting potential issues and vulnerabilities in the source code. By combining these approaches with the appropriate tools, developers can create secure Android applications and reduce security risks.

Last word

My final words are that I have tried to compile everything I discovered during my research on Android security—how to secure applications, services, and the operating system—into this book, presenting it in a structured way that I hope is useful, practical, and easy to follow.

However, the key point is that **threats in the software domain, especially in Android, are constantly evolving**. While the general categories of threats remain the same, introducing new software, features, and system updates means continuous changes in the ecosystem. Every update to the operating system, every modification to a library, and every new service introduced can shift the security landscape in either direction—making the system more secure or vulnerable.

I have emphasized throughout the book that **security is a living process**. It is not a one-time task but something that should be regularly assessed, revised, and enhanced throughout the lifecycle of a software product. Keeping our knowledge up to date is essential. We can strengthen our approach by practicing regularly and applying security techniques consistently. Of course, there may be techniques I have not covered—either because of limitations in my knowledge or to avoid unnecessary length.

The chapters in this book aim to guide Android developers, Android system developers, Android engineers, and Android architects—no matter their role—on how to approach security in the Android ecosystem.

I sincerely hope my efforts make the Android ecosystem more secure at every level, even in a small way.

I look forward to your feedback.

About the Author

Mohammad Hossein. Heydarchi is a curious and passionate software engineer with a deep interest in Android internals, system-level programming, and embedded development. He enjoys exploring the Android Open Source Project (AOSP), Linux, and the challenges of building secure, reliable systems from the ground up.

He shares what he learns on his blog, AospInsight.com[1], hoping it can help others on their own journeys through Android and security. His focus is on practical, hands-on knowledge—ranging from architecture and secure development to tools and techniques that strengthen system and app security.

He's always open to learning from others, exchanging ideas, and working together on meaningful projects. Feel free to connect with him on LinkedIn[2] to chat, collaborate, or simply say hello.

[1]https://AospInsight.com
[2]https://www.linkedin.com/in/heydarchi/

Abbreviations Glossary

AES - Advanced Encryption Standard
AFL - American Fuzzy Lop
AIDL - Android Interface Definition Language
AMS - Activity Manager Service
API - Application Programming Interface
ASLR - Address Space Layout Randomization
ASCII - American Standard Code for Information Interchange
ATT - American Telephone and Telegraph
BLE - Bluetooth Low Energy
BSIMM - Building Security In Maturity Model
CA - Certificate Authority
CERT - Computer Emergency Response Team
CFI - Control Flow Integrity
CI - Continuous Integration
CIP - Critical Infrastructure Protection
CIS - Center for Internet Security
CK - Cryptographic Key
COBIT - Control Objectives for Information and Related Technologies
CPU - Central Processing Unit
CRC - Cyclic Redundancy Check
CSF - Cybersecurity Framework
CVE - Common Vulnerabilities and Exposures
CWE - Common Weakness Enumeration
DAST - Dynamic Application Security Testing
DMA - Direct Memory Access
GATT - Generic Attribute Profile
GDPR - General Data Protection Regulation
GNU - GNU's Not Unix
HAL - Hardware Abstraction Layer
HFP - Hands-Free Profile
HIDL - HAL Interface Definition Language
HIPAA - Health Insurance Portability and Accountability Act
HMAC - Hash-Based Message Authentication Code
HTML - HyperText Markup Language
HTTP - HyperText Transfer Protocol
HTTPS - HTTP Secure
IDA - Interactive Disassembler

IDE - Integrated Development Environment
IDS - Intrusion Detection System
IOMMU - Input/Output Memory Management Unit
IPC - Inter-Process Communication
ISO - International Organization for Standardization
ITIL - IT Infrastructure Library
JADX - Java Android Decompiler
JAR - Java ARchive
JIT - Just-In-Time
JSON - JavaScript Object Notation
KISS - Keep It Simple, Stupid
KPS - Key Provider Service
LDRA - Liverpool Data Research Associates
MAC - Mandatory Access Control
MCU - Microcontroller Unit
MFA - Multi-Factor Authentication
MITM - Man-In-The-Middle
MITRE - MITRE Corporation
NDK - Native Development Kit
NIST - National Institute of Standards and Technology
OEM - Original Equipment Manufacturer
OTA - Over-the-Air Updates
OWASP - Open Web Application Security Project
PASTA - Process for Attack Simulation and Threat Analysis
PCI - Payment Card Industry
PID - Process ID
PIE - Position Independent Executable
PII - Personally Identifiable Information
PKCE - Proof Key for Code Exchange
QR - Quick Response (Code)
RBAC - Role-Based Access Control
ROP - Return-Oriented Programming
RSA - Rivest–Shamir–Adleman
SAST - Static Application Security Testing
SDK - Software Development Kit
SDLC - Software Development Life Cycle
SELinux - Security-Enhanced Linux
SHA - Secure Hash Algorithm
SOC - Security Operations Center
SOME/IP - Scalable service-Oriented MiddlewarE over IP
SP - Service Provider
SSL - Secure Sockets Layer
SSO - Single Sign-On

STRIDE - Spoofing, Tampering, Repudiation, Information Disclosure, Denial of Service, Elevation of Privilege
TEE - Trusted Execution Environment
TLS - Transport Layer Security
TPS - Token Provider Service
UID - User ID
URL - Uniform Resource Locator
UX - User Experience
VPN - Virtual Private Network
XML - Extensible Markup Language
XSS - Cross-Site Scripting

References

- **Google Documents** – https://developer.android.com/
- **Android Open Source Project (AOSP)** – https://cs.android.com
- **NIST Publications:**
  - *NIST Special Publication 800-218* – NIST Secure Software Development Framework (SSDF) Version 1.1[1]
  - *NIST Special Publication 800-53, Revision 5* – Security and Privacy Controls for Information Systems and Organizations[2]
  - *NIST Special Publication 800-160, Volume 1, Version 1.1* – Systems Security Engineering[3]
  - *NIST Special Publication 800-160, Volume 2, Revision 1* – Developing Cyber-Resilient Systems: A Systems Security Engineering Approach[4]
- **CVE (Common Vulnerabilities and Exposures)** – https://www.cve.org/
- **Common Weakness Enumeration (CWE)** – https://cwe.mitre.org/
- **OWASP Mobile Application Security (MAS)** – https://mas.owasp.org/
- **MITRE Mobile Matrix** – https://attack.mitre.org/matrices/mobile/
- **Guardsquare** – https://www.guardsquare.com/
- **SEI CERT C Coding Standard** – https://wiki.sei.cmu.edu/confluence/display/c/SEI+CERT+C+Coding+Standard
- **Saltzer, Jerome & Schroeder, Michael. (April 17, 1975).** *The Protection of Information in Computer Systems.*
- **Adam Shostack's Threat Modeling Resources:**
  - *Shostack, Adam. (2014). Threat Modeling: Designing for Security.* John Wiley & Sons.
  - **The Four-Question Framework** – https://github.com/adamshostack/4QuestionFrame
  - **AOSP Insight** – https://AospInsight.com/

[1] https://csrc.nist.gov/publications/detail/sp/800-218/final
[2] https://csrc.nist.gov/publications/detail/sp/800-53/rev-5/final
[3] https://csrc.nist.gov/publications/detail/sp/800-160/vol-1/rev-1/final
[4] https://csrc.nist.gov/publications/detail/sp/800-160/vol-2/rev-1/final

Appendix

Security Standards and Guidelines

Category	Standard/Guideline	Description	Industry Focus
General	**NIST Cybersecurity Framework (CSF)**	High-level framework for managing and mitigating cybersecurity risks.	General
General	**CIS Controls**	Set of 20 prioritized cybersecurity practices for securing IT systems.	General
General	**SANS Institute Guidelines**	Best practices for security training and certification.	General
General	**GDPR**	Regulation focused on data privacy and protection in the EU.	General
General	**COBIT**	Framework for IT governance and management.	General
General	**ITIL**	Framework for IT service management.	General
General	**CWE**	Database of common software weaknesses and vulnerabilities.	Software Development

Category	Standard/Guideline	Description	Industry Focus
General	CVE	List of publicly known cybersecurity vulnerabilities and exposures.	General
Core Security Frameworks	MITRE ATT&CK	Framework for describing attacker tactics and techniques.	Cybersecurity
Core Security Frameworks	OWASP	Best practices and guidelines for web application security.	Web Applications
Core Security Frameworks	OWASP Top 10	List of critical web application security risks.	Web Application Security
Security Standards	ISO/IEC 27001	International standard for information security management systems (ISMS).	All Industries
Security Standards	ISO/IEC 15408 (Common Criteria)	Standardized framework for IT product security evaluation.	Government, High-Security Sectors
Security Standards	PCI DSS	Security standard for organizations handling credit card information.	Finance
Security Standards	HIPAA Security Rule	U.S. standard setting requirements for healthcare data protection.	Healthcare
Security Standards	NIST SP 800-53	Catalog of security and privacy controls for federal systems.	Federal/IT Security
Security Standards	ISO/IEC 27017	Extension of ISO/IEC 27001 focused on cloud security controls.	Cloud Computing

Category	Standard/Guideline	Description	Industry Focus
Security Standards	SOC 2	Security framework for data protection in cloud and service organizations.	Cloud/Service Organizations
Security Standards	BSIMM	Maturity model for assessing software security programs.	Software Development
Automotive Standards	AUTOSAR	Security framework for automotive systems.	Automotive
Automotive Standards	ISO/SAE 21434	Road vehicles cybersecurity engineering.	Automotive
Automotive Standards	ISO 26262	Functional safety for road vehicles.	Automotive
Automotive Standards	UNECE WP.29	Vehicle cybersecurity regulations.	Automotive
Industrial Security	IEC 62443	Standard for security in industrial automation and control systems.	Industrial Automation
Industrial Security	IEC 61508	Functional safety of electrical/electronic systems.	Industrial
Aviation Standards	DO-178C	Software considerations in airborne systems.	Aviation
Infrastructure Security	NERC CIP	Security standard for electricity grid protection.	Electricity Grid
Threat Modeling	STRIDE	Threat modeling framework (Spoofing, Tampering, Repudiation, Information Disclosure, Denial of Service, Elevation of Privilege).	General

Category	Standard/Guideline	Description	Industry Focus
Threat Modeling	**PASTA**	Process for Attack Simulation and Threat Analysis.	Software Security
Risk Assessment	**TARA**	Threat Assessment and Remediation Analysis; a framework for assessing and mitigating risks in software development.	Software Development
Risk Assessment	**OCTAVE**	Operationally Critical Threat, Asset, and Vulnerability Evaluation.	Risk Assessment
Risk Management	**FAIR**	Factor Analysis of Information Risk framework.	Risk Assessment
Risk Management	**ISO 31000**	Risk management principles and guidelines.	All Industries
Development Guidelines	**MISRA C**	Guidelines for the use of the C programming language in safety-critical systems.	Embedded Systems
Development Guidelines	**CERT C/C++**	Secure coding standards for C and C++ languages.	Software Development
Development Guidelines	**SEI CERT**	Software Engineering Institute Coding Standards.	Software Development
Development Guidelines	**Google C++ Style**	C++ coding standards and best practices.	Software Development

A detailed STRIDE and TARA comparison

Framework	STRIDE	TARA
Main Focus	Software-specific threats	Threat agent & organizational risk analysis
Scope	Individual components/systems/services/applications	Organization-wide (People, processes, technology, assets, etc.)
Use Cases	Software development, threat modeling, security testing	Risk assessment, compliance, audit, security planning
When to Use	During software development/design	Strategic security planning
Key Elements	- Spoofing, Tampering, Repudiation, Information Disclosure,- Denial of Service, Elevation of Privilege	Threat Agent Library, Methods & Objectives, Risk Assessment, Countermeasure Development
Target Users	Developers, Architects & security engineers	Security teams and security strategists & managers
Analysis Level	Technical/Component level	Strategic/Organizational level
Implementation	More straightforward, technical	More complex, strategic
Output	Prioritized list of software-specific threats	Prioritized list of threats to organizational assets
Time Frame	Project-based	Continuous/Strategic
Resources Needed	Technical expertise	Broad security knowledge
Integration	Development lifecycle	Enterprise risk management

Useful tools

Category	Tool Name	Purpose
Static and Dynamic Analysis Tools	MobSF (Mobile Security Framework)	Automated analysis for static and dynamic app security.
	QARK (Quick Android Review Kit)	Automated source code analysis and flaw detection.
	AndroBugs Framework	Detects Android app vulnerabilities and misconfigurations.
	SonarQube	Static code analysis for identifying code vulnerabilities.
	Fortify SCA	Comprehensive static application security testing (SAST).
Reverse Engineering Tools	Apktool	Decompiling and recompiling Android APKs.
	Dex2Jar	Converts APK files to Java JAR for deeper analysis.
	JADX	Decompiles APKs into readable Java code.
	IDA Pro	Advanced binary analysis and reverse engineering.
	Frida	Real-time dynamic instrumentation and debugging.
	Ghidra	Open-source reverse engineering and static analysis framework.
Network Security Testing Tools	Burp Suite	Comprehensive tool for testing app communication security.
	OWASP ZAP (Zed Attack Proxy)	Active and passive scanning for mobile and web apps.
	Mitmproxy	Analyzes and manipulates network traffic in real time.

Category	Tool Name	Purpose
	Wireshark	Packet-level network protocol analysis.
Penetration Testing Tools	Metasploit Framework	Exploit creation and vulnerability verification.
	Drozer	Assesses vulnerabilities in Android app components.
	Kali NetHunter	Mobile penetration testing platform for Android devices.
General Vulnerability Scanners	Nessus	Comprehensive vulnerability assessment across systems.
	OpenVAS	Open-source vulnerability assessment and management.

www.ingramcontent.com/pod-product-compliance
Lightning Source LLC
Chambersburg PA
CBHW061354240926
51846CB00007B/1408